P9-AFD-310

BAD WOMEN

BAD WOMEN

Regulating Sexuality
in Early American Cinema

Janet Staiger

University of Minnesota Press
Minneapolis
London

Copyright 1995 by the Regents of the University of Minnesota

Portions of H. L. Mencken, "The Flapper," are reprinted by permission of the Enoch Pratt Free Library in accordance with the terms of the will of H. L. Mencken.

All rights reserved. No part of this publication may be reproduced, stored in a retrieval system, or transmitted, in any form or by any means, electronic, mechanical, photo-copying, recording, or otherwise, without the prior written permission of the publisher.

Published by the University of Minnesota Press
111 Third Avenue South, Suite 290, Minneapolis, MN 55401-2520
Printed in the United States of America on acid-free paper

Library of Congress Cataloging-in-Publication Data

Staiger, Janet.
    Bad women : regulating sexuality in early American cinema /   Janet Staiger.
        p.   cm.
    Filmography: p.
    Includes bibliographical references and index.
    ISBN 0-8166-2624-3
    ISBN 0-8166-2625-1 (pbk.)
    1. Women in motion pictures.   2. Sex in motion pictures.
    3. Motion pictures—United States—History.   I. Title.
    PN1995.9.W6S73   1995
    791.43'652042—dc20   94-46539

The University of Minnesota is an
equal-opportunity educator and employer.

To Kristin Thompson

Contents

Illustrations

Preface

Good girls go to heaven. Bad girls go everywhere else.[1]

The greeting card text quoted in the epigraph perhaps does not sum up life for women in the 1990s, but to some people it might have been an appropriate admonition for women in the 1890s. This book is about bad women, or more accurately, about cultural notions such as "bad women" in historical context. Judith Butler, Teresa de Lauretis, and Judith Flax, among other theorists, argue that "woman," "gender," and other such apparent realities are discursive constructions.[2] Specifically, I will be arguing that it is valuable to reconceptualize film history from the vantage point of its constitutive historical formations. At the time of cinema's beginnings in the United States, economic, social, and discursive conditions encouraged talk about women, men, sexuality, gender, and object choices. This talk about "woman" was symptomatic of changes in these conditions, but "woman" was a particularly useful concept upon which to focus. While this book will concentrate on a particular period of U.S. cinema (specifically 1907 to around 1915), the study has implications for other eras and media.

As someone writing and theorizing histories, I am increasingly convinced that contradictions in structural configurations provide useful sites for examining potentials for transitions into new social organizations. In the case I examine, however, that potential for change has only possibilities but no necessary outcome. That is, a necessarily progressive or conservative future is not embedded in a situation. It all depends on what people do—consciously or not.

In the latest book I wrote, *Interpreting Films*, I used a quotation by V. N. Volosinov as a significant theoretical premise. Volosinov writes that *"the sign may not be divorced from the concrete forms of social intercourse."* Not only is a sign embedded in its specific conditions and context, but at that very historical and contingent moment, a sign does not have any necessary inherent meaning. Volosinov believes that a sign has different meanings to different

xi

people, or even more important, people may struggle over its meaning: "Sign becomes an arena of class struggle."[3]

This contingency about meanings—and the ability to appropriate and re-inscribe a sign into a new context, thus transgressing and redefining the (ever permeable) boundaries of its signification—is a powerful political tool for anyone interested in social change. Consequently, reconceptualizing texts as complicated masses of ideas, neither internally unified nor externally stable in meaning to readers, becomes even more useful. As Stephen Greenblatt con-tends, texts ought to be seen as "fields of force, places of dissension and shift-ing interests, occasions for the jostling of orthodox and subversive impulses."[4] The struggle, to use Volosinov's term, is not complete once a sign is rein-scribed in a new context, creating a new meaning, since people making the reinscription have difficulty in imagining or predicting all of the consequences of the next configuration or how others will use that new configuration.

This work, then, is a continuation of those theoretical issues through an examination of how a historical context could provide the *possibilities* for a variety of *actual* (not hypothetical) readings of films by actual (not ideal) spectators. Although I will not be describing actual spectatorial responses, I will be providing a new interpretation of the complexity and productivity of the time frame of 1907 to 1915 and what that means for understanding film-going, spectators, and moving images. Once we have a better picture of the complexity of the period, we will be in a more advantageous position to theo-rize specific historical spectators and the production of culture among the various groups of people involved in making and viewing movies.

In his introduction to *The Cheese and the Worms*, Carlo Ginzburg surveys approaches to "ideas, beliefs, and world views of the lower classes" among a group of cultural historians.[5] He rejects the view that the lower classes simply pick up residual notions left over from coherent ideologies created previously by dominant classes. He also rejects "imposition" or "acculturation" theses—the positions that dominant classes cause by force the lower classes to take up certain ideas, or that the dominant ideas steadily wear away or erode those held by the subordinate classes. He rejects a "reciprocal" thesis in which lower-class ideologies and cultures are produced in a simple resistance to dominant ideologies and cultures. Instead, Ginzburg asserts a complex rela-tion among classes.[6] Aspects of subordinate cultures can have causal force with autonomous effects as well as affecting dominant cultures, and vice versa.

The case I will examine had some very contradictory aspects within it be-cause of the possibility of such autonomous effects. Take, for instance, the de-velopment of the social hygiene movement after 1906. I shall discuss how the movement was crucial in suggesting that the middle class *needed* to talk about sexual behavior. Such talk would seem possibly useful to the emancipation of women, at least insofar as the talk produced the representations that a repeal of reticence was imminent, as well as widespread criticism of the double standard. However, the historical context that provided the backdrop for that representation also had within its mix aspects that could connect the need to talk with racist discourses. Talking was vital if (at least some of) the middle class were to save its Anglo-Saxon heritage from the (projected) ravages of venereal disease. "Race suicide" thus intersected with "social hygiene." Fears of race suicide also connected with evidence available to the middle class that within their group couples were limiting the number of children they had in an effort to improve their social standing and take advantage of material goods increasingly available to them. Thus talk was also about new types of families and roles for a New Woman and a New Man. Conversely, the emphasis on family values had the potential to empower women asserting new definitions of territorial privileges and gender possibilities.

Thus I will treat a historical moment much as I will treat the films I analyze: each instance is heterogeneous, filled with strands and traces that have very different meanings and possibilities to individuals viewing those instances. Just as the films will not be treated as coherent—but rather as a site for talk—so are the meanings of history discourses and events to those living through them.

As a performance, this history writing is a contingent, subjective, evaluative, and judgmental act on my part. Throughout the book, I will imply that some of the events appear to me to have led to more progressive or at least contradictory situations while others operated to maintain the status quo. I judge as progressive texts and events that promoted egalitarianism and diversity. Conservative or regressive texts and events are those that created or reinforced hierarchies among peoples and intolerance for those who sought equity.

One current question in film history has been whether 1909 (more or less) marks the emergence in American cinema of a middle-class vision of sexual morality. Yes and no. The era around 1909 was a period of intense struggle within the middle class to define an appropriate version of and explanation for Woman and women's sexuality. This was produced as a condition of transformations affecting middle-class life and American society: shifts from small-scale farming and businesses to industrialism and monopoly capitalism, from rural to urban living, from nationalization to globalization, from a culture of production to a culture of consumption. What does appear in the following years could be said to represent the views of many middle-class individuals about the *limitations* for the New Woman of the early twentieth century. This New Woman is an idealized, contemporary version of the Good Woman, constructed in opposition to a New Bad Woman, operating within the ideological fallacy of a binary opposition derived from the long-standing notion of the virgin/whore dichotomy. This representation of the New Woman had specific features useful for the turn of the century and was a manifestation of what might function well for constructing socialized gender relations within twentieth-century American capitalism.

Yet the ideological vision also included the *possibilities* for Woman. Moreover, because no unified middle-class position existed, the representation was not a coherent and unified act of repression but indexed struggle instead. Thus the New Good Woman was actually a lot of New Good Women, counterbalanced by many New Bad Women. The more people represented Woman the more possibilities developed for complexity and contradiction. Rather than see Woman as Other (the "opposition" thesis), we need to understand Woman as a sign with multiple meanings.

In the specific case of cinema, prohibiting certain images about women and men and their relations was considered by some as important for the maintenance of good taste and social mores. Others believed that regulating the images through appropriate storytelling could be beneficial. For the former group, repression of some material was its goal; for the latter group, analysis of characters and behaviors was its aim. Eventually, the latter group's view emerged as the more powerful. Although some images (explicit representations of sexual intercourse) were not tolerated, other troublesome situations were dealt with by narrativizing them, explaining them, and then resolving them via an "appropriate" conclusion. This strategy was supported by important social and civic organizations with institutional credentials to claim legitimacy in speaking for at least a respectable part of the middle class. It also followed tactics well in place for similar representations in novels and the theater—specifically, rejuvenated melodramatic and realist aesthetics.

Talk was not only important in trying to control what might occur in the future but, as Michel Foucault has pointed out, talk created a dispersion of practices. In something of a "big bang" theory of discourse, Foucault writes that during the Middle Ages a discourse on sex was fairly "unitary." However, "in the course of recent centuries, this relative uniformity was broken apart, scattered, and multiplied in an explosion of distinct discursivities. . . . So it is not simply in terms of a continual extension that we must speak of this discursive growth; it should be seen rather as a dispersion of centers from which discourses emanated, a diversification of their forms, and the complex deploy-

ment of the network connecting them."[7] Without implying an origin to this
discursive practice, Foucault suggests that at certain moments powerful institutions constructed a very potent organization of discourses. Yet, even then,
some internal contradictions, some resistances to that power, some continu-
ities of alternative ideologies produced a disintegration and reconfiguration of
meanings and institutions. Talk participates in those social and discursive
events.

Women did a lot of this talking. In the media outlets available to them,
women made clear that they had views about their lives and the lives for
which they were responsible. Literature was a powerful means for women to
communicate with each other, as were essays in journals. A critical moment,
for example, in the social hygiene movement is when a woman such as Helen
Keller titles a piece about venereal disease " 'I Must Speak.' " Women also at
least tried to articulate their expectations. Despite the hackneyed question,
Rheta Childe Dorr was quite willing to tell people in 1910 *What Eight Million
Women Want* (the vote, equal rights).

This book tries to describe changing sets of conditions that produced a system of regulation of the content of cinema permitting a lot of talk about
women, men, sexuality, gender, and object choices. Although I shall not be
pursuing this here, I do see the same general pattern of activity surrounding
later events connected with content regulation of movies until the end of
World War II. That is, the pattern of activity is generalizable, although the
specific details of the events are not reproduced precisely. After World War II,
the film industry reconceptualizes its notions of audience address, other social
changes occur, and television takes up functions that cinema-going had served.
Henceforth, regulation of moving pictures operates somewhat differently.

Besides introducing my theoretical model, I survey in chapter 1 the economic, social, and cultural transformations occurring in the United States between 1880 and 1920 as part of the contextual background for the film industry's behavior about representing gender and sexuality. In particular, I
emphasize that economic and social transformations produced all sorts of diversity and inequities among different peoples. The consequences of that
stimulated reform and utopian thinking, but reformers were by no means unified. Populists, socialists, reformers drawing on religious strictures, and reformers turning to social science policymaking contended for the right to define the utopian future for America.

Chapter 2 focuses more specifically on the history of the representation of
"woman," especially the so-called New Woman. In this case (as in other instances of social change), "woman" is one of the signs mobilized to symboli-

cally represent this change, a sign to be struggled over. Writers of the period emphasize that the New Woman appears as a replacement ideal for the Victorian Domestic Woman, but her definition is often debated in opposition to the construction of the New Bad Woman. Consequently, just as no single, coherent representation of the Victorian Good Woman can be said to exist, neither does a single image of the New Good Woman. Talk may have been about trying to pin down consensus on that issue, but all talk did was proliferate possibilities.

From these social and ideological subtendings I move to the specific situation of the U.S. film industry. Through reviews and discussion in trade papers, chapter 3 describes general views and debates about what might count as troublesome pictures around 1907 through about 1912. These views boil down to three general guidelines and two theories of film viewing. In particular I discuss how films could introduce bad women (and men), how much sexual desire was permissible, how compromising situations were to be handled, and how nudity could be displayed. The specific narrational devices, I will argue, derive from both realist and melodramatic aesthetics, transformed into stylistic and formal systems that become part of the causes for and features of classical Hollywood cinema. They also fit in neatly with progressivist regulation strategies since they provide a motor for narrative action.

Chapter 4 tells the story of why and how the U.S. film industry introduced a form of self-regulation into its production and exhibition process. From an economic point of view, self-regulation was a method to manage competition. However, the type of self-regulation installed by the industry was probably about as liberal as it could have been at the time.

The last section, chapters 5, 6, and 7, discusses the consequences of this type of production of cultural meanings by considering three feature-length films of the period—*Traffic in Souls* (1913), *A Fool There Was* (1914), and *The Cheat* (1915). I chose these three films in part because they are well known by scholars. They all also feature Bad Women as protagonists. The New Woman is described as someone who knows good and evil and chooses her mate; the Bad Woman who goes astray is the indulged, the parasite, the one who does not think. Where good and evil were once matters of natural inclination or sin, now they are facts of individual agency or choice.

The three films exemplify each of these three types of Bad Women, but they also incorporate discourses about the New Woman. The older versions of a good woman will no longer be acceptable, and the films insist upon the value of a new, independent, intelligent, and aggressive woman, even a *desiring* woman. Thus, the films are not simple instances of patriarchal repression of women. A lot of talk exists within them, although some of that talk is indeed racist, nativist, and patriarchal. The talk reasserts a revised version of middle-class "civilized morality," a prescriptive system of the individual as unified and responsible. That regulation combines well with a narrative system in which character causality is created as the primary means for activating narrative events. Or, conversely, cinema is constructed to enhance that regulation.

In *The Classical Hollywood Cinema*, David Bordwell, Kristin Thompson, and I did not directly consider the ideology of textual systems, although we did raise that issue at the end of the book. I hope this book will give some directions as to how to make parts of that book correlate with questions about representation. In particular, I would stress that as far as I am concerned the creators of the classical Hollywood cinema chose to use within its primary dramatic form many features connected with early twentieth-century melodrama and realism, concomitant with liberal-humanist assertions of individual agency. One such feature was the illustration of social conflict through individualized and psychologized characters who are presumed to carry the weight of causality.

In summary, the function of this book is to contribute toward a historical understanding of the productive aspect of discursive constructions of woman as a cultural sign. I shall use Foucault's notion of a "transfer point" to describe this. Foucault conceives of discursive nodes as places for generating a resurgence of power and pleasure; I also consider the intersections as sites of potential transformations from one form of meaning to another.[8] A transfer point, like any generator in a revolution, is a valuable site to control. Images that disrupt norms, that display current norms, also set agendas for changes. These transfer points change historically. Thus, the theoretical significance of this book includes recasting representations about causality for the narrative forms of classical Hollywood cinema, about the diversity of images available for various spectators (of all classes, but particularly for the middle class), and about the opportunities for multiple interpretations to exist simultaneously within a culture.

I am sincerely grateful to many institutions and people for helping me with this project. The University of Texas Research Institute granted me a faculty research leave in the spring of 1992. This provided me the time to write the initial draft of the book. I also appreciate in general the support of the College of Communication and former dean Robert Jeffrey.

Archives and libraries are essential to such projects, and the field of film studies is fortunate in having particularly helpful ones at the Academy of Motion Picture Arts and Sciences, the Library of Congress, the University of California–Los Angeles, the Museum of Modern Art, the New York Public Library, New York University, the University of Texas at Austin, and the University of Wisconsin–Madison. This book could not have been written without the research and screenings of the annual Giornate del Cinema Muto. Unlisted in the references are hundreds of films made available to scholars such as me through that event. The explosion of research on this period of film history has been immeasurably assisted by this institution.

My students at New York University (1983–87) and the University of Texas at Austin (1987 to present) have helped me see cinema and this period in more complex ways. They have brought me readings and small period clippings. They have shared with me their research. They have remained colleagues even after they've left. Thank you all so much.

Trying out ideas is critical to finding out how to think about a historical problem. Two groups let me officially practice on them: the University of Texas Women's Studies Research Seminar (1991) and the University of Texas Law Library's "Lawyers and Popular Culture" Conference (1992).

The staff at the University of Minnesota have been spectacular. Thanks so much to Robert Mosimann and especially my editor, Janaki Bakhle, whose intelligence graces many passages in this book.

The discipline in which I work is filled with generous colleagues, ready to share support and constructive criticism. Over the years on this and related subjects, I have been blessed with the conversations (and in a couple cases the close readings of parts or all of this manuscript) of Richard Abel, Robert C. Allen, Tino Balio, John Belton, David Bordwell, Eileen Bowser, Edward Branigan, Charles Ramirez Berg, Ben Brewster, Ed Buscombe, Don Crafton, Susan Dalton, Mary Desjardins, William K. Everson, David Francis, Tom Gunning, Miriam Hansen, Rosemary Hanes, Ann Harris, Lea Jacobs, Mark Langer, Jay Leyda, Charles Musser, Lauren Rabinovitz, Robert Sklar, Vivian Sobchack, Paulo Cherchi Usai, Virginia Wright Wexman, and especially my terrific friends Horace Newcomb, Tom Schatz, and Kristin Thompson.

They say last is not least, and this is certainly the case here. This book is dedicated to Kristin for what she has given me professionally and personally. She's not just a good woman, but a great one.

1

The Repeal of Reticence

The first scene of the 1924 Paramount film *Open All Night* begins with an intertitle to establish the place and situation of the movie: "This is the story of one night in Paris—city of gay loves and unhappy marriages." A montage of views of a city verifies at least part of the intertitle's proposition. Intertitle two: "It begins in the apartment of Edmond Duverne, who loves his wife— not wisely—but too well—." A medium shot of a cigarette holder in the shape of a naked woman introduces a medium shot of Adolphe Menjou, playing Edmond. Edmond is looking through the windows with binoculars. Intertitle: "Edmond Duverne—shrewd enough to study women—but foolish enough to believe he understands them—." In a series of eyeline match shots, the film viewer and Edmond watch a scene in an apartment across the way. A brutish man drags his girl toward him, he takes his belt off, and as she moves off the edge of the window frame (just out of sight), he strikes at her. Edmond, still looking through his binoculars, sighs and shakes his head. Intertitle: "Ivory Lady, you can't beat your wife and hold her, too. A woman may be fascinated by a brute—but she can never respect him—." The ivory lady, Edmond's cigarette holder, does not reply. "—and without respect love cannot last."

Then the film crosscuts to a woman bathing. "His wife's name is Therese—Viola Dana." But Therese is scrubbing very slowly, for she is reading from a book: " 'You brute,' she moaned. 'You are hurting me—I love you.' " Therese closes her eyes and breathes and shivers. She reads on as Edmond enters the room: "Now he was beating her—beating her—. She moaned half in pain and half in ecstasy . . . exulting in his love." Therese moans.

"We are an hour late, ma Cherie," says Edmond.

"I'm not going. . . . If you were a man you would make me go. You would break down the door. You would beat me—*beat* me."

The first plot point has arrived. Will Edmond beat her? Will he "be a man"? Will she still love him or love him more? What does a woman really

1

want? And what should a man expect as a consequence of her desire? The rest of the film, of course, is dedicated to those very twentieth-century questions. *Open All Night* concludes that, indeed, Therese does want Edmond to be a brute, of a certain kind: "And so to Duverne came the realization that the more you learn about women the less you understand them."

The question I shall be asking in this book is not "What do women want?" but how can an explicit investigation of female sexual desire, one implying a certain mild degree of perversion, appear on the movie screen in 1924? Or rather, what cultural and social configurations in the decades before 1924 prepared American society and the U.S. film industry to broach such a query? Why were decent men and women looking through binoculars at windows across the way or at movie screens in their own neighborhoods to find out what women (and men) wanted? What counted as "bad" and "good" behavior by either gender?

Open All Night is itself not particularly out of step with everyday notions of what was happening in the 1920s. The roaring twenties had its jazz babies and the "It" girl; bathtub gin and gangsters populate our representations of the period. But the "flapper" is not a concoction of that era. It is, instead, an invention of the 1910s. In fact, H. L. Mencken introduces the term in the *Smart Set* magazine in 1915, before the start of World War I. His description is worth quoting almost in full:

> Observe, then, this nameless one, this American Flapper. . . . Youth is hers, and hope, and romance, and—
>
> Well, well, let us be exact: let us not say innocence. This Flapper, to tell the truth, is far, far, far from a simpleton. . . . The age she lives in is one of knowledge. She herself is educated. She is privy to dark secrets. The world bears to her no aspect of mystery. She has been taught how to take care of herself.
>
> For example, she has a clear and detailed understanding of all the tricks of white slave traders, and knows how to circumvent them. She is on the lookout for them in matinée lobbies and railroad stations—benevolent-looking old women who pretend to be ill, plausible young men who begin business with "Beg pardon," bogus country girls who cry because their mythical brothers have failed to meet them. She has a keen eye for hypodermic needles, chloroform masks, closed carriages. She has seen all these sinister machines of the devil in operation on the screen. She has read about them in the great works of Elizabeth Robins, Clifford G. Roe and Reginald Wright Kauffman. She has followed the war upon them in the newspapers.
>
> Life, indeed, is almost empty of surprises, mysteries, horrors to this Flapper of 1915. She knows the exact percentage of lunatics among the

children of drunkards. She has learned, from McClure's Magazine, the
purpose and technique of the Twilight Sleep. She knows exactly what the
Wassermann reaction is, and has made up her mind that she will never
marry a man who can't show an unmistakable negative. She knows the
etiology of ophthalmia neatorum [sic]. She has read Christobel Pankhurst
and Ellen Key, and is inclined to think that there must be something in this
new doctrine of free motherhood. She is opposed to the double standard of
morality, and favors a law prohibiting it. . . .

This Flapper has forgotten how to simper; she seldom blushes; it is
impossible to shock her. She saw "Damaged Goods" without batting an eye,
and went away wondering what the row over it was all about. The police of
her city having prohibited "Mrs. Warren's Profession," she read it one rainy
Sunday afternoon, and found it a mass of platitudes. She has heard "Salomé"
and prefers it to "Il Trovatore." She has read "Trilby," "Three Weeks" and
"My Little Sister," and thinks them all pretty dull. She slaved at French in
her finishing school in order to read Anatole France. She admires
Strindberg, particularly his "Countess Julie." She plans to read Havelock
Ellis during the coming summer.

As I have said, a charming young creature. There is something trim and
trig and confident about her. She is easy in her manners. She bears herself
with dignity in all societies. She is graceful, rosy, healthy, appetizing. It is a
delight to see her sink her pearly teeth into a chocolate, a macaroon, even a
potato. There is music in her laugh. She is youth, she is hope, she is
romance—she is wisdom![1]

The pleasures I have in this sketch of the 1915 ingenue are multiple. Here
is not the "whore" or the "madonna" so typically described as image for pre–
World War I filmic woman. Here is neither the threatening lower-class proletariat nor the vicious upper-class capitalist. This is a young, middle-class
woman, perhaps a bit indulged but "healthy." She is more commonly known
by her contemporaries as the "New Woman." Here too is mass media. The
New Woman has become the woman she is by reading newspapers, magazines, plays, novels, and nonfictional tomes. She goes to the opera. She also,
apparently, occasionally sees movies.

Another author describes the early teens as the age of the "repeal of reticence." Agnes Repplier, writing in the Atlantic Monthly (1914), is, however,
not very happy that "the 'Conspiracy of Silence' is broken."[2] As proof she
complains about an incident in a New York theater with "The Lure," in
which Mrs. Emmeline Pankhurst stood up and admonished the audience to
pay heed. "But whatever may be the standard of morality, the standard of
taste (and taste is a guardian of morality) must be curiously lowered when a
woman spectator at an indecent play commends its indecencies to the careful
consideration of the audience."[3]

Two views from the middle class, two opposing sentiments about social and cultural change at the turn of the century. Repplier, however, complains not so much about educating young women. She is more concerned about how that education should occur.

> It was never meant by those who first cautiously advised a clearer understanding of sexual relations and hygienic rules that everybody should chatter freely respecting these grave issues; that teachers, lecturers, novelists, storywriters, militants, dramatists, social workers, and magazine editors should copiously impart all they know, or assume they know to the world. The lack of restraint, the lack of balance, the lack of soberness and common sense, were never more apparent than in the obsession of sex which has set us all a-babbling about matters once excluded from the amenities of conversation.[4]

As Repplier put it, "There is nothing new about the Seven Deadly Sins." What was new, she thought, was *talking* about them. Or as another writer put it in 1913: it was "Sex O'Clock in America."[5]

Repplier criticizes every form of mass media for contributing to this chatter, and she does not neglect the movies. " 'White Slaves' " and " 'Traffic in Souls' . . . claim to be dramatizations of Mr. Rockefeller's vice-commission reports, or of United States Government investigations. 'Original,' 'Authentic,' 'Authorized,' are words freely used in their advertisements. The public is assured that 'care has been taken to eliminate all suggestiveness,' which is in a measure true. When everything is told, there is no room left for suggestions."[6]

This accusation, then, is about representation. And it is the one with which we are familiar. People are seeing and hearing more than they ought. To go beyond a certain degree of communication is tasteless. Discussion of sexuality may, indeed, be a good idea, but that discussion needs *regulation*. What is perhaps not so familiar in this accusation is that the disputations are not particularly class biased. That is, it is some middle-class reformers who are encouraging this talk, while other middle-class individuals advocate restraint. The dispute is not between the rich and the working class, it is among segments of the middle class as guardians of public morality, as seekers of power in terms of the directions of social and cultural change.

One of the lines of development in this book, then, is the relationship of cultural and social conditions in changing America to moving pictures as a major mass medium, one capable of facilitating the representation that a repeal of reticence was occurring, a repeal to be resisted by some members of the middle class but advocated by others. However, while this so-called repeal of reticence finds its subject to be human sexuality, sexuality is often merely the point of attack for discussing other changes. These changes result from the massive transformations from a rural, agrarian, national society to the urban, industrial, global world of the new century. As other historians have aptly described the era of 1880 through World War I, these years produced instabilities of a massive dimension. Immigration, feminism, free love, adultery, class warfare, and a multicultural urban life were widely perceived as threats to the (apparent) stability of the agrarian and small-town Anglo-Saxon republican atmosphere of the United States of the nineteenth century. That image is now recognized as romantic nostalgia for a utopian society that never actually existed, as a fantasy that sustained many American myths. Yet it was an image promoted by many during this period.

Moreover, other signifying systems by which individuals represented themselves seemed to be in flux. Middle-class ministers and merchants, bourgeois landowners, and lawyers believed they had provided the dominant social norms, founded on Christianity, to govern the behavior of the middle class, the landed gentry, and many of the working class. As historian T. J. Jackson Lears and others have argued, as the nineteenth century ended, the moralists' credentials to organize human behavior seemed to be fading in favor of those of the secular scientist.[7] New experts, without religious strictures, founded unprecedented doctrines to govern conduct, based on individuals' well-being within the social unit but also contributing to new senses of who they were. Lears and others use the term *the culture of consumption* to distinguish the transformation from personal identities based on occupation to those organized around consumption.[8] Lears also claims that this new self-definition produces a new moral authority, an "internalized" one. I will show how this representational shift to a culture of consumption reinforced certain types of psychologized characterization, narrational addresses, and plot constructions in the movies. The move to this type of causality is accomplished in part through the *regulation*—not censorship—of images of bad and good women.

Overt discussions in movies of female sexuality during this period were permitted and encouraged as morality tales connected not merely to reaffirming middle-class heterosexual, nonmiscegenous monogamy but also to prescribing appropriate behavior for consuming and helping expand the material wealth of the United States. Desire should be stimulated. This general desire can be coded as sexual. Thus, abstractly, bad women are those people who have yet to learn how to use their new freedoms in ways constructive to the regulated expansion of capital. The New Woman should desire (and purchase products), but within guidelines of balance and reasonableness. Her desire, moreover, is to be regulated by self-awareness. Inappropriate desire—of sexuality or of consumer products—could harm social stability. According to the dominant ideology, this "badness" may be accidental, because of the naïveté of the first- or second-generation immigrant, the country cousin, or the youthful store clerk. This "badness" may be intentional, a consequence of class envy or revenge, or just foolishness and lack of control over appetite. But self-consciousness and self-will could remedy the problem—thus the need to talk about desire.

Consequently, whatever the cause of badness—naïveté, jealousy, foolishness, weak will—for many middle-class reformers of the early twentieth century, a repeal-of-reticence solution was preferred over repression. The time of the repeal was the era of self-help, and some reformers believed that one of the best sources of instruction about personal behavior could be the mass medium of the moving pictures—as long as the right stories were told. Thus, movies could and did participate in this ideological transformation by serving up cautionary tales, fictional fables for educational purposes. However, movies also could fall victim to a contradictory problem for these reformers—for to instruct required representations of that against which the individual was being warned. Hence, how to regulate knowledge, to monitor consumption of the representations, but to investigate fully the issues were the tasks of any progressive text.

Many movies of the teens, then, need to be recognized as regulated, intensive investigations of "woman" and "female sexuality"—not only as meaningful concepts but also as positive and useful social signifiers that buttressed capitalism. The movies of the teens, and of the years thereafter, are also the product of the middle class's association of female sexuality with the new world of urbanization, consumerism, globalization, and, eventually, monopoly capitalism. The New Woman is thus a mobile signifier, acquiring fresh meanings in different contexts.

It is far too simple, then, to think, as some have suggested, that the earliest cinema provided a spectacle of forbidden sights to a proletariat, a spectacle shut down by the middle class from around 1909 on. It is better to recognize that while explicit *sexual actions* are prohibited from sight from the very start of cinema, as a repeal of reticence is encouraged by many in the middle class and as satisfying middle-class norms continue to be the target of film exhibitors, *sexuality itself* becomes a predominant topic. A far more subtle way to consider the contradictory trajectory of American film is to recognize that it is, in fact, the middle class as much as any class that puts sexuality on the agenda for twentieth-century discussion. That sexuality, however, is not limited to its most obvious referent; sexuality also stands in for other concerns.

Movies about heterosexual romance *are* about heterosexual romance, but they are also about other desires—some encouraged, others discouraged by monopoly capitalism in the United States.

For a film industry increasingly geared to appeal to the middle-class audience as its primary consumer, finding the right *regulation* of representation was a complex process. For one thing, the middle class was not uniform in its views about social and cultural changes. Furthermore, even if a group agreed to tackle the moral education of female sexuality, the negotiation between tasteful representation and regulation was tricky. In early American cinema, sexuality is not censored or repressed; it is studied. What is covered up—and then only visually—is only a part of that sexuality: the explicit physical act of copulation.

To achieve this showing and not showing, specific narrational techniques are employed to soften critical responses from more conservative or resisting members of the middle class. As Lea Jacobs points out about the "fallen women" genre, appropriate endings could ameliorate complaints from critics. Appropriate endings are those that obeyed the "rule of compensating moral values"—wrong choices could not be rewarded on earth.[9] Tom Gunning also argues that what helped make a movie "moral" was providing a clear representation of the internal thoughts and motivations of a character.[10] And, as I shall add, additional textual strategies involving sources of causality, types of character motivations, details claimed to be authentic, narrational voices judging character behavior, and comparative subplots also appropriately contextualized troublesome images into moral narratives. Sexuality could easily be studied if filmmakers followed the rules for its discussion.

The Early Cinema and Its Representation of Women

The first years of cinema (1895 to circa 1917) have provided fertile grounds for debating the nature of film as a cultural system. The early one-shot films may appear "primitive" to today's viewers because the referents for the images are lost. However, if the historical context and its spectator are considered, then photographic renditions of popular activities, contemporary events, and famous people and travel spots are quite legible. These moments of spectacle were rapidly narrativized into stories comprehensible to as many viewers as possible across class, ethnic, nation, and gender lines.[11]

Films were from the first days shown in middle-class entertainment centers—big-time vaudeville in the major cities, the opera house in smaller towns. In large cities, the expansion of exhibition sites to small, cheap theaters after 1905 increased access of movies to working-class and immigrant spectators. A nickel admission made movies a viable alternative to penny arcades, amusement parks, dancing halls, and the saloons. Thus, the native-born middle class became much more conscious about movie representations because of the broadening audiences likely to be influenced by them.[12]

It was not merely access on the basis of class distinctions that provoked concern; ethnicity, age, and gender differences were also at stake to the middle class. As Elizabeth Ewen introduces the issue, "Movies [for the immigrant in the 1900–1920 period] also became a translator of the social codes of American society which could now be unraveled, looked at, interpreted, made fun of, understood. They formed a bridge between an older form of culture inadequate to explain the present and a social world of new kinds of behavior, values and possibilities."[13] Ewen notes two contrasting categories: the immigrant, who at this time was likely to be from a different ethnic background than the average U.S. citizen, and the older generation, which tended to be more conservative.

In understanding cultural friction during this period, one of the most salient oppositions was generational conflict. "New kinds of behavior, values and possibilities" affected both the children of new arrivals and those of multigenerational residents. Young shopgirls who flaunted outfits that seemed exaggerated renderings of the haute mode challenged more reserved sensibilites. Seeing youthful clerks swagger through the city streets, picking up dance partners at public halls, and hopping trains to Coney Island or just lounging in lively restaurants bespoke of a new order to social life.

Figure 1.1 reveals this new age. It is a reproduction of John Sloan's "Fun, One Cent." Produced in 1905, the engraving shows five young girls (not boys) peering into movie kinetoscopes. Gender difference in this new culture is a fourth variable of middle-class concern in addition to class, ethnicity, and generation. A significant strand of research on early cinema describes the place of movies in the world of men and children, but especially women. Here I mean literally "the place," since the variable locations for watching films had social connotations.

Where people experienced their entertainment was meaningful. The legitimate theater, big-time vaudeville, and the city opera house were respectable institutions in which proper women and men could watch drama, variety shows, comedic skits, acrobatics, even movies. Other places of amusement, however, were tinged with an element of social danger, partly because of the inevitable commingling of classes or ethnicities in less expensive venues.

Figure 1.1 "Fun, One Cent," by John Sloan. (Delaware Art Museum.)

Women venturing out even in the company of other women might need to pay more heed to their reputations.

Lauren Rabinovitz lists some of the more troublesome public sites: cabarets, dance halls, parks, and nickelodeons. In Chicago around 1907, for example, the Riverview Amusement Park, a microcosm of the larger city, had safer and more risky regions. The "Bowery [was] a self-contained section along Riverview's boundary that included Salome-the-hootchy-kootchy dancer, a Gypsy camp and the 'girlie' show 'Paris by Night.' "[14] Rabinovitz suggests these distractions were "contained" within the public "family" sphere of the park in part by existing at its margins, but nonetheless reveal the possibilities of wide experiences for even the most virtuous young woman. Moreover, while the parks and movie houses "may have liberated women from familial constraints and Victorian sexual restraints, they exercised a new kind of cultural authorization of sexual objectification and of women's roles as consumer and consumed" (p. 71). Women in groups and in the company of young men could partake of available commercial leisures outside of the home, ones their parents may not have condoned.

In fact, as monopoly capitalism refined its strategies of expansion, marketing experts around the turn of the century began acting upon the recognition that women were *the* family members in charge of spending much of the household income. Targeting advertisements to those doing the consuming seemed a logical practice. Women had always been in the public sphere as consumers, but the new consumer culture began privileging and promoting that identity. Woman's attention and her needs were focal points for retailers. By the 1920s, argues Miriam Hansen, "women's status within the public sphere [had] shifted from a discourse of domesticity to an updated ideology of consumption, superimposing models of feminine virtue and female skills with appeals of pleasure, glamour and leisure, of sensuality, eroticism, and exoticism."[15] Hansen's observation seems particularly significant since the transition to this new ideology had to have been occurring in the teens.

Superimposing sensuality over femininity does not, however, liberate women in patriarchy to seek their own sexual and gendered identities. Rather, definitions of women continue to be constructed in relation to others. Now, however, sexuality as one signifier of woman's essence and agency does take on a more positive connotation. It indicates a range of possibilities: a lively, energetic, healthy, directed vitality—all necessary for a new age in capitalist expansion. Although I could argue that the representation of a repeal of reticence was necessary just to maintain the political economy of the United States, I hesitate to push the argument, since other factors are also involved in transforming attitudes about discussing sexuality (see chapter 2). At this moment sexuality still needs organization: a *regulated sexuality is the proper synthesis* of the prior terms that had separated sexual pleasure from maternal proprieties. Within bounds of a (heterosexual) marriage (or its likelihood), women could enjoy sexuality and sensual pleasures without being bad. It might even be good—for the economy and the country!

Thus, sexuality's representation should be understood through historical, not essentialist, terms. Following Michel Foucault and others, Stephen Heath exaggerates for emphasis the emptiness of the meaning of the term outside of its local context:

> Sexuality is without the importance ascribed to it in our contemporary
> society (Western capitalism); it is without that importance because it does
> not exist as such, because there is no such thing as sexuality; what we have
> experienced and are experiencing is the fabrication of a "sexuality," the
> construction of something called "sexuality" through a set of representations
> . . . that propose and confirm, that make up this sexuality to which we are
> then referred and held in our lives, a whole *sexual fix* precisely; the much-
> vaunted "liberation" of sexuality, our triumphant emergence from the "dark

ages," is thus not a liberation but a myth, an ideology, the definition of a new mode of conformity (that can be understood, moreover, in relation to the capitalist system, the production of a commodity "sexuality").[16]

As would be expected, Heath qualifies this statement, but his point is made: What we have available to us as knowledges of our own selves are constructed socially and culturally through representations. Furthermore, these knowledges are produced in relation to other, and fundamental, developments in society and the economy.

When "woman" is no longer defined only by her role in the mode of production (namely, as wife and mother) but now also as a consumer with a "lifestyle," *the cultural meaning of sexuality changes*. Sexual behavior is not studied through a perspective emphasizing just a mode of production (woman as bearer of children for the workforce); sexual activity needs to be redefined in relation to lifestyles (woman as working girl, consummate shopper, gourmet consumer). Thus, the foundations in the mode of production and consumption upon which sexual representations were established changed, and social identities were discursively redefined.[17] Such changes were potentially a good idea, and it seemed so to many people of the era.

If women are now in the public sphere—as both producers and consumers of the material wealth of industrial America—women's movements into areas previously not accepted may now be advantageous. Thus in Sloan's engraving, this new and risky indulgence is gently depicted. Surrounding the arcade where the girls gather are posters advertising the flicks: "Girls in their Night Gowns / Spicy" and "The Naughty Girls." Women are both subject and spectator—even if somewhat covertly—for these films.

Sloan was part of the new school of artists who were painting the everyday life of America, much as contemporary realist and naturalist writers depicted its range of classes and peoples. Sloan provided newspaper and journal illustrations for *McClure's* and *The Masses*, progressive journals of the era.[18] It is difficult to discern much of his personal view of this "fun," but assuming the image has some verisimilar credibility, I am struck by the expressions on the women's faces: they are laughing, clearly enjoying their access to a realm once, and probably still slightly, deemed off-limits to them. While some people might want to label the girls "bad," they might take personal pleasure in resisting that labeling. The women, seeing what they were not supposed to be seeing, and knowing that they were in a marginal zone, might well have been empowered to at least question the previous limitations of that access.

Did they learn anything new from the movies? Not much, I would think. "Sporty" films that still exist from the pre-1909 era show nothing about the human body that could not be seen just as well in respectable settings— museum paintings, live vaudeville, art photographs, or the more scandalous popular living pictures in which people dressed in tights reproduced famous paintings on the stage. Then, too, less appropriate places such as the margins of fairs could introduce young people to bodies of foreign dancers.[19] Perhaps the thrill was in the small narratives, through their tease and delay. But even when Suzie finally pulls down the curtain or the young miss straightens out her skirt on Twenty-Third Street, only the most perverse mind would be able to call "obscene" what actually had appeared on the screen (although it could be considered tasteless, perhaps, to an eye preferring reticence).[20]

Now, a bone of contention may have existed in terms of the effects of see-ing the previously unseen. Would individuals titillated by the possibility of watching the forbidden then flesh out fantasies in real life? Would young girls, now out on their own for an evening of amusement, adopt the behavior of "the naughty girls"? Scholars of film history contend that that was, indeed, the worry of the middle class.[21]

Two solutions for the middle class existed, however. One was to forbid any naughty representations. The other was to narrativize those representations. In fact, like Matthew Arnold's prescription for literary studies, some people argued that movies could be educational. Lary May summarizes the view: "Movies could function, as one reformer phrased it, like a 'grand social worker.' "[22] As I shall suggest, both views—favoring censorship and advocat-ing regulation—existed within the middle class. No one doubts the potential significance of going to the movies; what is in question is whether that is more harmful than good. Causal relations and appropriate solutions based on those assumptions are then debated. The middle class and the working class, with their varied cultural and social differences, were no more homogeneous in the 1910s than they are in the 1990s.[23]

Obviously, one of the major concerns about representation was the site of "woman"—more specifically, woman as human agent. What did a woman do? What did she want? Why did she act as she did? Woman's agency also in-voked questions of ontology—a woman's essence. As theorists have pointed out, trying to define the essence of woman by opposition also supposedly de-fines man, or, actually, vice versa, since in patriarchy man is asserted to be the original locus of meaning. Isolating and analyzing the transitory object (here "woman") is an ideological maneuver attempting to stabilize an eternal sub-ject (here "man").[24] Consequently, the *way* Michael Rogin approaches the image of woman in movies of this period is compatible with this book's aim. In an insightful analysis of D. W. Griffith's *The Birth of a Nation*, Rogin asserts that

> traditional patriarchical forms were under siege at the end of the nineteenth century . . . from what was conceived of as nature, from regressive forces as well as progressive ones. . . . And women, whether out in the world or confined to the home, stood for that regressive, disorganizing power. Partly, in their efforts at emancipation, they posed a threat to order in their own right. Partly they stood as a symbol and accessible scapegoat for more distant social and political disruptions. Instead of providing a refuge from modern disorder, the New Woman fueled it.
>
> The New Woman appears everywhere at the end of the nineteenth century. . . . As working girl, fashion-conscious wife, or lady of the night, the New Woman represented the modern city. But even where women stood for fecundity and reproduction . . . [they were also] imaged as monstrous and chameleonlike. [Their] permeable boundaries absorbed children and men.[25]

However, images that emblematize social change (such as the changing notion of "woman" or "mother") are also signifiers of meaning and prognostications for the future. I will argue that visions of woman or the New Woman are as multiple and conflicted as the narratives in which she appears, and she does not always stand for chaos and monstrosity. Some 1910s film stories may be about the New Woman as symbol of contemporary culture's disorder—such images are common in D. W. Griffith's films. However, to equate his images with the era's (as Rogin and Hansen do) is a mistake. The ideology of Griffith's films is one version (and not even a coherent one) of woman, but not the only version or even, I believe, the dominant one among movies of this period.[26]

In the cinema of this era, many other versions of woman and the New Woman exist, and among these are narratives about hopeful alternatives—for women and for society—and about *positive* possibilities of the New Woman, as well as chaotic ones. Furthermore, the hopes, as the films articulate them, are not necessarily tied to fecundity and reproduction, but sometimes to personal liberation from stale images of woman's nature and essence as maternal and domestic. The New Woman, thus, was sometimes productive for thinking about options and imagining utopias for women. In fact, positive, regulated representations of the New Woman might well serve the developing consumer culture.[27]

Taboo Topics

A fundamental upheaval in the social formation at the turn of the century provoked an epistemological investigation of representation. Both outright censorship and the more covert regulationist positions proceed along these lines. Locate images that are troubling, then either prohibit their appearance—even listing in written codes what cannot be tolerated and thus actually verifying the existence of that very thing not to be mentioned—or recognize it but punish it. This is censorship as fetishistic or sadistic behavior.

Research on early cinema has stressed censorship as a significant social response to some representations of woman and sexual activity, but scholars have recently argued that censorship is a complex act not reducible to a set of apparently restrictive laws imposed by specific governmental or industrial groups. In her *Cinema, Censorship and Sexuality, 1909–1925*, Annette Kuhn breaks with a former view that she labels the "prohibition/institutions" model. Such a model, she writes, considers "censorship as a *problem* of a certain kind," one of *"interference."*

Drawing from the work of Foucault, Kuhn proposes an alternative model, which I will label as the "eventualization/diagnosis" one. This model stresses an account of "the conditions of operation and effectivity of film censorship," of "processes and practices" (the eventualization).[28] Instead of seeing a law or a shot edited out of a final product as a static object, this model considers the activity of censoring to be determined and causal (the diagnosis). The model promotes the recognition of censorship as operating within broader social contexts than the specific institutions most obviously involved in prohibition. The object of inquiry consequently is not any specific board of censorship (such as the National Board of Censorship in the 1910s or the Breen Office of the 1930s) but the wider social and cultural ideologies determining those groups' activities.[29]

More important, the eventualization/diagnosis model stresses the productivity involved in censorship: "In certain circumstances, therefore, power and regulation can be productive, rather than—or as well as—repressive, operations. Regulation, in consequence, may be understood not so much as an imposition of rules upon some preconstituted entity, but as an ongoing and always provisional process of constituting objects from and for its own practices" (p. 7). What Kuhn implies is that censorship *creates* meanings. This position asserts the social and cultural significance of definition by denial and marginalization. Casting out is meaningful. It is thus as "productive" as explicit representation is, although in a more perverse way.[30] Kuhn prefers the term *regulation* to *censorship* because it "captures not only the instrumental and processual character of the power relations involved in institutional practices . . . but also the simultaneously productive and prohibitive logic of their operations."[31] Productivity occurs in the creation of meanings of what counts as resistance and transgression as a consequence of censorship or regulation.

In practice, two methods for regulating troublesome images have been generated from two different institutional sites: regulation through the excision of images (censorship) and containment through specific narrativization (regulation). These two notions, although theoretically distinct, tend to fall into line for the situation I will be discussing. The distinction in any case is somewhat slippery since filmmakers may choose to avoid images they know will not pass official censors, thus regulating them by excision. Moreover, some public legal bodies were more tolerant than others about the effects of narrativization to compensate for images that on their own might require prohibition. Nonetheless, the operational value of both terms lies in their status as historical markers.

Power is a key term in the eventualization/diagnosis model, for Foucault did not perceive equity among parties involved in defining categories of taboos. As Linda Williams interprets Foucault, "the modern compulsion to speak incessantly about sex" does not imply that the woman's point of view has ever been represented[32]—or, obviously in our society, lesbian, gay, or bisexual subjectivities either. "Women [have never] been the true subjects of sexual art or sexual knowledge" (p. 3) because the representations have always been within a "dominant male [heterosexual] economy" (p. 4; interpolation mine). Lea Jacobs concurs when considering the events in the early 1930s: "In my view, the pressure on the industry to regulate representations of sexuality is best understood as a function of a set of assumptions about spectatorship, specifically female spectatorship, current in the thirties."[33] Woman-as-object was to be investigated, while women (and men) as real spectators were to be protected—by patriarchy.[34]

Thus, productive as censorship of sexual behavior might have been in theory, the last two centuries in the United States speak to the dominance of some images rather than others, despite instances of resistance and transgression. Talk is not equally distributed among those who would speak. For example, pornographic films as a genre of codified practices responding to the productivity of censorship must be read ambiguously since they are not, until recently, productions from a woman's point of view.

Moreover, the history of their appearance is important to note. The earliest three films, well articulated in conventions of the genre, that Williams found in the Kinsey Institute for Sex Research in Sex, Gender, and Reproduction—Am Abend (circa 1910, Germany), El satario (circa 1907–12, Argentina), and A Free Ride/A Grass Sandwich (circa 1915–19, United

States)—arrive as the individual countries construct public and institutional methods for censoring movies. As far as we have evidence,[35] nothing more visually explicit than the physical display of a woman's nude body exists prior to the overt declaration of sexual copulation as off-limits (or at least beyond the movie frame). Only after censorship defined the sanctioned limitations of representation does the illicit appear.[36] Most people did not see pornography in this period; they did, however, see movies representing desire so explicitly that it could be imagined.

However, calls for control of images prior to 1910 were less directed toward supposed improprieties for visually displaying or implying nonsanctioned sexual behavior. Middle-class critics of the movies were much more upset about representations related to criminal behavior that were displayed on the screen. Reformers mentioned sexual indiscretions as worthy of concern, but they focused as much or more so on movies that might provide inappropriate occupational role models for young boys and girls. Censorship and regulation entered the movie business as much to guard against the genres of westerns, melodramas, and adventure and detective stories, which were seen as promoting criminal behavior among young people, as to prohibit the vice of pornography.

Woman and woman's sexuality were not taboo as topics but were a focal point for understanding a changing social order. As Christian Metz has diagnosed the cinema, our theaters have been "houses of tolerance," liminoid sites for social and cultural production.[37] And Williams reminds us that, "according to Foucault, then, the proliferating medical, psychological, juridical, and pornographic discourses of sexuality have functioned as transfer points of knowledge, power, and pleasure."[38]

If woman is situated at the intersection of one of these transfer points, a useful cognitive map is generated. Other signifiers can also be so located: man, for instance, or child, or Latino, or queer, and so forth. Each social formation finds specific bodies to identify as a transfer point, specific identities to privilege in trying to control and master social change, and identities to narrativize. Threats to social stability are ostensibly mobilized through a woman's sexuality, but covertly designed to investigate social transformations. Furthermore, plots often offer contrary or reformist versions of woman's agency. A conclusion to a film or a narrational voice may produce containment: female sexuality regulated in terms of both its proportionate desire and its object orientation. However, the struggle for that containment is filled with opportunities and options for individuals of varied sexes, gender identities, and sexual preferences. As I shall show, talking about sexuality in the movies was extremely productive for prewar America.

The United States at the Turn of the Century

In a 1913 essay, *Current Opinion* credits William Marion Reedy with saying that America was at "sex o'clock." Listing all sorts of instances of a "former reticence on matters of sex . . . giving way to a frankness that would even startle Paris," *Current Opinion* mentions exemplary events from the past three years: Reginald Wright Kauffman's stories about white slavery, Mrs. Warren's profession, the *Damaged Goods* drama about venereal disease, and John D. Rockefeller Jr.'s real-life vice investigations. *Current Opinion* queries, however, "Is this overemphasis of sex a symptom of a new moral awakening or is it a sign that the morbidity of the Old World is overtaking the New? Does it indicate a permanent change in our temper or is it merely the concomitant of the movement for the liberation of woman from the shackles of convention that will disappear when society has readjusted itself to the New Woman and the New Man? Has it struck sex o'clock permanently or will time soon point to another hour?"[39]

Taking up Reedy's position, *Current Opinion* agrees that in this new era "the emancipated woman, knowing good and evil, will choose her man rather than be chosen." Furthermore, it would be inappropriate to correlate the New Woman with those who " 'go astray' The sexually loose women are not the so-called advanced women. They are the parasite women, the indulged women, the women who do not think." Reedy and *Current Opinion* go on to argue two causes for sexual deviancy: poverty and "the hedonistic materialistic philosophy" that the rich are teaching the poor.

Dr. Cecile L. Greil, a "Socialist," is also quoted in the essay in *Current Opinion*. Greil believes that "vanity and love and sport . . . make more prostitutes than economic pressure and exploitation." Moreover, society forgets that adolescents are a "seething turbulent ocean underneath. . . . 'We surround that young, passionate, bursting blossom with every temptation to break down its resistant power, lure it into sentient pulsating desire and eroticism by lurid literature, moving pictures, tango dances, suggestive songs, cabarets, noise, music, light, life, rhythm, everywhere, until the senses are throbbing with leashed-in physical passion. . . . So one day the leash snaps, and another boy or girl is outside the pale.' " The only conclusion *Current Opinion* reaches is that "radicals and conservatives, Free-thinkers and Catholics, all seem to believe in solving the sex problem by education, but as to the method that is to be followed there are abysmal differences of opinion" (p. 114).

The method for salvation depends upon the assumed cause, and *Current Opinion* explicitly lists some possibilities: poverty, hedonism, indulgence, foolishness, natural sexual passion. Implicit causes are also embedded in the text: foreign mores affecting the United States, changing norms for women's behavior, media, and new entertainments. In describing postmodernism, Fredric Jameson uses the notion of a "cultural logic." I would like here to discuss the cultural *illogic* of turn-of-the-century America as it is displayed through the set of motifs that appear over and over again in public discourse about sexuality. These motifs involve oppositions of class (the rich versus the middle class versus the poor), nationality (Americans versus foreigners), ethnicity and race (Anglo-Saxons versus everyone else), sex and gender behavior, and age. This public discourse includes the reformist agendas of religious leaders and social scientists, both groups that claim a higher right to prescribe social solutions. Panaceas are suggested for all sorts of evils, but I shall focus on views about "bad women."

This is a "cultural illogic" because systems of representations are always within complex environments that prevent structured and totalized order, just as social life itself may be at odds with its self-representations.[40] The presence of residual and emergent practices complicate any attempt to represent a period with so much order as to render it perfectly intelligible. Although the period of 1880 to 1920 is often described as having certain general characteristics, coherence is not one of them. The era is one of major transition in American economics, society, politics, and, consequently, culture. Part of the transformation between 1880 and 1920 is the emergence of the woman as a worker in the public sphere. Kathy Peiss provides the details: "Young, unmarried working-class women, foreign-born or daughters of immigrant parents, dominated the female labor force in the period from 1880 to 1920. In 1900, four-fifths of the 343,000 wage-earning women in New York were single, and almost one-third were aged sixteen to twenty."[41] Moreover, the types of jobs women held moved them into a new heterosocial public sphere. Women had worked as domestic laborers and in small sweat shops; now they were in "department stores, large factories, and offices" (p. 35). Young working women's experiences were widened by intermingling among the sexes and with married people. "Adolescents formed social clubs, organized entertainments, and patronized new commercial amusements, shaping, in effect, a working-class youth culture expressed through leisure activity. . . . [T]hey sought adventure in dance halls, cheap theaters, amusement parks, excursion boats, and picnic grounds. Putting on finery, promenading the streets, and staying late at amusement resorts became an important cultural style for many working women" (pp. 56–57). Peiss aptly points out that the late 1800s New Woman was more an invention for the middle class that "questioned the 'natural' division of women and men's lives into separate spheres" (p. 163) while the single, working-class woman actually lived this new public life.

Historians of America describe modern culture as affected not only by shifting employment patterns related to gender distinctions but by the immigration of the late 1800s. The United States, like other industrializing capitalist nations, was already reaching out to peripheral nations. The "Orient" represented not merely an array of exotic places but also economic opportunities. This period indexes the transformation of the United States from a rural to an urban society, from a separation of the spheres of men (public) and women (private) to a publicly heterosocial situation into which women of various classes were encouraged to travel to lesser or greater degrees. It is also a period of economic growth and political influence favoring the globalization of American capitalist interests.[42] Thus, immigration and imperialism provide a wider variety of cultural options to traditional America. America was experiencing (and needed to experience) a much more diverse cultural exchange.

This is also a period in which class structures changed. Urban growth came from immigrants and from farmers, with the latter being more significant numerically. However, as urbanization developed, so did the middle class. Between 1870 and 1910 the entire U.S. population increased over two and one-third times. The old middle class, categorized by Richard Hofstadter as business entrepreneurs and independent professionals, grew at about the same rate, while the working and farmer classes tripled in numbers. A new middle class, however, multiplied eightfold. These were technicians, salaried professionals, clerks, salespeople, and public-service personnel. This new middle class in 1870 was about one-third of the total class; in 1910 Hofstadter puts it at two-thirds.

This change and growth did not come without conflict.[43] Although geographical mobility was great, not much upward class movement was possible for the lower class. The middle class experienced somewhat more mobility, with an appearance of improvement in occupational categories. Both the lower and middle classes accumulated property. This improvement had its costs, however. Wages were in most cases low, necessitating multiple members of the family to work if mobility was to be achieved. Employment conditions were generally unregulated, and laborers were still dependent on the goodwill of their employers for any social welfare benefits. Unionization was in its most turbulent and violent days of formation.

One-eighth of the population at the turn of the century owned seven-eighths of the wealth. These rich also began to behave differently. Lary May calls the changes in the 1890s "dramatic."[44] Previously, wealthy individuals were somewhat circumspect in their lifestyles; now, they built "lavish hotels, mansions, and museums along Fifth Avenue or the Lake Front" (p. 32). They also found their entertainments, as did the working class, in public, commercial establishments, making more visible the disparity between their leisure possibilities and those of the other classes, while at the same time the upper and lower classes began intermingling in the same entertainment sites. Theaters, new music and dance halls, fancy hotel restaurants with lobster dinners were the haunts of many wealthy people. But upper-class men also visited vaudeville, cabarets, dance halls, and movie houses. In New York City in 1905 no cabarets existed; by World War I, twenty were operating.[45]

A strikingly vivid example of both the split and the encounter between the classes was the scandal over the 1906 killing of Stanford White by Harry K. Thaw in one of these new public places—the roof café of Madison Square Garden. Both White and Thaw were upper class (White was an important architect; Thaw, the son of a Pittsburgh railroad millionaire).[46] The girl in the case, Evelyn Nesbit, was working class, supposedly an actress. Neither gentleman was a moral innocent. Thaw was described as "the most profligate" of Americans in Paris and was nicknamed "Mad Harry" (pp. 12–13). White had an apartment "decorated in unusual fashion" (p. 12). At the trial, Nesbit described the decor: "There was a red velvet swing. Mr. White put us [Nesbit and another woman] on this swing and we would swing up to the ceiling. They had a big Japanese umbrella on the ceiling, so when we were pushed up very high, our feet went through it" (p. 60). Nesbit claimed that, after a series of meetings, one evening White drugged her champagne, and she woke up in a bedroom lined with mirrors. Thaw argued that he had saved Nesbit from this horrible life by marrying her. Moreover, his attorneys made the case that Thaw suffered from "hereditary insanity" (a code for syphilis) and that he was justified in killing White because of "dementia Americana"—the "unwritten law" that a man whose wife has been violated by another man can take revenge. This case and the details of its testimony made the headlines and was common knowledge among all classes, genders, and ethnic groups. In 1907 a filmed version appeared: *The Unwritten Law: A Thrilling Drama Based on the Thaw-White Case*. Basically a reenactment of the most scandalous images, *The Unwritten Law* became one of the reference points for reformers who argued for censorship of the movies.

It is important to recognize the threat of such visible conspicuous consumption and gratification of desires. Class differences in terms of material goods were already obvious and dangerous enough, but such behavior by the rich was setting a bad moral example, particularly if it was preying on the poor. This case combined public leisure spaces in the new urban environment, unmoderated consumption, unbridled sexual desire, the abuse of the poor by the rich, the violation by trickery of a woman, and a sort of exotic eroticism (it was a *Japanese* umbrella!). The White-Thaw Case was but an exemplar of the dramatic changes being witnessed by a twentieth-century American, focused on the victimization of a woman who seems to have been led astray and the lack of remorse evidenced among the people involved.

Yet America's upper classes and their social mores were on the whole perceived less as a problem and more as enviable. Capitalist expansion into new markets might provide riches for many good citizens irrespective of their class background. By the conclusion of the nineteenth century, for all practical purposes the United States had reached the boundaries of its national territory. Furthermore, technologies such as the railroad, telegraph, and telephone made distances and time shrink and amalgamated regions into a nation-state. European countries had already reached out to control foreign sources of raw materials and new markets. America's version of its own imperialist age was now also under way.[47] The rhetoric of this expansion was to distinguish between Europeans' acquisition of territories and peoples to rule and America's mere support of its nation's trade. Additionally, a use of social Darwinism articulated a growing ethnocentrist belief that Anglo-Saxons were justified in taking advantage of primitive or failed nation-states since they were obviously more fit.[48]

However, that taking care of the "self" also produced internal and external racism. African-Americans were only one obvious group of perceived others against which to guard.[49] In his classic study, Oscar Handlin traces several waves of immigration, culminating in the late 1890s through 1914 with the arrival of Mediterranean and Slavic immigrants.[50] The concentration of these immigrants in the tight urban space of the new city life provided a good opportunity for seeing the increasing magnitude of ethnicities. Other groups also received xenophobic attention, especially the Chinese and Japanese.[51]

Beyond the antiradical theme (foreigners were the ones fomenting labor unrest) and an anti-Catholic, anti-Jewish religious distinction was a third, ethnic-racial one: "the old idea that America belongs peculiarly to the An-glo-Saxon race,"[52] or that Anglo-Saxons represented the highest level of hu-man development. During the 1890s, people as influential as Henry Cabot Lodge (the president of the American Economic Association), Nathaniel S. Shaker (dean of the Lawrence Scientific School of Harvard), and Francis A. Walker (president of MIT) articulated such views. In particular, Walker gath-ered statistics that indicated the birthrate for native-born Americans was lower than that for immigrants. The formation of ancestry societies dates from this decade.[53]

Although viewing the nation as a great melting pot was one response to the conditions of increasing multiculturalism, another was the intensification of racist rhetoric. Handlin writes about Madison Grant, an anthropologist at New York City's American Museum of Natural History, who published in 1916 *The Passing of the Great Race*. Grant writes, "These immigrants [Medi-terraneans, Balkans, Poles] adopt the language of the native American, they wear his clothes, they steal his name, and they are beginning to take his women." To permit assimilation was to encourage "racial hybrids": "ethnic horrors that will be beyond the powers of future anthropologists to unravel" (p. 185).

Indeed, the new culture of consumption seems to have reordered priorities for many of the middle class. Concerned leaders represented wives as no longer believing in their destiny as perpetual baby makers; rhetorics of self-improvement and quality of life justified birth control. In the positive version, the New Woman was educated to the widening world around her; she was also a perceptive consumer who rationally organized her domestic life through judicious ventures into the public stores and streets of urban America. This new identity as a careful consumer was often promoted throughout the cul-ture of the turn-of-the-century United States. In the negative version, the woman was abandoning her essential nature of mothering children.

Regulating consumption is necessary for capitalist expansion. Consump-tion supplies profits for its economic source, but it is wasteful for consumers to desire products not available or not to desire what is available. Consumption needs to be *stimulated*; it also needs to be *directed*. As capitalism expanded, and the necessities of life were satisfied, an obvious direction in consumption was toward personal comfort. Lears calls this the "flight from pain."[54] He also notes, however, that such a flight required an altered ideology. Formerly, "per-petual work, compulsive saving, civic responsibility, and a rigid morality of self-denial" governed the social behavior of the upper and middle classes.[55] After 1910, "a new set of values sanctioning periodic leisure, compulsive spending, apolitical passivity, and an apparently permissive (but subtly coercive) morality of individual fulfillment" was available to guide personal actions. Yet permitting personal desire to flow in any direction could not be accommodated to the needs of capitalism. "Freed from older constraints, each masterless man needed a moral gyroscope to keep him on course or else market society might dissolve into a chaos of self-seeking individuals. The destruction of old oppressive forms created new problems of social control."[56]

Lears hypothesizes that while the Protestant church was once a major, if not the major, institution for cultural hegemony in the United States, advertising now took its place—or advertising as the articulation of the common sense of the democratic and social whole.[57] In smaller and tighter social groups, "intersubjective comparisons [present] a limited set of role and behavioral models to guide tastes." In the modern, urban, global, and mobile culture of twentieth-century America, earlier connections were disappearing and an " 'open set' of intersubjective comparisons were available; advertising [became] one of the most important vehicles for presenting, suggesting, and reflecting an unending series of possible comparative judgments."[58]

The promise, then, of the new urbanization and globalization of America was also its danger. The multiplicity of consumption possibilities proliferated as did the disparity in wealth. Additionally, immigrant cultures provided *too many* options in *too rapid* a transition in capitalism to be easily handled. Failure to secure goods and experiences marked out as useful or even necessary could produce conflict between goals socially indicated as desirable and the actual means of realizing them.[59]

Desire had to be coordinated with the organization of capitalist production. Leach describes how by the 1840s and 1850s, shopping is represented as a *woman's* activity. He calculates that "by 1915 women were doing between 80 and 85 percent of the consumer purchasing in the United States."[60] Women as the major consumers were also perceived as potentially problematic.[61] Leach indicates that education about public consumption had to go hand in hand with its pleasures. "Through a multitude of display devices, merchants 'encouraged' women to 'indulge their own desires,' to buy without much thought or reflection." But middle-class women "were dependent on male incomes." Leach details several court cases in which husbands and wives charged each other with neglect—either of personal needs or of the family's ability to respond to unrestrained consumption.

In discussing this transformation, Leach concludes that the culture of consumption, or at least the activities of gratification via purchasing products, reconfigured the association of the public sphere solely with men. Merchants were quick to address their female consumers on whatever grounds might appeal to them. Department stores supported suffragette activities, letting their workers march in parades and selling suffragette supplies (Macy's was an official outlet in 1912).[62]

However, desire did exceed its regulation, producing cautionary fables of learning to avoid "bad" behavior along with the court cases. Simon J. Bronner argues that in *Sister Carrie* (1900), *The Damnation of Theron Ware* (1896), and *The Spenders* (1902) unrestrained or misdirected desires are involved in events leading to the protagonist's decline.[63]

The era at the turn of the century, then, provided both promise and danger. Diversity could produce new experiences; it could also produce unsustainable differences that might threaten the status quo held dear by some members of the middle class. Woman as the center of these changes—in actual fact as worker and consumer—would need to be directed to participate in this transforming social formation in ways useful to the expansion of capital in an orderly fashion.

Directed Social Change

Religious explanations for strife among individuals increasingly had little currency in a social formation witnessing these effects of industrial capitalism. The concept of a moral universe (perhaps mechanically wound up) was seriously challenged by theories of an amoral one, producing conflicting attitudes about assigning responsibility to individuals or the labels "good" and "bad." Even if robber barons were equated with the devil, they were also bringing the United States into dominancy within a world order. Was a prostitute a bad woman or a victim? Protestant religions, dominant in the United States during the nineteenth century, stressed the individual's responsibility for moral behavior. Some individuals thought reform was possible if reformers just appealed to "the sympathy of intelligent and educated people."[64]

During this time many individuals attempted to direct social change through reform activities. Robert H. Walker writes that reform has appeared in "a number of shapes and guises." As such "the reform record is a prime source for the discovery of cultural priorities." In theorizing the causes for reform movements, Walker writes that recognizing diversity and desiring equity are primary factors.[65] Reform in its manifestations at the turn of the century took a number of directions, but much of it is bound into the stakes that I have been developing: urbanization, resulting in an intermingling of classes; globalization, producing a recognition of ethnic and racial diversity; heterosocialization of labor, opening the occupations of worker and shopper in the public sphere to women. These are all grounded in such recognitions of difference.

Theoreticians of reform movements believe that two types of reform solutions predominate. One is a glance backward—arguing that in the past things were better (or at least not as bad). Lears associates this type with those he calls "republican moralists," although others, such as the avant-garde and even the populists, might be so categorized. This backward glance is an "antimodernist" view. The other reform type is a cautious embracing of the future or perhaps even a "cult of science and technical rationality, its worship of material progress."[66] In this "modernist" view, cities and technologies, if rationally organized and developed, will ease the burdens of drudgery, liberating individuals from hardship and illness.

Two major reform movements eventually had less success than a third. Populists and socialists were finally outreformed by progressives, but in 1900 the direction the nation would take was uncertain. Although the political astuteness of the populists has been debated, Hofstadter has analyzed the main currents of their positions and determined them to be utopian in hoping for a golden age of harmony among citizens, founded on the "agrarian myth" that such a civilization once existed. Socialism was another political option during the period, well into World War I. Although a postwar change in the economy gave the appearance of declining inequities, overt suppression by the government also contributed to a temporary submerging of those views. Ultimately, the progressives, aligned with the new middle class, would dominate social policy.[67]

At this time, utopian proposals and reform movements flourished in response to social conflict. In the years between 1889 and 1912 approximately one hundred utopian (and dystopian) novels were published. The best-known example is Edward Bellamy's *Looking Backward*, published in 1888.[68] Charles J. Rooney Jr. has studied these books, locating the occupations of the writers and surveying their contents. He indicates that the favorite occupation for utopian writers was journalism, but "teaching, politics and reform, business and invention, the ministry, medicine, and engineering" are also represented.[69] These careers in large part index the growing professional middle class. Rooney also has listed the problems and solutions these utopian works presented, the most common being greed and selfishness (in 76 of the 106 books surveyed). Thus, the individual becomes the focus for reform as much as any larger structural or institutional condition.

Other economic problems needing reform included the decline in charity work, conflicts between the classes, the power of monopolies, and a scarcity of capital.[70] In fact, Kenneth M. Roemer thinks that other than "the labor question," the "religious" question was among the strongest concerns in this fiction. Utopian writers thought American religion had become "irrelevant," not dealing with secular evils or the advances of science. Many theologians agreed, and the "social gospel" movement tried to respond.[71]

Social sciences were also stimulated by reform thinking and ethical duty. The participation of American sociology in directed social change will be especially significant for what happens to the movies in terms both of individuals involved and of broader notions of how to educate and regulate society. The official founding of the American Social Science Association in 1866 included in its constitution the following objectives: "to guide the public mind to the best practical means of promoting the Amendment of Laws, the Advancement of Education, the Prevention and Repression of Crime, the Reformation of Criminals, and the progress of Public Morality."[72] These duties articulate the arguments of reformers: "morality, rationality, and feasibility." According to Günther Brandt, early American sociology "regarded diversity of beliefs and interests as inimical to social order and advocated the rule of public opinion enlightened by the findings of science."[73] The examination of a visible diversity became sociology's domain. Some individuals, such as Lester Ward, attributed variation in classes and their behaviors to the environment, while a minority considered lower classes inescapable but still the responsibility of the rest of the population. During the period of 1890 to 1914, the term *social engineering* achieved currency. By 1910, some four hundred schools and universities were teaching courses in sociology.[74]

Progressivism as a movement seems to include both the professional and the amateur, both the scientist and the moral reformer. Robert Wiebe agrees that all sectors of the middle class found in progressivism hope for a better order. Wiebe believes that the older middle class tended to envision a return to entrepreneurial capitalism and individual opportunities for success. The newer middle class yearned for a rationalized economy, intelligent administration, and lessening of social unrest.[75]

Between 1898 and 1917, progressivism emerged as the leading reformist discourse. I assume progressivism was a particular version of the more general reform response to diversity and inequity.[76] Many scholars believe that the phenomena of progressive reform activities were strongest among the urban middle class. As such, progressivism can be considered a liberal reaction to head off more serious structural upheaval, which was the threat from other organized reform groups such as populists or socialists.[77]

The ferment of radical labor movements and the generally hostile environment of slum tenements, impure foods, and inadequate health care required state intervention for progressives. Using the government when necessary to discipline people who were evil or misguided (depending on the causality attributed to the behavior) became part of policymaking in lieu of any fundamental structural changes in economic or political arrangements.[78]

Rationality, morality, and feasibility were sometimes called "efficiency," a term modern businesses also liked, and covertly indicated how middle-class progressive professionals could see others in the upper class as the enemies while perceiving themselves as saintly entrepreneurs.[79] Beyond the class bias in some progressive activity, Hofstadter also suggests that nationalism was implicit in late progressivism. When President Wilson went to the peace conferences after World War I, he went without demands. This was because "the United States was to be a kind of non-Europe or anti-Europe. Where European institutions were old, static, decadent, and aristocratic, American institutions were to be modern, progressive, moral, and democratic."[80]

Progressives, like other reformers, used journalism and fiction to proselytize their vision of a social harmony. Lloyd's *Wealth against Commonwealth* (1894, on Standard Oil), Steffens's *The Shame of the Cities* (1904, about bossism), and Ida Tarbell's *History of the Standard Oil Company* (1904) were instances of investigations of corruption in big business that, in an era of competitive journalism, produced great interest on the part of readers ready to read lurid tales. A combination of realist, naturalist, and melodramatic aesthetics, the "reality-based" narratives portrayed corruption, often by focusing on stories of specific people harmed by the machines of industry. By 1906, President Roosevelt, believing such reporting was beginning to undermine society, attacked the activity, labeling its practiioners "muckrakers." Although other intellectual journals such as *Atlantic Monthly*, *Harper's*, *Century*, and *Scribner's* had produced such essays, aggressive new mass market serials, particularly *McClure's Magazine* but also *Hampton's*, differentiated themselves by this brand of reporting. *McClure's* may not especially have been a voice of progressivism (some of its essays invoked arguments connected with the social gospel movement and social Darwinism), but its target was corrupt law and law officials. Additionally, *McClure's* used an appeal to "inside dope," authentic information gathered much like sociologists' fieldwork data, which gave a sense of scientific realism to the narratives.[81]

Given the economic and social conditions of the time, it would seem obvious that the middle class would want to regulate movies, although the precise methods might be debated. I will assume for starters that socially constructed identities change from emphasizing the self in terms of production to also envisioning one's self as a consumer. The public sphere is at this time becoming increasingly heterosocial; the private sphere also is being redefined away from productivity and toward personal satisfaction of all desires. This configures a redefinition of the good woman into the new good consuming woman who is knowledgeable, public, and willful. Woman's agency as well as its necessary containment is expressed through cultural representations. This opportunity for defining the New Woman was less a class conflict than a contention within a less than homogeneous middle class. The changes witnessed in the period from 1909 to 1917 in cinema are not due to the imposition of a Victorian middle-class culture but because of contradictory debate in the broad dominant social formation about one signifier of transforming America, namely woman.

Finally, then, talk was important. Foucault stresses how the Catholic confession of the medieval ages is replaced in the twentieth century by a science of sexuality. Thus while attempting to regulate desire, talk about practices and possibilities are dispersed.[82] Throughout this analysis, I will describe how some very influential people counsel talk, including individuals such as Helen Keller and film producer Alice Blaché, who states that the only way to solve social problems is through discussion. Filmgoing participated in the transformation of American culture as a cultural site for this talk. This book, then, is about the sense of a repeal of reticence and the part movies played in that transformation.

2

Sex O'Clock in America

If media are indicative of changes in social norms, one place to determine the cultural stakes for a group is in its "scandalous" literature. In this chapter I will examine some of the literature deemed "lurid." The representations of woman are important for considering the disruption of established norms in two ways: making the norms visible and setting the agenda for change. These images, then, act as transfer points for new mappings of cultural order. Beyond that, I will consider several forces that ultimately produce a new attitude about woman.

Lurid Literature

I have chosen to briefly discuss four scandalous novels published between 1886 and 1893 for several reasons. For one thing, Frank Luther Mott indicates that these books were "hot" at the time because of their representation of sexual issues. Moreover, although they derive from long-standing conventions in women's fiction, they were also *best-selling* volumes, suggesting that their content was widely circulated.[1] The books are Lily Curry's *A Bohemian Tragedy* (1886), Mrs. Amélie Rives-Chauler's *The Quick or the Dead? A Study* (1888, reprinted from *Lippincott's Monthly Magazine*), Laura Daintrey's *Eros* (1888), and Madame Sarah Grand's *The Heavenly Twins* (1893). In the case of the first three, Mott writes that critics blamed European writers such as Zola, Balzac, and Tolstoy for stimulating debased views of life. Whatever the literary precedents for the books, they also display a dissatisfaction with traditional roles assigned to women and suggest alternative possibilities for the future.

Additional reasons exist to focus on these four books. Women wrote all of them. I might have considered some scandalous literature written by men, but I was interested in what women were saying and reading among themselves. For example, I might have looked at Stephen Crane's *Maggie: A Girl of the Streets* (1893), Theodore Dreiser's *Sister Carrie* (1900), or David Graham

Phillips's *Susan Lenox: Her Fall and Rise* (1917). However, not only are these novels authored by men and written later than the ones I will be considering, but they were less widely read as well as censored. Additionally, the four novels I will discuss have melodramatic and comedic aesthetics (not a realist one) motivating their address—a significant issue to which I will return in chapter 3. The books are, finally, evidence of the circulation of a diversity of views among middle-class women about their desires and "essence," and hence proof of the struggle occurring over the meaning of woman by women.[2]

Curry's *A Bohemian Tragedy* forecasts some early film dramas. A married man has an affair with a young woman, claiming he loves her, but he will not divorce his wife. The young woman dies, apparently from the circumstances in which she finds herself. Retribution occurs when the husband dies accidentally (or by the hand of God), and the wife, now aware of the man's perfidy, manages to reconstruct her life by remarrying a better person.

To a modern reader, the immorality seems restrained and descriptions oblique. However, the reader of the 1880s could probably fill in those gaps. Adultery by a husband and premarital, unsanctioned sex by a decent young woman were topics seldom treated in earlier U.S. literature. What is somewhat surprising is that events occur without much moralizing by an omniscient narrator. Retribution comes through a morally just universe. Hence, this is a melodramatic treatment of a topic about which little discussion had occurred in printed form. It introduces a subject that had been part of the "conspiracy of silence."

The Quick or the Dead by Rives-Chauler can best be described as brooding eroticism. It vividly articulates a woman's physical desire for her lover while hinting at the bankruptcy of social and religious restraints. Barbara Pomfret returns to her home in Virginia where three years earlier she and her husband Val resided. Val died two years ago. Barbara misses him terribly and feels his presence in the house. " 'Oh, Val' she whispered,—'oh, Val! Oh, darling,—mine!—mine!—mine! Touch me, come to me, here in the darkness,—here where you used to love me' " (p. 439). She spends a lot of her time walking.

One day Val's cousin Jack (sometimes Jock or John) Dering visits, and since he is Val's cousin, Barbara finds Jack remarkably similar to her dead husband. Increasingly Barbara and Jack spend time together. A series of courtship scenes ensues, punctuated by Barbara's turmoil over her belief that she is sinning against the dead by desiring Jack. A critical plot point occurs: Jack is going to New York. Barbara rides with him to the station, and the romance heats up to physical contact behind the driver's back.

Jack breathes, "Je t'aime!—je t'aime!"

" 'Oh, no,' she whispered, bracing herself away from him by means of her hand against his knee under the fur robes. He drew off her glove and held it there, his pulses throbbing riotously, his eyes on hers." But Buzzy, the driver, accidently intervenes, and Jack leaves on the train.

The narrative strategy of delay, of incremental stairsteps to greater passion and some danger, signals this book as a forerunner of the romance novels avidly consumed by many women readers today. Indeed, the readership for novels at the turn of the century was also predominantly female, and the appeal of this narrative is quite comprehensible. Unfortunately, its ending is less so.

Barbara and Jack agree to write, but she interprets his letters to indicate that he might not really love her. In her uncertainty about her emotions and continued recollections of Val, she visits the church rectory and Mr. Trehune. Not knowing precisely what motivates her questions, Trehune counsels her that Val waits for her to meet him in heaven. So Barbara writes to Jack that they must no longer meet.

However, and a good thing for the plot, she reads in the paper that a John Dering was hurt in an accident. Barbara telegraphs, Should I come? Dering replies, It was a cousin who was hurt. She responds, "Then come to me!" Jack returns, and the reader is given a very passionate scene.

"Suddenly Dering turned, leaning over the arm of his chair, and resting both hands on the arm of hers. She could see his lips quivering, and the dilation of fiery eyes and nostrils." Does she love him, he asks, or was it merely pity? "I love you," she replies, and she is sure of it. No, no, "It was pity—," Jack worries.

"Jock! kiss me!"

"It was pity. You were sorry for that cruel letter. You were—"

"Jock! kiss me!"

"You thought you would atone. . . . "

"Jock! kiss me!"

The scene continues for several more "kiss me" 's until "he released her pliant waist and lifted her face to him with both hands." The chapter ends.

Chapter 19 begins, "After this interview followed a week of delight such as is sometimes granted to two mortals, one of whom obtains a love long fought for, one of whom yields to a love long fought against." However, some force— social, authorial, aesthetic—prohibits a happy ending. Barbara is locked in a church and, terrified, breaks off the relationship. She considers herself still married to Val.

The eroticism, the best and a good deal of which I have reproduced, is the driving conflict underlying the novel. Norms of monogamous fidelity *even be-*

yond death, reinforced by the church, seem the antagonist to Barbara's happiness. The narrational voice implies that Barbara's choice is wrong because she needs to separate monogamy from metaphysics, but the narrative obviously could not permit Barbara to obtain her earthly well-being. Perhaps the counterexample that Barbara sets serves as a better object lesson about marriage, sexuality, and obligation, that a woman has a duty to herself as much as to any man. Furthermore, religion and its representatives are questioned as a source of help in these matters. The advice is represented as out of touch with a woman's sensibilities and needs, perhaps even inhibiting a wise going on with daily life. The quick or the dead? The narrator implies that the former is a better choice. Here again, we have a new kind of talk about women and sexuality.

Eros by Daintrey makes no pretenses about its subject. This book is about adultery, sexuality, and divorce. Mamie Remington is in a passionate affair with Oliver Dominus, but he will not marry her because she wants too much. So she marries Shapiro who is loved by Marie who is loved by Caryll. When Mamie thinks Dominus loves someone else and Shapiro's bank is a failure, she deserts and divorces Shapiro. She lives with Dominus in Paris until Dominus's wife is alerted and confronts them. In the conclusion, Shapiro meets and marries Marie, Caryll kills himself, and Mamie remains in Paris.

Eros is a version of the vampire genre, already a common plot at the end of the century. The novel's interest lies in its representations of a bad woman and her aggressive sexuality. Examples of Mamie's behavior include motifs of animals and devils: "it was the union of the tigress with the tiger" (p. 13); "it was this animation which enslaved him, exhaling from her person like small caressing curls of infernal flame from that of a voluptuous fiend" (p. 15); "she was now a cobra measuring her spring" (p. 15). She is described as a snake, a tiger, and a sphinx (p. 57). Mamie's motivations are secular. She indicates that she will pursue Shapiro so that she will be rich. Women are fools to seek love. *Eros* clearly takes the final, moral position that Mamie's insatiable desire deserves to be punished, but along the way liaisons and desire are freely represented for the reader's pleasure.

The most intriguing of the four novels is Grand's *The Heavenly Twins.* According to Terry Lovell, the book was a "runaway best seller" in both the United States and Britain.[3] Three plots provide the narrative progression, each one somewhat replacing the former in narrational emphasis rather than intertwining among themselves. All three plots focus on a female protagonist who finds herself in a dilemma created by the role assigned her by society. These three women are Evadne, Edith, and Angelica. The middle plot is

Edith's, which Lovell indicates was the most scandalous to the novel's readers. Edith bears a syphilitic child and dies from dementia—both events attributable to her husband's promiscuity before and during their marriage. Although the etiology of sexual diseases was common medical knowledge from the middle of the century, Grand's novel, like the drama of Ibsen, was an early fictional treatment making public what had previously been only privately distributed knowledge.

Edith's story sets the negative example. However, Evadne's and Angelica's stories bracket Edith's, providing the reader with alternative characters. Furthermore, both Evadne and Angelica are explicit forerunners to the New Woman. Evadne is a nineteen-year-old who seems meek and dutiful, but "she wanted to know" (p. 3). The problem is that her father is very old-fashioned about women. Everything he says she ends up quietly questioning—so she learns a lot. "It was a notable thing that in almost every instance it was her father's influence which forced Evadne to draw conclusions in regard to life quite unlike any of his own, and very distasteful to him. He was the most conservative of men, and yet he was continually setting her mind off at a tangent in search of premises upon which to found ultra-liberal conclusions" (p. 11). Her father thought women should confine themselves to housework. He thought they should avoid arithmetic. So Evadne studied arithmetic to see what was so hard. She read books about medicine and anatomy. Everything Evadne studied returned her to the question of "the position of women." " 'Withholding education from women was the original sin of man,' she concludes" (p. 24).[4]

Like many other young women, Evadne does fall in love. Yet, on her wedding day, she learns that Major Colquhoun has had sexual liaisons with many women so she refuses to consummate her marriage, although she does agree to an outward appearance of wedlock. Her precise motivation is unstated but innuendos suggest that it is because of her knowledge of medicine rather than desire for virginity in a man.

Evadne's plot permits two compositional possibilities. For one thing, it remains a question as to whether Colquhoun will ever succeed in making her change her mind (she does not). For another, his career permits Evadne to enter social situations in which discussion of contemporary topics repeatedly returns to women's issues. Two examples are insightful into how conversations in *The Heavenly Twins* promote reformist alternatives to the fictional world being represented. Mrs. Sillenger addresses Mr. St. John: " 'I wonder men like yourself, Mr. St. John'—Mrs. Sillenger began in her quiet diffident way, 'continue so prejudiced on this subject [of women]. How you could help in the

moral progress of the world, if only you would forget the sweet soporific, "poetry of the pulpit," as Mrs. Malcomson calls it, and learn to think of us
women, not as angels or beasts of burden—the two extremes between which
you wander—but as human beings—' " (p. 181). Here the narrational voice
not only chastises men for their oppositional and reductive imaging of
woman, but attributes the cause to religion. As with *The Quick or the Dead?*,
The Heavenly Twins does not find comfort in religious platitudes; the help is
right here in secular choices.

In another instance of conversation, a character praises Evadne: "I don't
know, of course, but I'm no judge of character if she does not prove to be one
of the new women, who are just appearing among us, with a higher ideal of
duty than any which men have constructed for women" (p. 193). Again, in
the contrast between the sexes, the narration promotes self-determination by
women. Furthermore, the new woman is progressive and labeled positive, and
self-awareness and knowledge of that forbidden by "fathers" is promoted. Earlier, Evadne's parents are discussing her and her views: " 'Well, I don't know
where she got them,' Mrs. Fraling protested, 'for I am sure *I* haven't any. But
she seems to know so much about—*everything!*' She declared, glancing at the
letter. 'At *her* age I knew *nothing!*'

" 'I can vouch for that!' her husband exclaimed. He was one of those men
who oppose the education of women might and main, and then jeer at them
for knowing nothing" (p. 103).

A minor version of Evadne is Angelica, one of the twins who were *not*
Victorian cherubs. She and Theodore (Diavolo) were nicknamed the little
"devils." "Like Evadne, [Angelica] was consumed by the rage to know, and
insisted upon dragging Diavolo on with her" (p. 126). Their escapades provide some of the humor to the novel, but its joyful first half turns less so in the
second part. Distressed by the death of Edith's baby, Angelica marries an older
man. A major portion of the latter half of the novel is the slow revelation that
a young boy visiting Diavolo's tutor is Angelica in disguise.[5] The stunt, perpetrated in part by boredom, in part by desire, turns tragic as the tutor dies as
an indirect result of the discovery. Angelica believes she has killed him, and
her plot line—so filled with possibilities—comes to a conclusion.

Meanwhile, Evadne, unable to fulfill her marriage and crushed by Edith's
situation, ends up in "hysteria." She, however, is permitted some degree of
happiness. Colquhoun conveniently dies of a heart attack. Evadne marries Dr.
Galbraith and has two children. Despite fits of depression and worries about
her children's future, Evadne faces tomorrow with a somewhat upbeat outlook.

John C. Burnham writes that "the well-publicized 'revolution in morals' of
the 1910s and 1920s involved primarily changes in the nature of acceptable
and expectable female behavior."[6] What these fictional accounts reveal are
changes in possible visions of what women will *accept* and what men ought to
expect. Not only are traditional roles, with traditional institutions setting the
norms, declared inadequate, but behaviors and actions commonly associated
with those roles are also considered inadequate. All four novels indict the
predicament of the late nineteenth-century woman. If an unmarried woman
is trapped by her belief in a young man's words, succumbing to the passion of
love, her solution is death (as in *A Bohemian Tragedy*). If a widowed woman
accepts the routine counsel of the church, she will lose her chance for a reasonably satisfactory life (*The Quick or the Dead?*). If a married woman discovers her husband is an adulterer, she has to hope he dies so that she is free to
remarry (*A Bohemian Tragedy* and *The Heavenly Twins*). If a woman is caught
by patriarchy's contradictions—a double standard, a prohibition against
knowledge—she may expect her children and herself to die horrible deaths
(*The Heavenly Twins*). If she rebels, calling men to account for their treatment
of women as chattel, she is labeled a snake or tiger or devil, and is punished
with social ostracization (*Eros*). If she flirts with gender roles, her lover will be
unable to tolerate the deviation from norms of femininity, and she will lose
him (*The Heavenly Twins*).

Alternative possibilities are submerged but they do persist. They often appear in implicit counterexamples. If Barbara had responded to her own feelings about Jack, she might be happily remarried. If Evadne had divorced
Colquhoun, her opportunities for raising children and living a fruitful life
might have happened much sooner. If Edith had been warned about the
transmission of sexual diseases and had been able to inquire about her husband's past, she and her child might not have died. If Angelica's world had
provided more alternatives, she might not have resorted to the traditional
tactic of marrying a man she did not physically love. One of the four novels
places great weight on the appropriate value of sexual pleasure for women.
Not only is Barbara not punished for her sensual feelings, the novel implies
that not following through on those earthly passions is sad. Furthermore, her
aggression toward Jack, at the right moment, is rewarded with "delight."

These four examples of lurid literature indicate at least a minority view
about what women should accept and men could expect in this time of social
change. In particular, some women writers were talking about the limitations
of roles perceived as traditional ones for women, as well as faults in the institutions defining those roles. Women were presented with alternatives such as

the suggestion that they should follow their own intuitions (not the rules given to them by others), pursue knowledge, and in this modern world consider once-forbidden practices (for example, seeking a divorce, adopting different-gendered characteristics).

Given this context, I will specifically trace the transformation of norms about sex talk through a more precise historical chronology and logic than has previously been offered. Rather than make the New Woman (in all her versions) an abstract consequence of some forty years of change, I want to try to pinpoint several critical struggles that permit a more complex resolution. Moreover, I want to emphasize that this transformation occurred amidst a debate among factions in the middle class, not by an easy consensual overturning of older views.[7] This occurred at *just the time* when movies were threatened with restrictions against talking about such matters such as sexuality—around 1905. The complexity of influences provided the dynamics for envisioning a New (desiring) Woman, and this chapter will continue diagnosing the causes for why woman was to be central in the narratives of American movies.[8]

Woman's Work

The disparity between prescriptions and reality, between images and the ability or desire to fit those images, can be enormous. Apropos of woman, according to Barbara Welter, during the first half of the nineteenth century, representations of "true womanhood" (a prescription) included "four cardinal virtues—piety, purity, submissiveness and domesticity."[9] An absence of the second virtue, purity, was "unnatural and unfeminine." All women—upper, middle, or working class—were to try to attain these features. To encourage and reinforce these representations as hegemonic, bourgeois Victorian society used the institution of the family headed by the husband and the duties of child rearing to rationalize woman's place as subordinate in earthly affairs but simultaneously transcendent in spiritual matters. As the era proceeded, the home belonged to the private sphere, protecting the woman and her children from evil outside its haven. The evil beyond its shelter was business, relegated to the secular, and man's public life. Women who worked had to be especially careful not to be degraded and contaminated by the public sphere's corrupt nature. The consequence of these representational moves, as Stuart Ewen puts it, was that "Victorianism elevated the patriarchal home into a spiritual sanctuary against the realities of the productive sphere. Women's work, within the Victorian code, had also moved from the productive to the spiritual."[10] Moreover, the ideology constructed the image that being protected at home was the obvious choice or the better situation.

This segregation of sexes in the "cult of domesticity" had its consequences, as do all such restrictions and regulations.[11] Women's forays into the public streets were permitted and even encouraged when they were on God's duties, and women found numerous reasons for God to have called them there. Benevolent charity work, help to the sick and poor, and civic duties gathered women together in public associations to improve civilization. Thus, the grounds of religious directives and women's work could be deployed to authorize greater power in both the homes and in public to do the job "her great Creator has assigned her."[12]

In this way, the first cardinal virtue of piety could be used to justify special focus and privileges, even dominating (if not refuting) two other cardinal virtues—domesticity and submissiveness. Women's activities in reform projects between 1822 and 1848 (and the abolitionist movement) reinforced some women's views that they needed equal rights or at least the vote to fulfill their designated mission. Shortly after the Civil War, women turned again to their own situation in an effort to improve their ability to succeed in civilizing American society for the sake of their families and children.[13]

Women's organizations included, in addition to suffragette groups, the women's clubs that developed in the 1870s and 1880s for discussion and civic action. In 1890 the General Federation of Women's Clubs merged from various groups, and the effect was a better communication network for sharing ideas across the nation. The federation had one million members in 1912, and its activities included studying culture as well as social reform. Likewise in 1890, women led the organizing of the New York Consumers League and in 1899 the National Consumers League. Important issues for these reformers included the spiritual guidance of others and protection of the sacred home and children.

Furthermore, as women's organizations developed, women's influence expanded territorially. From the late 1860s, several women's groups urged "domestic feminism," bringing women's "moral sensibilities to bear on the social problems of America."[14] Gwendolyn Wright recounts that "in 1910, the president of the General Federation of Women's Clubs declared that their platform was protecting 'women and children, and the home, the latter meaning the four walls of the city as well as the four walls of brick and mortar.' "[15] It took little for women to recognize that morality and adherence to prescribed behavior had some connections to safe cities and better economic conditions. Women contributed to the running of settlement houses, using a model of the home to create a civilized haven. Consumer leagues lobbied for pure and better products and fair wages for women, shorter work hours, and better work conditions. Women's civic groups provided authorized models for organizing women's labor groups. The Women's Trade Union League was formed in 1903.

Frustrations mounted in this contradictory state of affairs, in which women were discursively assigned to "another place," that of home and sacred duties, while they were simultaneously expected to reform public life, created and controlled by another sex. *Women and Economics,* the brilliant examination of women's conditions in the social arrangement of dependency upon men's incomes by Charlotte Perkins Gilman, is still relevant today, yet it is quite conceivable that it could have been written in 1898. Gilman rehearses the emerging stress for a domesticated woman: a woman's "living, all that she gets—food, clothing, ornaments, amusements, luxuries,—these bear no relation to her power to produce wealth, to her services in the house, or to her motherhood. These things bear relation only to the man she marries, the man she depends on,—to how much he has and how much he is willing to give her."[16] Gilman recognized how social behaviors constructed gendered behavior: "To the boy we say 'Do'; to the girl, 'Don't'," and what men leave for women, they call "feminine" (p. 53). The first two decades of the twentieth century were a period of intensified struggle to resolve such contradictions. As consumers women entered the public marketplace, as working women they produced in the heterosocial work sphere, and as civic reformers they cleaned up the city.[17]

"Feminists" (a term appearing around 1913) were among the more radical women promoting additional goals beyond the vote and better wages. In 1914, Marie Jenny Howe theorized heterodoxy; in February 1914, at the People's Institute at Cooper Union (New York City), early feminist meetings were held. Speakers on "What Feminism Means to Me" and "Breaking into the Human Race" included Gilman, Rheta Child Dorr, George Creel, and Max Eastman.[18] These individuals argued for equality in all respects for both sexes.

Furthermore, despite the suffragists (whose activities need to be examined critically)[19] and feminists, women's positions were still quite confined to specific areas of the public sphere. Gains in occupational choices were made here and there, but the gains could also become liabilities. The first woman hired to work at the Boston Public Library started work in 1852; in 1910, about three-fourths of U.S. librarians were women. As Leslie Woodcock Tentler reminds us, the feminization of some occupations did not lead to equality. Rather the occupation become a secondary one. Women did not compete for men's jobs; instead, they were assigned to a "separate labor market, one characterized by low pay, low skill, low security, and low mobility."[20] Thus, the diversity between the sexes permitted inequities through controlled access to the labor market, in which some jobs were redefined as suitable for (only) women, and thus feminine (for example, schoolteachers, secretaries, librarians, store clerks, nurses). Such a domestication of some public occupations permitted capitalism to both exploit the woman in terms of her labor as well as constrain her economic mobility.

Women who lived outside the home had to live in dormitories or board in private homes.[21] Shared apartments such as would become options in a few more decades were not yet socially acceptable possibilities. Apartments seemed to indicate an alteration in the value of the family. Industrialization cut into the family as a unit producing and consuming together. The family was no longer a production unit as much as a consuming one, and, occasionally, not a very happy one. The power of a patriarchal family to define moral behavior weakened in relation to external agencies and new types of kinship groups. Advertising created an even wider social network.[22]

While advertising might at times try to hold up the value of the family, ideological discourses at the turn of the century also reasserted the value of the male as head of the household but within the transforming notion of the family. If a New Woman was appearing, so was a New Man. Margaret Marsh describes a cult of masculinity promoted in the early 1900s by Teddy Roosevelt, one stressing health and vigor for race perpetuation. Furthermore, men's contribution to the home was redefined in terms of "companion marriages" in which the husbands were counseled to spend more time in the household, interacting with the family in its activities.[23] Yet gender characteristics were as segregated and essentialized as before, perhaps in a counterreaction to the breaking down of what counted as men's and women's spaces. Indeed, turn-of-the-century discourse promoted both genders' interaction in "public" and "private" spheres.

However, although the virtue of piety produced new situations for women, the most fundamental virtue of *purity* would end up being the most significant attribute that would empower women in the new morals revolution. As I shall discuss in the rest of this chapter, it is ironic that images of purity, which may have held women in check in the Victorian era, should also be the arena *through* which women realized a major transformation in possibilities for their situation.

The Norm of Reticence

In this era of major discursive and social transformation, moral decisions became scientific, social, or personal ones. Men who once knew about sexuality and could sin (desire in them was considered natural) now needed to abstain from premarital relations or at least take specific prophylactic precautions. And women who were innocent about sexual activities and sexuality now needed education in sex hygiene to protect themselves, their children, the race, and the nation. This discussion of sexuality would influence how movies regulated gender and desire by the early teens.

The stories of Victorian women scandalized by hearing the word "leg" still have some currency, although how widely spread this revulsion was is questionable. In discussing Victorian England, Ronald Pearsall emphasizes that a strict morality and excessive restraint applied mostly to the middle class. He believes the upper class was quite casual about sexual matters. The middle class did what it *thought* the upper class modeled for them. Pearsall does not argue that the middle class had no interest in sex. Instead, the regulation was productive: thousands of pornographic photographs and engravings were generated, and newspaper details of scandals could produce circulations in the tens of thousands. Carl Degler insists as well that the Victorian reticence to speak about sexuality should not be mistaken as a hostility toward it. As Agnes Repplier described in her article about the changes she was witnessing in the early teens, what distressed her was the tastelessness of discussing sex, not the act itself. Thus, although Victorian England and the United States took the view that public discussion of sex was rude or uncouth, their actual practices seem to suggest that sexual pleasure in middle-class marriages was quite often assumed or at least expected.[24]

Sexuality in general seems to have been positively considered by some Victorian authorities. Degler surveys medical evidence of the late 1800s and concludes that not only did urban middle-class women experience "passion" but, at least within the circumscribed sphere of their relation with their physician and medicine in general, counsel about sexual arousal was given, even in printed form. Dr. George Haphey's *The Physical Life of Woman: Advice to the Maiden, Wife, and Mother*, published in 1869, included recommendations about sensible sensuality. Haphey even thought it wise to foster passion since he believed conception probabilities were higher when aroused. That opinion was not shared by everyone, but by the 1880s some writers were even claiming that suppressing sexual feelings could produce illness. This is, of course, the position Freud and other new sexologists would take.[25]

Even if sensual pleasure was accepted or encouraged, that would not necessarily alter the norm of reticence about such matters. What could account for moving away from silence to "sex o'clock" (or at least creating the appearance of such a change)? An important cause, I think, is that European colonialism and American imperialism along with the science of anthropology introduced Victorians to diversity—cultural, social, *and sexual*. According to Elizabeth Fee, "until about 1860, marriage, the family, and sexual roles were assumed to belong to the natural condition of man, institutions beyond and above any mere geographical or historical accident. Between 1860 and 1890, however, social anthropology demonstrated that the idealized family of the Victorian middle class was dictated by no law of nature, that monogamous marriage was only one of various human sexual possibilities and that women were not necessarily born only to domestic and decorative functions."[26]

I believe that an unintentional consequence of the urbanization and globalization of America was the all-too-apparent observation of alternatives in which sexual deviants experienced no earthly retribution. In fact, these foreign sinners might be happy and successful. Such a recognition, however, could produce its own rationalization, such as the view that other cultures were primitive or degraded versions of the middle-class Victorian world. In any case, a fascination with the deviation, whose investigation was authorized by the science of anthropology, permitted increased public exploration of the exotic disguised as rationalized inquiry.[27]

Another cause for moving away from reticence was resistance to women's situations. John S. Haller Jr. and Robin M. Haller argue that some women withheld sex or created an image of themselves as frail so that they could control their lives, including the number of children they would bear. This choice about motherhood was reinforced from the developing consumer culture: regulating birthrates could have personal advantages such as reducing the toil of domestic life, improving standards of living, and even differentiating oneself from other classes and cultures. By the late 1800s, middle-class women apparently used and disseminated to one another a variety of methods of birth control to limit reproduction. Gilman decried that women had been virtually enslaved by the notion of motherhood, or "matriolatry" as she called it, and advocated emancipation from it.[28]

By the late 1800s, "voluntary motherhood," as birth control was euphemized, was openly talked about by some suffragists, reform groups, and "free love" radicals. Other such radical ideas were also openly advocated by women and men. Free love, not surprisingly, was somewhat shocking, particularly when its supporters argued for an "integration of body and soul." Victoria Woodhull in the 1870s pursued the idea that " 'true love' sex . . . involved mutual desire and orgasms for both parties." Some radicals supported divorce and remarriage. Thus, such a proliferation of functions for sexuality helped provide the conditions favorable for believing that marriages were more about pleasurable consumption (for oneself) than production (of many children). This would be fine, of course, as long as every family had at least some children. Consequently, this new notion of proper birthrates would need to be regulated.[29] These subversions of motherhood-and-nothing-else and sex-for-reproduction instead of sex-for-pleasure provoked reactions that included, for example, the Comstock Act, which attempted to prohibit mailing obscene materials, including birth control information. The legal prohibition on birth control information would be challenged after 1910 by Margaret Sanger, Emma Goldman, and others.

While diversities of cultures became familiar to late nineteenth-century Americans and women resisted and disputed common norms about sexual and gendered behavior, science tried to separate sexual facts from myths. Medical and social science experts took up the research task of understanding women's sexual behavior. Odd theories were promoted one hundred years ago. For instance, physicians counseled against overstimulating women's brains with too much education because they thought that women's neurasthenia was caused by thinking. Or at least doctors noticed a relationship between a decline in reproductive instincts as women turned to intellectual activities, a decline that the doctors illogically attributed to a physiological cause rather than to women's willful choice.[30]

In fact, observers began to perceive more diversity in gender characteristics once they started trying to delimit sex differences in terms of anatomical sex, social gender attributes, and sexual practices. In the 1890s, some doctors attacked women who were advocating women's rights for being tomboys and behaving aggressively, even suggesting that these women had hermaphroditic tendencies. S. P. White in 1890 declared aggressive women to be among the causes for "the increasing problems of homosexuality and gynandry." At this same time, perhaps due to the concentration of population in the urban city or the scientific desire to notice it, people began seeing homosexuality not as a sporadic sexual practice but as a subculture with its own places for gays and lesbians to gather and its own norms and protocols for behavior.[31]

Both Jeffrey Weeks and Arnold I. Davidson write that during the 1800s, women (and men) might be defined by the features of their bodies (for example, by anatomical sex), but distinguishing *sexuality* as a theory of physical or emotional pleasure related to the sexual act did not occur until late in the century. At that time psychology distinguished between an anatomical sex and a psychological sex. The long-standing body and mind split encouraged separating out desire and its satisfaction.[32]

Sexology as a field of inquiry may have been most generally defined by Freud's theories, but at the turn of the century other writers were more popular, or at least more available for the public's attention. One of these individuals, mentioned by our Flapper of 1915, was Havelock Ellis. Ellis's actual publications were banned in Britain and only carefully distributed in the United States, but synopses of his ideas and interviews with him were widely disseminated. Ellis presented sexual activity as natural and delightful. He approved of premarital relations, with multiple individuals, and of masturbation as a way to relax. One of his lovers, the women's activist Olive Schreiner, agreed with him that women's sexual feelings were as strong as men's and should be cultivated. Schreiner's call for sexual "parity" became part of the rights for which many women lobbied. Ellis did consider homosexuality as a "sexual inversion," and thought it was congenitally produced. Thus, Ellis provided no affirmative view for homosexuality or bisexuality.[33]

In his study of sexology and theories of sexuality, Lawrence Birken argues that the twentieth century's intensive investigation of sexuality is a product of the move to a consumer culture. As capitalism through advertising multiplies the reasons to purchase products, locating those causes in individual tastes and preferences, by analogy sexuality is another site of personal life for which science must account. The "laws" of sexuality needed analysis, as did the differentiation between "productive and unproductive desire." Birken believes that the early sexologists tried to "regulate the idiosyncratic consumer" to avoid wasteful "spending" (a euphemism exceptionally revealing of this equation) when resources were (thought to be) limited.[34]

Certainly, sexology, and the consideration that women might have desires of multiple kinds, reinforced the vision of women as consumers with a variety of specific tastes. The desiring woman was apparently a recognizable and moderately acceptable social image by the first decade of the twentieth century. According to Nancy F. Cott, "Feminists did not make very clear what were meant by women's sex rights beyond the basic acknowledgement of erotic drives, which might be said by 1912 to be a staple of sophisticated urban discourses"; at least they knew they ought to have those rights to desire. Cott further remarks that "even a *Nation* reviewer that year maintained, as for the rights of women to a frank enjoyment of the sensuous side of the sex-relation . . . no sensible person now disputes that right, but only, as in the case of men, the right to make it a subject of common conversation."[35]

Unfortunately, this new view of the existence (and possible advantages) of sexual desire in women was not sufficient to have broken any dominant norm of reticency. The free lovers, sexologists, and so forth were a small fraction of society and insufficient to legislate a repeal. It took a threat to alter general public imagery that reticence about discussing sexuality was appropriate, and this threat hit right to the most sacred aspects of the Victorian domestic ideology—the home and the children, the nation and the race. The threat was disease.

Those Who Go Astray

Around 1905 when Americans ascertained the etiology of veneral diseases, the final stroke creating sufficient alarm to break the "conspiracy of silence" fell. Reticence, which was once a tasteful choice by proper men and women, now was represented by many to be a complicity directed against society's future. Giving up the secret, however, was an inadequate response. At this point it was to capitalism's advantage to acknowledge sexual feelings and even exploit pleasurable sexuality as a feature within companion marriages (thus maintaining patriarchal monogamy). Sensuality could be mobilized as drives directed toward consuming a variety of luxury products and services. The cause for this change in hegemonic representations was the pestilent effects of venereal disease, spread by prostitution.

After decades, even centuries, of tacit acceptance, prostitution became a focal point for reform. While prostitutes were represented as fallen women, religions counseled restraint or continence for men. When prostitutes spread diseases that could destroy Anglo-Saxon families, then they were truly dangerous and required prohibition. Thus, as science replaced religion as the guardian for dominant society, moralists used scientific findings to justify more restrictive approaches to the "social evil" problem. These restrictive methods included regulation and even suppression of prostitution. In reaction against the moral reformers, some progressives advocated education—the social hygiene movement—as the best policy. It was the social hygiene movement, starting about 1905, that ultimately made possible the acceptance of talk about sexuality, dispersing even more widely than just among the radical few information about a bewildering array of sexual practices and sexual preferences.

In the middle of the eighteenth century, women fell into either of two categories—virtuous or not.[36] Sometimes categorization was based on an assumption that an innate feature of women was their sinfulness; at other times the hypothesis was that they had a weakness of will. A third possibility, also correlated to self-control, was feeblemindedness. Finally, a long-standing theory was the fatal seduction and betrayal of a woman (as in, for example,

The Scarlet Letter). In all these cases, religion and individual morality were both accuser and salvation.[37]

Sometime during the development of the women's reform movements in the 1860s and 1870s, the thesis began appearing that women were being forced into prostitution. Drawing on contemporary social theory, people argued that economic causes contributed to women's occupational options, and some reformers believed that prostitution was evidence of men's economic dominance. Thus, the coercion was forceful only in a figurative sense.

Other narratives explicitly mention trickery, drugging, kidnapping, and bondage. As Laura Hapke notes, such tales are a transformation of the older seduction theme: "The seducer was replaced by the white slaver, the madam, and the environment itself."[38] As this explanation developed, it became mixed, I would argue, with some actual occurrences but also with sexual fantasies. Hapke remarks that the story permits denial of illicit desires by women while still playing to certain erotic pleasures. As shall become apparent in chapter 5, these narratives of physical coercion had great force in the public's imagination, particularly after 1905, as both "true stories" and fictional accounts of women tricked or captured *by syndicates* and then held in brothels against their will warned citizens of dangers surrounding young women who ventured out into public areas. Moreover, the places of greatest danger to women were the places they were now increasingly frequenting: the department stores, hotels, restaurants, dance halls, parks, theaters, movie houses, and public streets.

Two additional theories for the causes of prostitution appeared as the consumer culture took hold. By the late 1800s, reformers and social scientists encountered evidence that women were willfully attracted to the work because prostitution paid better than other jobs available to them. These working women were tempted by consumer goods offered for sale and wanted to purchase them. Prostitution seemed a good and quick way to improve one's economic status.

Moreover, however, some women admitted to a certain degree of satisfaction in the work. Obviously, Old New England religious restraints were no longer sufficient in preventing women from going astray! If evil men did not capture them, a fancy dress or even personal satisfaction might. Women's activist Rheta Childe Dorr in *What Eight Million Women Want* (1910) describes nice women's consternation upon learning this. She details that in 1888 the Massachusetts Bureau of Labor investigated the prior occupations of 3,866 fallen women in twenty-eight U.S. cities and discovered that 32 percent of the women had no prior occupation and 30 percent had been *domestic* servants. Dorr continues, "It never tried to find out *why* housework was a trade dangerous to morals." Women's organizations did ask this, and concluded that the cause was quite obvious: "Annie Donnelly became a dance-hall habitué. Not because she was viciously inclined; not because she was abnormal; but because she was decidedly normal in all her instincts and desires." Annie Donnelly had *normal* instincts and no adequately supervised alternatives for social exchange with men.[39]

When society considered prostitution or sexual activity outside of marriage simply a matter of sin, people could ignore the behavior, employing moral and religious ideology as their means of restraining the conduct among most of the populace. However, when people thought women were by happenstance just falling into the trade or even beginning to consider prostitution as a viable occupation to achieving upward mobility, then moral governance in this new urban, global, and secular society was shown to be inadequate.[40]

Furthermore, moral restraint had always been directed somewhat un-equally, aimed as it was primarily toward only one of the sexes, women (who bore the family's children), while men were tacitly protected by the double standard. Calls for sex equality began sounding serious, especially if they were associated with moral undertones. Many of the requests for state legislation to prohibit prostitution came from women's civic and reform organizations and suffragists.

Coercion was also a social, not individual, reason for state legislation, es-pecially when foreigners were presented as the major villains in these stories. It is not clear to me precisely when such tales begin circulating, but by the late 1800s, reformers were avidly attempting to destroy prostitution in major cities because they associated it with immigrants and slum bosses.[41] A spec-tacular case of this, to which I shall also return in depth in chapter 4, is that of the Reverend Charles Parkhurst. A Presbyterian minister in New York City, Parkhurst was elected president of the Society for the Prevention of Crime in 1891. In the next several years, from his pulpit, Parkhurst attacked Tammany Hall (the New York Democratic party's social club and political machine) and the New York City police for profiting from payoffs related to vice, particularly protection money from prostitution and gambling. These charges produced the creation of the Lexow Committee, which substantiated his accusations; a series of reform mayoral candidates; and much legislation directed toward shutting down opportunities for illicit commercial sexual behavior.[42]

Parkhurst's work fed into the next wave of coercion narratives, which ap-peared within the space created by muckraking journalism. In the first years of the twentieth century, not only were foreigners involved in running urban prostitution, so went the tales, but also there existed an *international white slavery* network. In 1907, George Kibbe Turner, writing in *McClure's*, argued that Chicago's prostitution was run largely by Russian Jews. Ernest A. Bell in *Fighting the Traffic in Young Girls; or, War on the White Slave Trade* (1910) attributed the network mostly to French Parisians, but also to Jews, Italians, Sicilians, and some Austrians, Germans, English Americans, and Greeks.[43] Vice commissions studying the accusations of the existence of a national or international white slavery organization were never able to find serious evidence to confirm these speculations, although cases of local gangs and instances of coercion by lovers and pimps do seem to have been common. Yet prostitution linked to the foreign and criminal element fostered a sense of duty to protect the honor of Anglo-Saxon American women.[44]

Finally, though, the best justification for state legislation was the realization that prostitution and the double standard permitted the spread of venereal disease to innocent victims—the wives and children of men who let their passions, however natural they might be, rule them. Where morality had failed to constrain behavior, medical science was the accuser. This is precisely the pronouncement made in *The Heavenly Twins* (1893), and this public discourse—that men's behavior had consequences for the race and nation—motivated a legislated response.

The knowledge of syphilis and gonorrhea had been established as early as 1837, but it was not until the mid to late 1800s that causes for diseases related to syphilis or its hereditary possibilities, including insanity, were diagnosed. Likewise, gonorrhea's connection to various ailments, including women's sterility, was undetected until the same period. It was after 1900 before a clear agency for syphilis was determined. The Wassermann test in 1905 was medicine's surveillance tool. Experts were unsure of exact proportions of the VD epidemic; one study around 1900 estimated that 75 to 90 percent of prostitutes were infected.[45]

Given the seriousness and extent of the disease problem, turn-of-the-century America considered a combination of four options to the disease threat. One was strict counseling of continence combined with new attitudes about the so-called natural necessity for men to have sexual relations. This "purity" movement started around the 1890s and had great appeal to religious individuals and also to those who held another modern idea—creating one's own destiny through, as T. J. Jackson Lears puts it, an "internalized mode of moral authority."[46]

A second option was regulating prostitution—controlling its operation

under municipal authority to prevent payoffs and requiring medical inspec-
tions. However, a third option was strict prohibition. Some reformers and social scientists turned their attention to gathering data to analyze the true
causes of prostitution so that proper solutions could be put into place. Volatile
debates between moral reformers and liberal progressives ensued. Some progressives argued that regulation (tried from the 1870s) was sufficient and that
prohibition was not feasible. They advocated various other regulatory laws to
protect against innocent contraction of venereal diseases. In 1899 Michigan
passed the first state law barring marriage if one of the individuals had such a
disease. By 1913, seven other states also had such laws.[47]

However, other progressives and women's groups, combined with moral reformers, argued that regulation was flawed since it contained unacceptable
double standards. What was sinful or dangerous should not be tolerated, said
the reformers. For progressive and women's rights people, regulation was directed toward women and thus a violation of the movement toward equal
rights (and wrongs) for both sexes.

This regulation/prohibition debate is symbolized by the 1902 New York
City Committee of Fifteen report and its aftermath. The Parkhurst campaign
continued through the 1890s. In 1900, a group of fifteen concerned New York
citizens began investigating the correlations between hotels, liquor licenses,
and prostitution.[48] This committee included George Foster Peabody, Jacob H.
Schiff, and Charles Sprague Smith (founder of the People's Institute, which
was later to step in to regulate motion pictures). In 1902, the committee published a report, *The Social Evil*. In it was a historical review of prostitution,
which the committee declared was "coextensive with civilized society."[49] Because of this, the committee believed that it would be impossible to prohibit
prostitution although it might be controlled. Having established that the
cause was the "male factor" (in a supply-and-demand equation), the group
also believed that women were "attracted, rather than forced, into prostitution" (p. 7). Some women were orphans without strong family ties, who
drifted into the profession; others were impoverished women who did it occasionally; but typical of modern America was the tendency to "experiment"
because these women thought "individual happiness is the end of life" and
their work was boring and not rewarding (pp. 10–11). Although the committee was concerned about moral and criminal issues, their major worry was the
extensive effect of disease. Thus they advocated "reglementation" by the government: (1) *repression* via suppressing "flagrant incitement to debauch"
(p. 147), (2) *prevention* via improving family situations and institutionalizing

minor (under eighteen) offenders, and (3) *sanitation* via making available pro-phylactic protection through public dispensaries.

This modern and liberal approach did not appeal to many people. Yet as vice commissions continued their work and as social scientists surveyed pros-titutes, the causes cited were increasingly economic and social. Furthermore, muckraking journalism and cautionary tales produced from around 1907 sen-sationalized the problem. It was at that point that the international white slavery theme was seriously introduced, reinforcing the disease scare with ra-cial threats. An early narrative in the series was Turner's "The Great City of Chicago: A Study of the Great Immoralities" (*McClure's*, April 1907). He followed it in 1909 with "The Daughters of the Poor: A Plain Story of the Development of New York City as a Leading Center of the White Slave Trade of the World, under Tammany Hall" and "Tammany's Control of New York by Professional Criminals" (*McClure's*). Other reformers, progressives, and muckrakers also discovered the problem. Among them, Clifford G. Roe pub-lished *Panders and Their White Slaves* (1910) and *The Great War on White Slav-ery* (1911, a.k.a. *Horrors of the White Slave Trade*); Ernest A. Bell, *Fighting the Traffic in Young Girls; or, War on the White Slave Trade* (1910); Reginald Wright Kauffman, *The Girl That Goes Wrong* (1911) and *The House of Bond-age* (1911); and O. Edward Janney, *The White Slave Traffic in America* (1911). I shall return to these narratives in chapter 5; however, these stories and nov-els produced a sufficient stir so that after 1910 almost every major U.S. city commissioned its own vice commission along the lines of New York's Com-mittee of Fifteen. The normal strategy was to present a scientific survey of the causes and effects of prostitution, a confirmation or denial of the existence of white slavery, and recommendations of various kinds.

The fourth option to solving the problem of prostitution, also promoted by liberal progressives, women's groups, and even some moderates, was "social hygiene"—the movement's term for widespread dissemination of information about sexual activities, disease, and prophylactic protection. In 1905 Prince Albert Morrow founded the American Society for Sanitary and Moral Pro-phylaxis "to prevent the spread of diseases which have their origin in the so-cial evil." Physicians and reformers joined the Society, of which 30 percent were women. Education and publicity were its solutions, and it particularly encouraged sex education in schools for children. Morrow also took a prohi-bitionist stance. In 1910, he was elected president of the newly organized American Federation for Sex Hygiene. Meanwhile, the American Purity Al-liance, whose president in 1904 was O. Edward Janney, in 1908 added education as an objective. In 1912, that purity group and the American Vigilance Committee combined. The American Vigilance Committee counted among its members Jane Addams, Grace H. Dodge, Roe, and Janney (both wrote white slavery exposés in 1911), as well as a director of investigation, George J. Kneeland (he had worked for New York City and Chicago vice commissions). The year 1913 witnessed the merger of the American Vigilance Committee with the American Federation for Sex Hygiene into the American Social Hygiene Association. In this merger transformation, the purity stance of home education gave way to *public* sex education.[50]

Among the major supporters of the American Social Hygiene Association was John D. Rockefeller Jr. Rockefeller became involved in the social evil problem in 1910 when called upon to chair a grand jury investigating white slavery. In 1911, he established the Bureau of Social Hygiene. Its first duties were to establish a women's reformatory and a laboratory that was to scrutinize and catalog social scientific data about every admission.[51]

Additionally, the Bureau sponsored four major studies of prostitution: Kneeland's *Commercialized Prostitution in New York City;* Abraham Flexner's *Prostitution in Europe;* Raymond B. Fosdick's *European Police Systems;* and Harold B. Woolston's *Prostitution in the United States.* Using information from the reformatory, Kneeland studied its criminals. His work did not discount some degree of organization of prostitution but could not find evidence of white slavery, and certainly not on an international scale. Instead, women reported to him that family life, married life, and personal and economic reasons led to their activities. Kneeland summarized the value of such a study as "leading to lines of action not only more scientific and humane but also less wasteful than those at present followed." Flexner's study stressed an economic model: the problem existed because of the demand from men. Until demand ceased, prohibition would not work. He also urged against regulation because it fostered a false sense of security about disease.[52]

Although not specifically part of the social hygiene movement, a series of articles in the *Ladies' Home Journal* in 1906 also indicated the new attitude supporting public discussion about the social evil and VD. *Ladies' Home Journal* was targeted to northeastern middle-class families but also to individuals in a middle- to lower-income bracket who were upwardly mobile. The magazine stressed modern homemaking skills and had a civic reform agenda centered around preserving and improving the family and race.

Essays about the right way to approach the social evil began appearing, including a 1909 article by Helen Keller about children's blindness. In " 'I Must Speak': A Plea to the American Woman," Keller writes that ignorance was no longer tolerable: "What is the cause of ophthalmia neonatorum? It is a specific germ communicated by the mother to the child at birth. Previous to the child's birth she has unconsciously received it through infection from her husband. He has contracted the infection in licentious relations before or since marriage." The *Ladies' Home Journal* also published counsel from Florence Kelley, secretary of the National Consumers' League, about how low salaries tempted working women into sin and how concerned citizens should work for justice for their plight. Women were urged to tell their children how babies were made so that youth would not learn this from stories in the streets.[53]

Other major middle-class journals and associations also promoted public dissemination of the health consequences of the social evil. In 1911, the *Survey* reported that the 1910 Chicago Vice Commission's study counseled as a primary remedy "wise teaching of sex hygiene in the schools." In 1912, the National Education Association resolved to endorse sex education in public schools. Although it had a troubled season, Eugene Brieux's drama, *Damaged Goods,* appeared in 1913 on Broadway. Part of the play's ability to be presented without official suppression was the legitimization achieved though the authority of official bodies sponsoring it, including the *Medical Review of Reviews* Sociological Fund. An endorsement by Rockefeller and an appearance before President Wilson, his cabinet, and the congress also served to legitimize the play.[54]

Although this new emphasis on public discussion of sexual behavior and sexuality was crucial in providing a sense that a repeal of reticence was occurring, the discussion had its costs. As John C. Burnham points out, Morrow and the social hygienists used fear as one of their major tactics. Specifically, Morrow employed visual exhibits of the ravages of VD to scare people into continence. Additionally, many advocates of social hygiene promoted prohibition of sexual activity outside of marriage rather than reevaluating the place and direction of sexual behavior within human lives. Steven Schlossman and Stephanie Wallach put it elegantly: for Morrow and company, "if reticence was no longer possible, purity was."[55]

Moreover, Roosevelt's remarks around 1906 about race suicide and, starting the same year, publicity that venereal disease could be passed to wives and children fed into one another. The white slavery scare from 1907 on may have had other causes, but Turner's argument initially hinged on accusations that foreigners and Jews ran these rings. This xenophobic motif was prominent in the tales. To perceive the social hygiene movement as a healthy reaction against reticence would be to miss the racist reasons for some of its advocates' support. As the former president of Harvard University, Charles W. Eliot, wrote in *Current Opinion* in 1913: "We have got to remove this evil [prostitution], or this country will not be ruled by the race that is now here. The family life of the white race is at stake in its purity, in its healthfulness and its fertility."[56]

Criticism of these regressive and suppressive views did occur. Havelock Ellis in 1914 particularly criticized the white slavery scare as unproductive, and another writer in the *Survey* linked the slavery narratives with stock melodrama. A *Forum* essayist declared in 1915: "The 'Comstock Law' has become a synonym for the 'obscenity law,' and 'Comstockery' is an Americanism for our whole system of sex-censorship, at once suggesting to our minds all that which we think is thereby suppressed." Taking a stance that Foucault would have appreciated, the writer continued that obscenity was in the individuals' minds; that the name Anthony Comstock called up everything against which he stood. Thus, *his* name should be censored.[57]

Walter Lippmann argued in 1914 in *A Preface to Politics* that if the cause of prostitution was lust, suppression was hardly a solution. What would be more constructive would be "transmuting the sex impulse into art, into social endeavor, into religion." Furthermore, do not "confine sex to mere reproduction"; "treat sex with dignity and joy."[58] This positive view of sexual activity was not one shared by any kind of a majority of U.S. citizens, but it did permit some individuals to consider options and the role of sexuality in the lives of twentieth-century Americans.

The New Woman

At the beginning of chapter 1, I reproduced Mencken's 1915 description of the Flapper. Although I have not accounted for all of the references that Mencken's audience would have understood, many of them have now been placed into the historical context of the early teens of America. The Flapper was the most recent version of the New Woman advocated by *The Heavenly Twins*. She was also the woman described by Gilman in 1898: "So the 'new woman' will be no less female than the 'old' woman, though she has more functions, can do more things, is a more highly specialized organism, has more intelligence. She will be, with it all, more feminine, in that she will develope [sic] far more efficient processes of caring for the young of the human race than our present wasteful and grievous method, by which we lose fifty per cent. of them, like a codfish." She was Evadne, a woman with perhaps a higher ideal for herself than any man might have given her. Even the *Ladies'*

Home Journal had its more skeptical version of the New Woman by 1907: the New Woman was involved in social responsibilities and suffrage activities, but at the cost of being intemperate. Furthermore, this New Woman should be a phenomenon only among the educated class.[59]

As later commentators would remark, society had a variety of New Women, not a stable representation with which everyone was comfortable. As Kathy Peiss summarizes the diversity: "For some, the New Woman was a mannish, political, and professional woman who had entered the public sphere on its own terms. For others, the New Woman was a sensual, free-spirited girl—in the 1880s a 'Daisy,' by the 1910s and 1920s, a flapper. The latter figure embodied another set of contradictions: she was at once an independent wage-earner, making her own way in the world, and a beautiful, romantic girl, seeking marital fulfillment."[60]

The security of the notion of a pious, pure, domestic, and submissive woman, if that image was ever stable during the Victorian era—and I doubt that it was—had certainly become uncertain and even unstable enough to provoke something of a crisis by the time moving pictures were ready to tell narratives. Miriam Formanek-Brunell describes the development of a "New Kid doll" and a wave of boy dolls distinguished from girl dolls between 1902 and 1912. The girl dolls exhibit new types of behavior: being mischievous, sassy, and rebellious.[61]

The displacement of social and sexual behavior on the sign of Woman was necessarily an *alogical* move. Trying to make that association logical and the images stable was a doomed project (and still is). The project was more than a simple opposition to man; it was a *productive* act. Moreover, as I shall discuss in the analysis of three films from the era, the attempt made for good drama, but the institutional rules *and* opportunities for constructing those stories need to be established.

3

Troublesome Pictures

At the turn of the century people argued about what should and should *not* be said or shown during the first years of the American cinema. Here I will survey the discussions, in some cases merely noting the prospects for further research on how audiences viewed these early movies in relation to notions of good taste and propriety. Although I raise an economic reason (making money) for the breaching of boundaries into the tasteless, improper, immoral, and even dangerous, I do not try to analyze either the more general social or psychological causes for such a breach or, except most briefly, the specific historical conditions that might account for these particular infractions. My purpose, instead, is to set out some of the norms of representation operating at the time of the move to a national self-regulation system. Because the norms were not agreed to by everyone, the more conservative people pressured legal authorities and the industry to insist upon officially instituting rules that would reproduce their views about representation.

Beyond this is a description of the logic and causes for the rules for filmic representation that were then negotiated with the self-regulation board that came into existence in 1909. This beginning of an arrangement for institutionalized self-regulation by the industry around the first months of 1909 as a means to stave off an extraindustrial control of content is described in chapter 4. However, I suggest that the consequences of the 1909 arrangement were minimal, since the National Board of Censorship operated from a perspective compatible with the dominant ideology that defining the good and bad woman was an acceptable, even valuable, topic for moviemaking as long as it was done within specific guidelines. The board merely put a check on those who might try to breach the guidelines. As I shall indicate, the board should be seen as attuned to progressive liberal views about representing sexuality and thus reflective of the developing dominant ideological positions described in the previous two chapters. From the perspective of an eventualization/diagnosis approach to these events, the board is simply a manifestation of newly hegemonic views among the middle class about talking in regulated ways about sensuality and women.

What constituted the guidelines for representation was evident in public discourse about movie content prior to the board's institution. While it established itself as having some credibility to represent the views of the dominant groups, conservatives and even some members of the board complained that it was not strict enough. In this chapter I describe the protocols that reviewers in the period between 1907 and 1912 accepted for permitting troublesome material to be incorporated into, or even emphasized in, the plots of the films, and I link this to the development of wider melodramatic and realist aesthetics.[1] If moral reformers and progressive crusaders could see films as capable of harming their viewers, they also hypothesized that films could teach people important social lessons. Thus, they held specific theories about film viewing evident in the rules they constructed and the narratives they encouraged to be made.

Three situations about what could and could *not* be shown require examining: (1) films that should have been troubling and were (the obvious case); (2) films that might not be expected to have been a problem but were; and (3) films that might have been and were not, mostly because they abided by rules already established for presenting certain types of content.

"An Outrage upon Public Decency"

Between 1892 and 1909, thousands of short one- and two-reel films were produced by manufacturers in Europe and the United States for exhibiting in kinetoscopes, amusement parks, vaudeville theaters, civic clubs, opera houses, and nickelodeons. Several individuals have considered films prior to 1909 in terms of what might be called provocative or salacious content: the baring of an ankle, peering through keyholes at people in their bedrooms, the unintentional revealing of a woman's underclothing, the reproducing of a burlesque act that may have appealed to elements of voyeurism. These films may not have been more than a bit of fun for many customers, but to others, they represented inappropriate or outright obscene material.

At the turn of the century, law enforcement of representations was primarily a local matter. Cities had different means of regulating entertainment. Sometimes administration was a police matter; at other times, agency was in another wing of the mayor's or city commissioner's office. National regulation or censorship per se did not exist except insofar as district courts or the U.S. Supreme Court might rule on lower-court decisions. The Comstock Law specifically addressed *interstate* transportation *through the mails* of lewd materials, which thus did not affect films. Later, interstate transportation of fight films was federally prohibited. So at first questions of obscenity or salaciousness were matters of only local concern.

Some of the earliest troublesome pictures were reproductions of women dancers. In the peephole kinetoscopes that were installed in penny arcades or kinetoscope shops as early as 1894, films were less than one minute long. Showing the gyrations of Dolorita, Carmencita, and Fatima nicely fit the technology's limitations. These dancers were part of the recent fad of reproducing oriental and exotic cultures. At least two of the dancers had performed for their purported benefits at the Chicago World's Fair and Columbian Exposition in 1893. However, some local officials found these movies an "outrage upon public decency."[2]

In his study of American burlesque, Robert C. Allen argues that after the 1850s, stage entertainment in the United States was increasingly split into segments related to class and gender. Among these were (1) the theater (including ballet, opera, and legitimate drama) for the upper classes; (2) the concert saloon or burlesque (including cheap vaudeville) for working men; and (3) sanitized vaudeville for the middle-class family. The theater sphere became respectable for women to attend (and even perform in), while the burlesque sphere was appropriate for men only, particularly those in the working class but also middle- and upper-class men who were out carousing for an evening.[3]

Allen indicates that the ways women were permitted to display themselves in each of these spheres differed, as did the middle class's view about that display. One good example of the difference was in the "living pictures" trend. Toward the end of the nineteenth century (although it started much earlier), reproducing famous scenes associated with important historical events or famous stories was popular stage fare. It was also common to reveal various parts of a woman's body, although in vaudeville or the theater the model was always covered in flesh-colored tights. In these spaces living pictures carried a cultural meaning of high art; in burlesque, such a display of the body was salacious.[4] By opposition, the female performer in burlesque had taken on the deviant cultural position of the "low other," a transgression, inversion, and grotesque antithesis of normative social roles.

Allen's discussion suggests that it was not so much the degree of nudity (or the representation of nudity) that determined the meaning (art or cheap thrill) as it was the *context* for its appearance and what that context connoted. Nudity or the display of the anatomy of the body had meaning not in itself but within the circumstances of its representation. Furthermore, however, the stylization of the presentation of the body, its narrativization within a story, and its address to the spectator could reinforce or contradict the context of nude exhibition. According to Peter Gay, a "doctrine of distance" permitted Victorians to "display attractive nudes without offending the discreet and the respectable." All sorts of nudes in statues, paintings, photographs, and engravings were examined and admired by individuals of both sexes. Moreover, by the end of the century, respectable wide-circulation magazines such as *Munsey's* reproduced paintings with nudes and photographs of bathing girls and star actresses in tights. Lois Banner recounts that around 1900 public discourse about women's bodies was common enough that the variety performer Frankie Bailey was widely considered to have the ideal legs for a woman. Thomas Waugh describes the popularity of male nude photographic postcards from 1900 on, and connects this to the developing physical culture promoted by Roosevelt and others.[5]

Why then were the exotic dances a problem? After all, on the surface they had at least two claims to middle-class protection. For one thing, these performers danced at places as acceptable as the Columbian Exposition. Additionally, these dances were *narrativized* as reproductions of foreign cultures. They should have been educational (and probably were!) but became a problem mainly, I think, because the cultural distance asserted was insufficient to successfully counteract the movements of the women's bodies and the creation of a story about sexual relations. The threat of (low) primitivism and the (low) sexuality associated with primitivism overwhelmed the claims made by context, even at the fairs. Allen notes that the "hootchy-kootchy" phenomenon, as it was called, had troubles when it first started off in the 1890s; after arrests, the acts were toned down until they could be safely exhibited at least on the fringes of expositions.[6] Moving the dances to a kinetoscope only enhanced the likelihood for trouble. At a kinetoscope it was difficult to establish a patina of "distance" from the event. Thus, the officials responding to movie reproductions of these acts were simply operating within normal middle-class views dominating local regulation of theater and burlesque.

According to Allen, taking off layers of garments started about the same time as the Cooch dance (and film), around 1896. Narrative pretexts for such acts did attempt to authorize these displays of disrobing acts. The dance of the Seven Veils was one story line. After all, this was a reproduction of a biblical event. Other pretexts were legitimated by appeals to realism: "preparing for a

Figure 3.1. *Trapeze Disrobing Act.* The act begins with a blouse removed.

bath, donning a swimsuit in a bathhouse, or, perhaps the most common device by the early 1910s, getting ready for bed."[7] These acts were further safeguarded by having translucent screens separate the performers from the audiences. Even then, the models only stripped to flesh-colored tights. Not until the 1920s were tights finally discarded on the public stage, although nude acts existed in brothels during the 1800s.

One of the best examples of a movie reproduction of these acts was *Trapeze Disrobing Act* (Edison, 1901) in which a woman on a swing gradually strips off part of her clothing to the obvious delight of her male audience (Figures 3.1 and 3.2). Scholars report that one of Edison's major competitors, the American Mutoscope and Biograph Company (AMB), produced quite a few of these films, partially as a strategy of business survival in the early years of moviemaking. European examples also were imported, including Pathé films, which presented frontal female pictures of women (usually in tights but occasionally without them). Examples would include *The Corset Model* (AMB, 1903), in which a young woman models a corset for two women; *A Fire in a Burlesque Theater* (AMB, 1904), which displays burlesque queens in tights climbing down ladders; and *Model Posing before a Mirror* (without tights) (AMB, 1903) (Figures 3.3 and 3.4). These films were, indeed, "underground," and it seems hardly questionable that anyone doubted the wicked nature of

Figure 3.2. *Trapeze Disrobing Act.* The artist finishes in her tights.

their representations, or of those movies of explicit sexual copulation, which appeared soon thereafter.[8]

Even though a market for these existed among men (of any class), limiting business to these consumers would not make sense. By 1909, the U.S. film industry had sufficient capital and distribution networks to support at least three national trade papers aimed at exhibitors, as well as to command significant news sections in general entertainment papers. The size of the business alone indicates the decision made by the major manufacturers to pursue a broad audience, not only one segment of the population.[9]

I shall return to the economic and institutional rationales for the film industry's continued pursuit of its business in chapter 4. However, I do want to rehearse here the basic *economic* imperatives governing the filmmakers' choices. Mass production in capitalism operates from an economic tension between (1) standardizing production to achieve rapid, predictable, and economical manufacture of goods, and (2) differentiating its products to secure consumption. Purchasers of movies are offered a certain formula (based on genres, stars, and production values) and some innovations (through creative variations on the formula).[10]

In the United States, once the mode of production was large enough and production practices were routine (around 1917), competition primarily ex-

Figure 3.3. *The Corset Model.* The woman models the latest in corsets.

isted in the latter realm—product differentiation. Capitalist businesspeople had already learned that cutthroat competition was actually not always the best way to make money. Tacit collusion could create artifically high prices. While it was profitable to exploit current and permanent consumer interests, including interests in sexuality, that exploitation could have a loss factor if the audience took the exploitation to be not creative but objectionable. The difficulty when dealing with potentially troublesome material (such as sexuality) has always been to go far enough to maximize differentiation but not so far as to become trapped in situations in which sizeable numbers of consumers reject the product.

What we have in the first years of U.S. cinema is an initial testing of the waters to determine what types of representations will constitute permissible formulaic treatments of nudity, eroticism, sexuality, and so forth. But the same testing was occurring for other troublesome aspects of narrative, particularly crime.

"Bordering on the Sensational or Immoral"

Sorting out the limits to and procedures for securing a wide audience for various controversial subjects took a while to figure out. For example, one of the

Figure 3.4. *Model Posing before a Mirror*. The model displays her figure.

first films discussed in the *Moving Picture World* (established in 1907) as creating a stir was *The Unwritten Law* (Lubin, 1907), based on the Thaw-White
murder (described in chapter 1). Houston, Texas, police closed a showing of
the film even though the exhibitors offered to cut "the mirrored bedroom
scene."[11]

This censoring event will stand as a prototype for how the business would
work for the next several years. Officials either on their own initiative or because of customer complaints would enter theaters and seize films deemed immoral or dangerous. Exhibitors might offer to edit out objectionable portions,
and if they were so permitted, the film in its cut form might then be shown.
Obviously, this was a lot of bother, but given the local nature of the regulation
it was merely part of doing business in early moviemaking.

Exhibitors could perhaps on their own predict what might be trouble and
take their chances in showing a movie. However, since the distribution system did not permit advance screenings of the products (at this point exhibitors basically took what they could get or had standing orders for a certain
number of reels per week), theater managers were on their own to contend
with local officials. With the start-up of the trade papers in 1907, exhibitors
had two advance bits of information. For one thing, they began to have some
idea of what the forthcoming movies were about. Additionally, they learned

whether people elsewhere had trouble with any specific title. The news items and early reviews in the trades even articulated and stressed details about films that might cause difficulties.

The Thaw-White movie was definitely a film that provoked problems. Basically a series of intertitles interlaced by single-shot scenes of the famous moments in the case, *The Unwritten Law* is typical in narrative structure and narrational tone for the time. For example, the intertitle "Preparing for the Stage" prefaces a scene in which Nesbit is taught how to dance. In "The Boudoir with a 1000 Mirrors," White drugs her champagne. The walls are decorated with paintings of naked women. Characterization is minimal, but audiences could fill in the gaps since the story was front-page news that year. The resolution provides some interior development and sympathetic treatment of Thaw: while residing in the Tombs prison awaiting trial, he dreams of killing White and then of being with his mother and his wife. Awakening, he slowly heads off to the trial where—via the wonders of the movies—he is acquitted, and he rushes into the arms of his Mother and Nesbit. (This is not what eventually occurred.) A compact narrative, with some narrational strategies to create emotional empathy with the protagonist through explaining his motives, the film is not far off from what Hollywood cinema would eventually become.

The police in Superior, Wisconsin, stopped *The Unwritten Law* at the Grand Opera House. Reporters indicated that "the house was packed with an audience two-thirds women, and as the first picture was thrown upon the screen depicting an artist's studio the interest was intense." In New York City, the authorities were self-appointed. A nickelodeon operater reported that representatives from the Children's Society raided his establishment. Upon their testimony, he was fined one hundred dollars because four boys under the age of fourteen were watching "The Great Thaw Trial." Two scenes were considered as "imperilling the morals of young boys": Nesbit's drugging and the shooting of White on the garden rooftop. Within a few months, editorials in *Moving Picture World* called for the manufacturer of the movie to withdraw it because it had no "redeeming feature" and everyone showing it was having trouble.[12]

Other movies also caused forceable action. Police arrested a theater owner in Saint Louis in April 1907 for exhibiting "suggestive pictures," including "one of extreme licentiousness, showing a young woman in various stages of retiring for the night." Exhibitors were warned that the police intended to continue raids on such movies.[13]

Reports about salacious pictures do continue for the next few years, but generally, they are rare compared with the other major complaint about rep-resentation.[14] Police and citizens seemed awfully concerned about movies showing crimes. As early as May 1907, Jane Addams proposed that instead of "suppressing these places [nickelodeons], they be placed under the proper su-pervision and regulation" so that they could be beneficial rather than show "subjects bordering on the sensational or immoral." Addams had two con-cerns. One was that movies could affect children and adult criminals and an-other was that the theaters could be dangerous places to meet the wrong sorts of people. To prove her point that a regulated show could be beneficial, she opened a nickelodeon at Hull House in June 1907.[15]

In Chicago, the Juvenile Jewish Protective League also wanted movie houses policed and age limits for attendance enforced. Its concern was that nickelodeons were becoming "schools of crime where murders, robberies, and holdups are illustrated. The outlaw life they portray in their cheap plays tends to the encouragement of wickedness." When the Chicago City Club investi-gated the effects of moving pictures on youth in June 1907, they discovered that boys could see movies in all sorts of places, from penny arcades to high-priced houses. The club's report stressed all the types of crimes in the films, including gambling and murders, but it did not mention any content related to sexual behavior. In October 1907 Chicago's delegated censor, Lt. Alex-ander McDonald, stopped fourteen films for fear of their leading a "weak mind into an evil path." Although the titles are all I have to go on, only one or two suggest narratives that might provoke titillation through sexual mate-rial. The rest are clearly crime plots.[16]

The concern was specifically directed toward children (or childish minds). In an editorial about *Highwayman* (Pathé, 1907), the writer explained why it would be all right to show the film at Hammerstein's but not at a nickel-odeon: the two places were different. Children could be admitted to the latter exhibition site.[17] City after city went on record as intending to police films for the safety of children's impressions.

Although today it would not be difficult to imagine what might count as salacious material in terms of sexual content, it is more difficult to appreciate the extent to which some citizens were disturbed by representations of crime. Take, for instance, the film *The 100-to-1 Shot* (Vitagraph, 1906). A young man must find the money to save his fiancée's home. With a deadline in place, he rushes to the race track and bets a long shot. Winning the prize money, he returns in the nick of time. In the literature on early cinema, this film is prized as an early example of motivated point-of-view editing. That is, during the race the film cuts forth and back from the young man watching the horses run to the race itself. The film also has crosscutting, in which shots in different spaces are edited to represent simultaneous action in disparate locales.

Now listen to a manager of a large theatrical circuit worry in early 1908 about the wrong kinds of movies:

> In the first place, the immoral film must be banished. Scenes of drunkenness and debauchery—the tippling of vagabonds and the revelry of chorus girls— should have no place in the theatorium. Melodramas with the suggestion of prostitution or illicit love, with suggestions of criminal methods, or suggesting the commission of horrible crimes, must be done away with. Pictures which teach children to deceive their parents and encourage them to commit dangerous pranks should not be manufacturered. I am not one of those who believe that crime should be altogether eliminated, but the more horrible and disgusting features of it should not be glorified or paraded. There is no greater source of danger to the moving picture business to-day than such films as "The Hooligans of Paris," "The Indian's Revenge," or "The 100 to 1 Shot," which teaches the youth of the country that "playing the ponies" is the way to retrieve the fallen fortunes of one's family. These are old films, but their horrors and false morality linger especially in every mind.[18]

The 100-to-1 Shot was a dangerous film, at least to that observer!

Other films now considered to be outstanding examples of developments in narrational procedure were similarly viewed by some people to be inappropriate subject material because of their illustration of crime. The Chicago police censored and suppressed The Lonely Villa (Biograph, 1909, directed by D. W. Griffith) despite the praise the film won in New York City. The Lonely Villa depicts burglars attempting to break into a home while the husband is away, putting the wife and children into jeopardy. The family is saved in the nick of time. (As I shall suggest in chapter 4, Chicago and New York City were different in important ways, indicating the need to recognize the diversity existing among communities in the United States, not merely among individuals within the middle class.)[19]

Unfortunately, people seemed to have evidence that their theory of cause (seeing movies) and effect (reproducing the crimes seen there) was accurate. As early as May 1907, Moving Picture World reported that two young women, aged fourteen and ten, were caught in Chillicothe, Ohio, trying to steal some gems. Their explanation was that they had seen in a film how easy it would be to do it. Another story came from Los Angeles in August 1908. Charles H. Loper confessed to murdering his "friend and patron," Joe Vernett. "Loper told the story in all its gruesome details with little show of feeling of any kind.

He declared that ill success in a number of undertakings had caused him dis-couragement and that attendence at a number of moving picture shows where nothing but murders and burglaries were depicted had put it in his mind to kill."[20] A *Washington Post* reporter is quoted as writing that even if the hero beats the villain, one wonders what would be the effect of "action and simu-lated crime" on "impressionable and unformed minds."[21] As shall be con-firmed in the case of regulating pictures in New York City, it seems that breaking the law, gambling, and violent acts were more directly contributory than were sexual representations to requests to regulate the movies.[22]

Now if it is surprising to what degree crime films rather than representa-tions of sexuality were troublesome, some of the reasons given for negative responses to films confrontational to many sensibilities were also surprising. The rationales for disapproving some films are important for illuminating rules of presentation. Take, for example, another Lubin film, *An Unexpected Guest* (1909). Actually quite sophisticated in its storytelling, the plot is the tale of a young man who wants to marry a young woman. The young man's father intervenes and with a trick makes each person think the other has per-mitted the ending of the relationship. The young woman is pregnant, how-ever. On the eve of the young man's marriage to a more acceptable mate (at least in the eyes of the father), the young woman, dying in a hospital with the baby in her arms, writes the fiancée, who arrives in time to have the baby delivered to her care before the young woman passes away. The fiancée re-turns to confront the young man, who takes responsibility for the child. See-ing his mature response, the fiancée reconciles with him.

From the point of view of traditional expectations about what might count as a moral movie, some proper narrative action has occurred. The young woman who bore the child dies. Although it is a sad resolution, she cannot live in shame. The young man, who the audience recognizes did not really abandon her in the knowledge that she was pregnant, acts appropriately upon discovering the truth. The fiancée also responds with maternal love, and a monogamous couple with a ready-made child will conclude the tale.

Now listen to the reviewer of *Moving Picture World* who is charged with guiding the exhibitors about the forthcoming product as well as with coun-seling the manufacturers on behalf of the exhibitors:[23]

A Lubin which seems to be somewhat uncalled for. To place upon the screen the story of a young couple who loved not wisely but too well, and then to have the fruit of that love produced at the man's wedding to another woman seems too much of an imposition. The photography is good and to a certain extent the picture may interest those who are thoughtless,

but there is a certain degree of delicacy which should be observed about
such matters that is plainly violated here. The picture serves no useful
purpose. It is not instructive and cannot be called entertaining. The reason
for its existence is not plain and the silent drama would be improved if the
picture was never shown again.[24]

Although the resolution was appropriate—death to the fallen woman—the
purpose (the morality lesson) was unclear. The young woman made a mistake
and she did "pay" for it, but her death is not clearly narrativized as a consequence of her behavior (the film is ambiguous as to the cause). Moreover, no
other lesson was taught in the story, except perhaps to warn fathers against
interfering in their children's love affairs.

Teaching the value of waiting until marriage for gratifying sexual desire
and maintaining that desire within marriage so that unwanted "guests" did
not arrive were social cautions that seem unquestioned by both the manufacturer and the reviewer. In contrast, however, the reviewer apparently believed
that merely providing a realistic reproduction of the fact that premarital sexuality did occur, producing "fruits" of that love, was insufficient justification
for a narrative. One requirement of a story to be transmitted to a general audience was the necessity for some type of *prescriptive* function; mere description was an inadequate rationale for narrating.

In chapter 2, I pointed out that lurid literature and various new theories
about free love and women's sexuality indicated that conflicts existed in attitudes about people's behavior. The response to *An Unexpected Guest* illustrates that while the expectations for monogamous sexual activity existed so
strongly that they were not questioned, the reality of deviance was an inadequate rationale for a narrative. Progressives or social scientists who turned to
empirical evidence to understand individuals' behavior did so with the reformist desire to determine solutions for what they perceived to be problems.
Policymaking (a sort of reform enterprise couched in terms of scientific procedures) underpinned the collection of social facts. *The social fact of premarital
sex was not worthy of narration in its right, but only in the context of directing social
behavior in appropriate ways.* Thus, the quoted reviewer's implicit evaluative
criteria are in line with developing liberal middle-class views about representing and regulating images: description is inadequate without prescription.[25]

In *An Unexpected Guest* the protagonists made no unbecoming choices
(except perhaps to take chances with sexual intercourse), so it is not clear
what lesson might have been learned. Moreover, the focus in the plot is directed more to the reactions by the young man and his fiancée than toward
the first young woman. No real character conflict—internal or external—is

established so that rewards or punishments can be meted out through a moral and, hence, educational resolution. The characters' behaviors are explained as due to a misunderstanding. Therefore, they can hardly be "blamed" for what happened. Nor can any moral growth occur from a nonmistake.

Reviews during the period of 1907 through 1912 illustrate this regulative assumption about the function of narrative. Narratives were tools for constructing social consensus and controlling deviance. Moreover, the narrative required characters who not only understood their own behavior but made decisions. Finally, the resolution was to indicate the proper retribution or reward for their acts as a consequence of that understanding. Even then, however, movies with crime and violence within them might have had such excessive images of how to commit wrongdoings that even a rationalized narrative was insufficient as a compensation, especially for young or weak minds. In that case, the transgressive scenes or entire films were to be unavailable to viewers.

"Instructive and Entertaining"

If a story was not instructive, it could still be acceptable if it were entertaining. Both Dr. Keenan of Boston and the reviewer of An Unexpected Guest use the same two criteria (even in the same order) as minimal requirements for storytelling. Many reviewers stress that some movies were morbid or depressing, and therefore not to their liking. They wanted to enjoy the movie. Yet any move to create such pleasure could also surely edge a plot toward the sensational or immoral.

If some films were obvious problems, others unexpectedly troublesome, perhaps the most surprising situations are those in which reviewers and audiences accepted representations that traditional scholarship might lead us to expect would be provocative. Here I shall discuss four types of potential problems in which narrative and narrational conventions apparently authorized by representational norms operated to make the dangerous situations instructive and entertaining—at least to many viewers. Although I could develop more than these four, these seem most commonly to have stimulated reviewers' evaluations in the subject area of sexuality. These four potential problems entail the representations of bad women and men, women's and men's sexual desire, compromising situations, and nudity. I will return to these issues in chapters 5, 6, and 7. Here I want to survey what norms for regulating images were already in place before and during the start of an official self-regulation (circa 1909).

Films about bad women and men not only might prevent some people from going astray, but they might also help those now in trouble. Some regulationists of prostitution urged families to accept fallen daughters back into the fold rather than forcing them to remain on the streets. A "fallen woman" in 1910 might be saved.[26] For example, The Lost Sheep (Vitagraph, 1909) is praised by the reviewer for its potential "moral teaching" that a woman seduced and abandoned can return to her family and is thus "not without its value," although this version of the story "is depressing in its influence, and the technical quality is not up to the standard of the Vitagraph."[27] Another instance of tolerating plots with fallen women is the reaction to The Scarlet Letter (Kinema-Color, 1913). Based as it was on Nathaniel Hawthorne's novel (already within canonical literature), the film was considered by its reviewer to have been well done, as eventually Hester and Dimmesdale experienced enough penance for their crimes.[28]

A fallen person had to show, however, a sincere conversion to the upright path. The Call (Biograph, 1910) was about "the spiritual rebirth of a 'coochie' dancer" who "is no better than she ought to be." Various events lead the coochie dancer to forsake the life of the ten-cent side show. After marrying a young farmer, she remains at his home, but when the show next returns to the area, she deserts him to rejoin the troupe and a "sinister" man. Variety's reviewer observes, "An attempt is made in the girl's extenuation by showing that the sinister person has hypnotic influence over her, but she had already shown her inclination." She does reject the life just as she is about to enter the show, "but she makes no reparation for the deceit she practiced against the people who had befriended and saved her. The pantomime of the Biograph's leading woman, which has frequently been commented upon, is the redeeming feature of the reel. Otherwise it is laid out none too well, and is not wholesome in theme."[29] In other words, characters not only had to direct their choices appropriately, all errors must be accounted for.

Not surprisingly, the use of the imprimatur of high art could be a supportive context justifying borderline content with bad women and men. Here context and the Victorian "doctrine of distance" sanctioned the subject matter. An exhibitor wrote to Moving Picture World in 1908 that he was upset about some manufacturers who "force a diet of bloodshed, drunkenness and adultery on the children of America." Better, he thought, were movies such as Michael Strogoff, Othello, Nero and the Burning of Rome, and Genevieve de Brabant.

Of course, these plays are not devoid of bloodshed and domestic infidelity, but they carry with them the prestige of genius, which is the excuse for their production. They are constructed by artists who knew how to use these elements without making them disgusting. Murder and adultery are important elements in "Francesco di Rimini," but between that and "The Poacher's Wife" there is a gulf as wide as between a Bougereau painting and a three-sheet poster showing the undraped beauties of the "Hot Girls from Hotville."[30]

The exhibitor did go on to remark that even *Francesco di Rimini* might have been toned down somewhat.

As I discussed earlier, the context of the exhibition of material was critical in its evaluation. Here knowing that the plot source had prestige as high art and thus an already established aura of "distance" in its earlier theatrical presentations was important, although the exhibitor also claimed that the narrative treatment by the filmmakers was influential in making the salacious subject matter tolerable, or even rewarding.

Filmmakers might be at risk, however, if they toyed too much, and inappropriately, with an original source. One reviewer for *Sampson and Delilah* (Pathé, 1908) thought generally the film was good, but it might have been better to cut out the last scene, "which is biblically incorrect, offensive to good taste, and spoils the climax." Three big no's: inaccuracy, unwise social address, and bad narration—nothing is left to redeem the scene.

The phrase "offensive to good taste" occurs often and seems to mean that the filmmakers lingered over gross details or even exaggerated them for sensationalism, in which case the viewer apparently became more conscious of the details than the narrative plot. This idea of a film being "offensive to good taste" is difficult to pin down, but the term does appear often in relation to scenes of death or physical violence. If Tom Gunning's thesis is accurate— that spectacle is submerged into narrative in order to satisfy social standards —these movies would be good instances of the tension between spectacle still "surfacing" to the visible despite the attempt by filmmakers to narrativize such material and make it acceptable to a wide audience. Spectacle of the wrong nature could not be indulged in by a viewer.

An educational lesson, character agency, "high art" sources, and restrained treatment of spectacle might not even be enough to save some films for some reviewers, and here I want to stress the variety of opinions circulating about borderline cases. Of *Sins of the Father* (Lubin, 1911) one reviewer wrote: "This picture affects one very powerfully. In brief, it tells of the failure of a brilliant son and of his approaching imbecility because of the dissipation of his father. He makes his mother promise that she will give him poison when she discovers symptoms of this malady. The last scene fades with the mother undecided what to do. A strong ending. The film preaches a highly moral sermon upon the effect of heredity, and it might have been suggested by Ibsen's 'Ghosts.' "[31] Given the current propagation of the social hygiene movement, which I discussed in chapter 2, the film seems indicative of one position in the debates about the social evil. Education is necessary and people need to recognize the effects of the double standard.

Not everyone agreed with the social hygiene movement, and that *Moving Picture World* presents an alternative review for *Sins of the Fathers* is unusual.[32] Another writer argues, "The subject is disgusting at best and Ibsen has used his marvelous dramatic powers to make it horrible and revolting. To film such an atrocity is to sin both against art and decency." The movie was also "literary piracy."[33] The second writer took the contrary position that reticence might be better, even accusing the *moviemakers* of sinning.

Stories of sexual licentiousness might not only be charged with being tastelessly revolting; they might also be accused of being foreign to American sensibilities. *The Wages of Sin* (Vitagraph, 1908) was reproached for its "ill-chosen subject": "The story is of foreign conception and repulsive to American ideals." A *Daring Maid* (1908) "borders on the vulgar and should be retired. It may go to Europe, but severe criticism is heard in first-class houses here. The less the American public has of such broadly suggestive subjects the better."[34] Here and elsewhere, foreign films or their topics could receive a "nativist" treatment typical of the period.[35]

Prostitutes, fallen women, or otherwise bad women (and men) could be portrayed in the movies around 1909. However, several rules were to be obeyed: (1) the narrative should have some lesson dependent on character agency; (2) individuals ought to have some choices to make so that the progression and resolution of the plot are consequences of their actions; (3) contextual features such as the source of the plot could provide sufficient legitimacy for the subject matter, although subrules existed, such as authenticity to the source and tasteful narration—restrained and not too depressing, disgusting, or morbid.

A second potential problem was the representation of sexual desire. This was probably the most difficult area to police. The uncertainty about instruction is whether or not it is appropriate instruction. To show desire would require configurations of image and plot arranged so that viewers did not begin to play out their own fantasies while watching the characters. The narrative conclusion of a plot of desire may reassert social norms through a vaguely motivated resolution or a tacked-on morality, but an awful lot, for the characters and for spectators, could happen on the way to the end.

In these moving pictures the *agency* of desire was permitted as long as actions did not eventually cross the border over into the sensational or immoral—a line then being debated and challenged because of the social transformations that were occurring. Such plots were productive in terms of instruction *and* entertainment in *many* films of the era. One of my favorites is *The Picture Idol* (Vitagraph, 1912), a story of an adolescent girl who has a crush on a movie star. The reviewer recounts the tale:

> A school girl, played by Clara Kimball Young, falls in love with a picture hero, played by Maurice Costello. The girl's parents (Mr. Eldridge and Mrs. Maurice), as well as her school sweetheart (Mr. Morrison) are troubled. The father goes to see the picture idol and they make up a plan to disillusion the girl. His table manners made laughs, but didn't quite cure the girl; so they made up one of the boys as the idol's wife, and got four kids to come in from the street. This did the business.[36]

I shall return to the subjects of cross-dressing and gender identity switches later. However, *The Picture Idol* and its reviewer seem to think that, while young women have sexual desires and fantasies, they recognize the limits of marriage.

Sexual desire in teenagers was a common plot device in Vitagraph movies of the period. The company also made *Love Sick Maidens of Cuddletown* (1912) and *Hearts and Diamonds* (1914). In *Love Sick Maidens of Cuddletown*, young girls pretend they are sick in order to have the handsome doctor come visit them. As an intertitle expresses it, "The epidemic spreads." The women ask the doctor to touch their foreheads, take their pulses, and generally make body contact. The disease resolves itself when, as before, the girls discover the doctor already has a wife. However, prior to the climax, the audience is treated to images of young women desiring a man, without apparent social concern. In fact, their behavior is perceived as natural and amusing; its common acceptance is shown by the film review of *Love Sick Maidens of Cuddletown*, which chastises the movie only for lack of originality.[37] Another Vitagraph movie, *Hearts and Diamonds*, is of interest because both of its plots are romances with physicality between courting partners represented as ordinary. One scene even depicts the protagonist's two daughters with their beaus sitting together on a couch kissing. They do stop when Dad comes in the room!

Movies started with images of kissing between individuals. An early Edison film, *The May Irwin–John C. Rice Kiss* (1896), is a close-up shot of a famous comic play in which a man and a woman kiss. Kissing apparently became not only an act but an art. During this era of film exhibition, better-class houses were providing musical accompaniment and sound effects as background information for the film images. In 1909, one theater seems to have had enough kissing in its movies to have developed conventional treatment of the action:

> Ever kissed or been kissed, reader? Of course you have. You remember the first you gave her or she gave you, don't you. Of course you do. The art of osculation is inherent in all created beings. Some savages, I believe, kiss by rubbing noses. Animals kiss. Ever see two dogs at the game, or cats? There is a great deal of human nature in man, still more in woman, and considerably more of it in animals.[38]

Although the writer's theory of the increasing degrees of passion in men, women, and animals seems contrary to some standard opinions prevalent in 1909, he accepts sexual pleasure as normal.

Well, actually he does not quite. For the writer describes a recent practice at the theater of having the musicians punctuate screen kisses with sound effects. A certain uneasiness must have been operating for him to have mentioned this, even though the audible representations were clearly for humorous pleasure. Part of the discomfort such representations generated was mitigated through laughter, and the filmmakers and audiences of the period seem to have enjoyed playing with touchy situations for comic purposes.

A third potential problem was the borderline possibility of a character ending up in a compromising situation. In the case of comedy, it was important that audiences knew that a mistake was unintentional or even nonexistent, merely the imagination of another character. This is the situation for *The Blue Garter* (Lubin, 1909). Although Lubin films often come in for trouble, the reviewer of *The Blue Garter* liked this one. A man finds "this interesting piece of feminine apparel," but his wife does not believe his story. The reviewer thought the comedy was well-constructed: "We laughed because we saw catastrophe after catastrophe coming. The humorous situations anticipate themselves."[39] Here the narrativization of a possible breach works because the audience knows that the protagonist has not actually violated any social rules about men and women's clothing.

Misunderstandings between husbands and wives about such possible mistakes are also a frequent plot device, and the thought of adultery (or at least adventuresome behavior) by one or the other provided not only dramatic but also comic potential. *The New Neighbor* (Keystone, 1912) is described as a "comedy of errors in which a young husband is obsessed with much groundless jealousy of his wife and comes to amusing grief for his folly. The fun is extremely lively."[40]

Intimate but unrevealing garments were acceptably risqué. *The Pink Pajama Girl* (Vitagraph, 1912) works on this premise. After changing to her nightclothes (the pink pajamas), the young girl accidently locks herself out of her apartment when going to mail a letter. Her boyfriend discovers her in that attire. The reviewer thought the movie was "a first-class comedy picture."[41]

At least two Vitagraph films paved the way for Roscoe Arbuckle and other comedians of the midteen years to employ the device of cross-dressing. *One Good Joke Deserves Another* (Wilfred North, 1913) stars John Bunny as a middle-class husband whose wife is very jealous. As part of the plot, the wife dresses as a man, but her husband recognizes that it is her. In response, he and two other men dress as women. Events proceed until each disguise is revealed.

Another such comedy was *A Florida Enchantment* (1914). This is an extensive treatment not only of cross-dressing but also of gender switching. The premise is that a seed turns people into the other sex. A young woman eats one, and begins shaving, acting roughly, and being attracted to women. Later a man ingests one as well and behaves with the gestures we associate today with the term "effeminate." His movements are bouncy; he delicately wipes his brow; he conveys an interest in fashions. An intertitle expresses his feelings: "Oh heavens I must be going. I'm so nervous." Eventually, he dons women's clothing and is chased by men. The film takes the easy way out, however. Our heroine wakes up: it was just a dream.

I have been unable to find reviews of *One Good Joke Deserves Another* or *A Florida Enchantment* in *Moving Picture World*.[42] While one explanation might be that the films were so troublesome that *Moving Picture World* would not admit to their existence, that is not likely. In February 1912, *Moving Picture World* called attention to Whitney Raymond, who "enacts a remarkable female impersonation in Essanay's bright comedy entitled 'The Lemon.' . . . Mr. Raymond is a handsome young man, and his portrayal of the mysterious 'woman' in the above mentioned photoplay will certainly cause the ladies, who view the production, much wonderment as to how he manages to appear so strikingly in feminine finery."[43] *Moving Picture World* accompanied the article with a photograph of Raymond in women's clothing. Furthermore, the continued employment of the device in later films suggests its acceptance, if not outright enjoyment. Most important, cross-dressing was a common act in vaudeville at that time, and thus within bounds.[44]

It is the case that *Variety* hated *A Florida Enchantment*. The reviewer goes so far as to say that it was "the worst program the Vitagraph theatre has yet presented." However, the review seems to suggest that the critic thought the film paled in comparison with what a good acting troupe might have done with the same story: "As a comic opera with the late Della Fox in the principal role, maybe yes, but cold and dispirited before the camera, it is only a senseless mess. None of the actors gained distinction in it. . . . The picture should never have been put out, for there's no one with any sense of humor whatsoever, or intelligence either, who can force a smile while watching this sad 'comedy.' "[45] When the industry moved to self-regulation in 1909, none of the codes had any suggestions about improprieties regarding cross-dressing or gender dissonance. These sexual practices would receive attention in later expressions of the codes, however.

A *Florida Enchantment* is interesting because it does not just make cross-dressing a performance, as with the masquerades to fool people. It narrativizes two transformations to the other gender and creates a narrative tension around the ambiguity of gender characteristics and sexual orientation for its comedic premise. That the activities were used for the sake of humor or curiosity underlines some potential discomfort in such situations. The arena of sexual mores among individuals in the realm of stereotypes of gender identities and confusion over gender roles, particularly in connection with homo- or bisexual overtones, deserves more attention than I am able to give it here. I note, however, that it is being raised within films, implying the general productivity operating from treating sexual difference and gender characteristics in binary terms (man/woman, masculine/feminine).[46]

While some dramatic films used women's rights movements as material for narrative, suffragettes were occasionally a source for comedy. *The Suffragette's Dream* (Pathé, 1909) is described as a comedy "which shows a woman going through all the stunts to which suffragettes are addicted. The men are made the burden bearers, and the millennium truly arrives. But it all ends very suddenly when her husband returns, finds her asleep in her chair and dinner not ready. The millennium vanishes, and she goes meekly about her business. The picture excites a roar of laughter from beginning to end, and is really funny."[47] Similarly, *The Suffragette Tames the Bandit* (Frontier, 1913) shows the uneasiness with which suffragette activities were met. In this case, the suffragette is kidnapped, but the villains are surprised about what they took: "She immediately goes to work on them and they offer to hand her back, without any ransom. One of the freshest comedies shown for some time and should not give offense to followers of the cause."[48]

The final remark is indicative of the general advice operating by the early teens. As I suggested earlier, at this point in the history of motion pictures, the manufacturers believed that their best method of profit making was to appeal to everyone. Although later (after World War II), distribution and marketing techniques encouraged targeting those who were most likely to attend pictures, in 1909 the sophistications of demographic research were not in place. Guides to screenwriters continually cautioned that no one should be offended by any movie. Comments such as "this story hardly will concern the men in any audience," although it might divert women "who find entertainment in a slow tale of a gossiping female interfering for no apparent motive in the charitable work of a neighbor" are telling.[49] Offense, bad taste, impropriety—these are the code words for breaching normative boundaries for part or all of the audience. Compromising situations could be considered in dramatic or comedic form as long as breaches in the norms are unintentional or easily rectified in a conclusion: it was a misunderstanding and did not really happen; no one was hurt by it.

One of the best possibilities for trouble, one might imagine, was the problem of suggesting nudity. Erotic dances and disrobing acts in which female anatomy was implied (even if covered by tights) solicited the viewer to construct in his or her mind a narrative about sexual intercourse. These films met with official censorship. Narrativizing the display of a body *into some other story line*, however, was one way to create a motivation for the display so that the filmmakers might appeal to the "doctrine of distance." The trick was positioning the body so that it was, indeed, subordinated to the (moral) story line.

An instance in which this failed is *The Acrobatic Maid* (Pathé, 1908). One reviewer wrote, "A knockabout comic which introduces an original scheme to extract laughs from the audience, and it succeeds. Perhaps this sort of film is as good as anything which can be produced in the way of a comic, and it may be worthwhile to speak well of this one." Another reviewer thought not. "This film can perhaps suit the Moulin-Rouge of Paris but is not a very proper film to show to an American audience. If some ignorant spectators laughed at the exhibit of women showing their limbs in their tumbling acts, many other persons, especially ladies, could hardly refrain from disdain."[50]

If done right, however, showing body limbs might not even provoke mention. *Mr. Bolter's Infatuation* (Vitagraph, 1912) is the tale of Mr. Bolter thinking that a "dancing girl" (she wears the short dress and tights typical of a burlesque chorus girl) is enamored of him from their brief encounter. The film's reviewer does not even hint that the woman's appearance or her attire might be delicate subject matter. In fact, Mr. Bolter is the object of the joke since the dancing girl tricks him into coming to the city to meet her at the Hotel des Imbeciles.[51]

The same type of situation occurs in The Deacon's Troubles (Keystone, 1912). According to the review, "The deacon, as a leading light in the Purity League, starts out to reform the theater. But he falls in love with a Salome dancer and gets in trouble with the other members of the League."[52] Playing jokes on strict older women also appear. In Odd Pair of Limbs (circa 1908), "two mischievous boys steal a pair of false calves used to display women's hosiery from the window of a department store" and put them in strange places, surprising people who take them for real. This includes placing them "so they appear to belong to a sour visaged old maid asleep in a hammock." Variety's reviewer—sometimes tough to please—thought it a "capital laughing series."[53]

It became apparent in my viewing and reading of reviews of the movies that much of men's anatomy was generally considered to be innocuous. Yet one problem did show up in a comedy, and in that case it bordered on the offensive for the Moving Picture World reviewers. In The Gangsters (Keystone, 1913), "Fred Mace appears as the leader of a gang of toughs, who make things lively for the police force. A favorite pastime of the gang is stripping trousers from the members of the force. This renders the film a little rough in presentation in some houses."[54] The reviewer may also have been writing about the lack of respect for the police, but the direct connection between the specific behavior and the judgment suggests that moving toward revealing anatomy normally concealed was part of the trouble.

If some aspects of the body could be used for comedy, the suggestion (or fact) of nudity could occur in drama if done tastefully. In 1911, Vitagraph filmed Lady Godiva. As the photograph accompanying the trade announcement indicates (perhaps mostly to encourage exhibitors), while the heroine is as naked as the original story says she was, her long hair discreetly covers her breasts and pubic area. Probably anticipating concerns, the reviewer also emphasizes the tastefulness of the presentation: "Tennyson's poem on her sacrifice has furnished the scenario for this picture, which is a very fine piece of art and picture-craft, full of spiritual significance. The impression it makes is distinctly human and tender. The audience seemed to be clearly moved by it." The same gesture of reassurance occurs for Dante's Inferno (Helios, 1912): "It is clean and moral to the point of austerity. Nowhere is there even the faintest trace of an appeal to the morbid or sensational."[55] Dante's Inferno is quite explicit, with no use of body tights to cover the naked men and women. It was, however, also an Italian import, thus gaining additional sanction from its European origin.

By 1914, a full frontal depiction of a female *in motion and without tights* appeared in an American-made moving picture—although very discreetly.[56] Lois Weber, a woman director of solid repute by that year, filmed *The Hypocrites* (Bosworth) as a moral fable in a narrational mode something akin to *Pilgrim's Progress*. Within a framing device of a minister's thoughts, the fable illustrates how truth as a virgin is ravished by the hypocrites. Of particular concern here is the literal representation of truth as a naked woman who walks among the sinners. The film anticipates the possibilities of its reception. An intertitle remarks, "The people are shocked by the nakedness of Truth." Weber, an activist in some women's movements, certainly knew the chance she was taking, and she managed to succeed in large part. "Sime," the reviewer for *Variety*, writes particularly to reassure exhibitors of the tastefulness of the nudity:

> To get right to the sensation of this four-reeler, it is the figure of a naked girl, about 18 years of age, probably designated on the program as "The Naked Truth" walking and flitting through the woods. Even the most fastidious can find nothing offensive in this to carp at, it has been so well handled. Although a couple of times the young woman walks directly toward the camera, there is no false modesty exhibited, and a shadowy trick by the camera does not permit of the nude figure too long in sight at any time.[57]

"Sime" does note that some uncertainty existed at a preview of the movie, but it is "a pretty idyllic pastoral picture of faultless taste" and has "the essence of sweetness in purity." In any event, just to be sure, the film's distributor, Paramount, chose to road-show the film: the company rented high-class houses, provided printed programs, and generally treated it as a legitimate theater exhibition. The film was banned in Chicago, however, indicating that even these precautions were not always sufficient for cities with stricter views about representations.[58]

The narration around nakedness, as well as the moral and didactic content, could motivate the representation of nudity as chaste. Thus, in itself, the body could often be displayed. Only if the context or story solicited from the viewer the wrong type of narrative tale would nudity be deemed salacious. These then were the types of individual rules operating around 1909. A diagnosis of their sources and cultural logics follows.

Reading Theories and Troublesome Pictures

This study reveals that a set of norms about representation within a narrative guided evaluative judgments about the propriety of specific images or actions.

These norms involve issues of narrative (for example, what is being said about reality, character psychology, and causality of events) and narration (for example, how images are embedded within the narrative, how closure is achieved, how narrational voice is employed). These norms of representation also exist in both dominant realist and melodramatic aesthetics of the period and, I will argue, constitute important influences on the formal, narrational, and ideological features of the classical Hollywood cinema. Furthermore, two conflicting theories of how spectators might learn from movies were applied to the cinema, resulting in the set of guidelines established around 1909 as the ad hoc production code for institutional regulation of the content of motion pictures. The two theories also explain some of the continuing contention about representing troublesome pictures. In other words, this is the movie industry's constitution of the rules for talking about women and sexuality, for breaking the norm of reticence and investigating woman.

Where are these rules coming from? Are they just ad hoc made up by the reviewers? Obviously not. The essay from which the evaluation of *Dante's Inferno* came was entitled "Gauging the Public Taste." No doubt exists that a diversity of opinions existed around 1909 about what was or was not tasteful or appropriate in still or moving pictures. Accounting for these differences requires considering two domains of diversity in public opinion. One is the range of views about sex and sexuality held within the middle class at the turn of the century. The other is that at least two theories about how spectators view movies were operating simultaneously. One theory I will call the "total picture" point of view. In this view, immoral or improper behavior could (and ought to) be displayed, although protocols for doing this existed. One rule was to be sure a moral lesson was apparent so that "uplift" and directed social change might occur.[59] A framing of the tale by a moral prologue perhaps would be good, but most assuredly the conclusion must end with a principled resolution that would teach youth and wayward souls about restitution for good and evil actions. This *prescriptive*, reformist function for storytelling not only permitted *but encouraged* the representation of material that would otherwise normally be out of bounds. *It stimulated and directed talk about sex, sexuality, and gender characteristics.*

Such a narrativization of problems of boundaries and definitions did require a bit more than a proper ending in which the good are rewarded and the bad punished. As I have illustrated, character agency and choice had to motivate the initiation of the impropriety. Furthermore, the resolution was to derive out of the conflict produced by that act. Mere coincidence was unacceptable. Screenwriting books of the era assert over and over again that chance might be involved in the activation of a conflict but it definitely could not resolve it. The ideological function of such a rule is quite simple: both religion and some social science theory of the period placed moral agency within the realm of individual action. To be saved required personal intention. Hence, willful characters had to be the cause of their own doing or undoing.

This total-picture theory assumes that the short-term effect of any infractions of norms would be outweighed by the larger rules operating, especially those about resolutions derived from characters receiving their just deserts. In fact, the point of storytelling was to show that agency had its consequences, so it was necessary to represent such violations.

The total-picture theory is counterbalanced by a pointillist position: proper resolutions are insufficient guarantees for insuring in spectators moral behavior and recognition of ethical lessons. The part might have much more significance than the whole. A child or weak mind (or even an adult) might view a salacious or criminal act and ignore the ending. Or the salacious or criminal act might encourage an alternative narrative, one filled with improper sexual fantasies or scorn toward authorities.

In the history of the regulation and censorship of moving pictures, these two theories have continually been at odds, and arguments for and against specific approaches for handling troublesome pictures derive from epistemological philosophy and empirical evidence about what people think and experience when they watch movies and other media. Still the rules about what some people believe others ought to think and experience cannot be enforced, and perhaps those rules even provoke resistance. This means that proving one position or the other to be "true" would be difficult. Much of the debate in contemporary theory still comes up against the wall of discerning the interiority of the human individual in relation to social systems. As I shall show in chapter 4, the first debates about formalizing rules for what could be shown on the screen were underpinned by these two reading theories. Although the total-picture theory basically prevailed, those holding the pointillist theory have never stopped trying to intervene.

Melodrama and Realist Aesthetics

Although the rules for telling acceptable stories were being articulated in the press, the protocols were not ad hoc or medium specific. They derived from procedures for appropriately narrating stories in novels and drama. Moreover, filmmakers did not immediately figure out how to transpose those tactics to movies. They created the means gradually, between 1895 (but more intensely after 1907) to around 1917. Here I am interested in connecting the development of the classical Hollywood narrative with current views about realist and melodramatic aesthetics, their relation to the filmic narrative form, and the creation of a "moral" narration acceptable to middle-class reformers holding a "total picture" theory of using movies for regulating and directing social change.

The work of Christine Gledhill, Marcia Landy, E. Ann Kaplan, and others has significantly improved the understanding in film studies of the relations between literary and dramatic forms of melodrama to the history of cinema.[60] Kaplan describes the theoretical shift from thinking of melodrama as a set of textual features to conceiving of it as a historicized aesthetic experience (connected to certain recurring devices).

Most writers associate the rising dominance of melodrama in theater with the development of the bourgeois class in the eighteenth century. As Gledhill describes it, "The tragic action [of the neoclassical drama] was increasingly internalised as individual error."[61] In the place of tragic value "emerged the notion of 'poetic justice' and a new moral mission for the theatre. The theatre took on an educative role through the power of example and appeal to the 'sympathetic emotions' of what was understood to be an essentially benevolent human nature." As the dramatic form developed, it incorporated other aesthetic features, including spectacle, song, and violence. Gledhill notes that in the 1800s, melodrama enjoyed the strategy of "externalis[ing] the inner states of characters" through "costume, makeup, gesture and facial expression."[62]

At the end of the nineteenth century, melodrama faced a theatrical competitor: realism. By the mid-1800s, numerous theatrical troupes had turned to subject matter depicting the lives of the bourgeoisie. This change in subject matter affected representation and included creating authentic, three-dimensional sets and props and promoting an invisible fourth wall viewing space. In both the United States and abroad, realism also had an impact on theatrical and film acting styles.[63] Where realism used conversation to indicate the interiority of a character, melodrama employed visual and musical means. Gledhill points out that an argument has been made that toward the end of the 1800s, realism "coincided with a re-masculinisation of cultural values" and picked up such a linkage by also stressing in its subject matter " 'serious' social issues or inner dilemmas, recentring the hero and claiming tragic value for the failure of heroic potential."[64]

The realist novelists in the United States also fit the description by attending to social issues and further developing the internal psychology of the individual character. William Dean Howells, widely considered an archetypical realist, produced work from the 1880s in such a vein, and Howells was very much a moralist. In describing Howells's beliefs about modern tactics of writing literary fiction, Horace Newcomb summarizes Howells's praise of the work of Turgenev: "In his hands sin suffered no dramatic punishment. It did not always show itself as unhappiness, in the personal sense, but was always unrest, and without the hope of peace. If the end did not appear, the fact that it must be miserable always appeared."[65]

Beyond Howells came the next generation, the naturalists—Stephen Crane, Frank Norris, and Theodore Dreiser. Two of these writers produced their versions of the "bad woman," but in an original way. Crane published *Maggie: A Girl of the Streets* in 1893; Dreiser, *Sister Carrie* in 1900, both in tune with the recent outbreak of interest by reformers in prostitution. The two novels were perceived as indecent and received limited first printings. Although Newcomb is not attempting to explain the difficulties the novels had in the public arena, his discussion of Dreiser's approach to *Sister Carrie* is illuminating. Newcomb emphasizes that Dreiser sets up Carrie as threatened by the city, by fate, by forces beyond her so that the reader is requested to fear for her. This appeal to empathy solicits acceptance of Carrie's choices as the "lesser of two evils." Moreover, the novel concludes without any poetic justice except the irony that Carrie is alone.[66] In my opinion, the dominant middle class was not yet ready (if it ever has been) for such a structural reading of human behavior.

In his major discussion of this era of U.S. literature, Jay Martin argues that some of the realist and naturalist aesthetics are picked up by the muckrakers. Attributing the success of muckraking fiction to contradictions in the move to urbanization and the middle class's observations of the rich (on one side) and the poor (on the other), Martin writes, "Disguised as social analysis or statistical scientific investigation, the muckraking movement became the literary outlet of American naturalism." Strategies in the fiction included a "polarizing" of good and bad to provide "placebos for American fears and frustrations."[67] The taking up of naturalism by muckrakers had good cause: Crane published short fiction in *McClure's* in 1894 and 1896; Norris worked for *McClure's*, covering the Spanish-American War in 1898. Norris was also the reader for Doubleday, Page (earlier Doubleday, McClure) who recommended publication of *Sister Carrie*.

While realism and naturalism as aesthetics responded to the social changes of the late 1800s and early 1900s, melodrama also changed. John G. Cawelti's work on the "social melodrama" of the era provides an important historical analysis of the aesthetics. Cawelti defines the "social melodrama" as combining older melodrama with "a detailed, intimate, and realistic analysis of major social or historical phenomena."[68] He writes that this formula appealed to moral fantasies and "poetic justice" while being revitalized to seem socially significant. The social melodrama required, however, a "proper order of things": it was "dependent on a sense of what is a proper, acceptable, and plausible means for insuring the triumph of virtue in spite of the terrible strength of vice" (p. 269).

How did it achieve that plausibility? It did so by changing its explanation for causality. Cawelti claims that the first period of the social melodrama (in the early 1800s) tied religion and social order together. However, during the second phases (mid to late 1800s), religious skepticism developed. Perhaps "divine providence" was not "the cornerstone of society," nor was it necessarily socially advantageous for women to be totally domestic and submissive. Cawelti argues that stories about women being saved or innocents martyred but going to heaven did not resonate with melodrama's audiences.

Two aspects to the older melodrama formula changed. One was "new forms of melodramatic action, and . . . ways of treating society. . . . Later melodramatists concerned with social change developed stories in which the protagonist was morally regenerated by a new and better understanding of what was happening to society" (p. 276). These stories might involve, for example, a minister abandoning a traditional religion that had no relevance to current social needs while adopting a more socially responsible doctrine. Or a capitalist could recognize the errors of materialism and find happiness serving society. Cawelti contrasts this approach to character and society with the procedures of Crane, Norris, and Dreiser, "in whose works there is no possible resolution between traditions of Christianity and the new naturalistic determinism" (p. 277).

A second change was the development of strong women heroines: "They also worked out new patterns for resolving the tensions created by the changing conceptions of the feminine character and of relations between the sexes. . . . A morally sympathetic portrait of the new woman" was possible. An "official heroine" had to remain pure, but she could have a "certain degree of wildness," "an increasing physicality and sensuality in her makeup" (p. 278). This heroine still found her place with the right man by the end of the story.

Gledhill has recently argued that she believes it is best to think of the classical Hollywood cinema as derived from both melodramatic and realist aesthetics, and that Hollywood cinema even helped make those aesthetics viable

for the middle class of the twentieth century. Gledhill summarizes the situation thus:

> Hollywood inherited that transformation [of melodrama and realism],
> producing a cinema in which the melodramatic and the realistic—the
> metaphoric and the referential, the psychological and the social—mesh
> together. . . . American cinematic narration and characterization are capable
> of externalizing in mise-en-scène, star personae, or musical orchestration
> melodramatic desires emanating from sets of personal traits and which satisfy
> demands for psychological realism.[69]

Hollywood makes films employing both aesthetics or films in which combi-
nations exist.

These descriptions of specific changes in literary and dramatic aesthetics
contemporaneous with the appropriation of narrative strategies by fledgling
film companies fit well with the explicit and implicit rules for representing
good and bad in films from about 1907 through around 1912. I want to stress
especially the importance of two features of that transformation. One is my
belief that as religion lost dominance to social scientific explanations of human behavior, the idea of "villains" was difficult to hold. Instead, humans
become "victims," capable of being understood and for whom sympathy could
develop. That does not, however, permit the acceptance of nonsocial behavior. Instead, even greater stress is placed on human agency and action as determining the judgment of one's outcome. Morality is behavior *in the face of
an amoral universe*.[70] Hence "bad" is redefined as the failure to act in the right
way even upon recognizing the proper choice. The rule of "poetic justice" is
contingent upon the individual's behavior *after* knowing what the stakes of a
choice are. Such a morality, which fits neatly with Christian theology as well
as reformism, easily works into a narrative plot of the classical three-act formula. Plot points are moments of character decision in relation to events.

Additionally, tremendous weight is given to character psychology and
development—manifested either through external means (the older melodramatic practices) or through internal ones (such as in realist practices). When
plots, "morals," and ends center on characters, then clarity in exposition of
character is crucial.

In his discussion of the development of D. W. Griffith's filmic practices
between about 1908 and 1910, Tom Gunning argues that one of Griffith's
strategies was to use a "moral voice." Gunning asserts that "in pre-Griffith
cinema the devices of filmic discourse are rarely used to convey moral judgments. Moral positions are simply implied in the presentation of stereotypical

situations . . . and the conventional response filmmakers could expect from audiences. The films, in effect, use no rhetoric to persuade or convince through their filmic discourse; they cannot 'depict a powerful lesson.' "[71] As he describes the way Griffith creates such a "moral voice," Gunning proceeds to equate it with the device of editing shots so that a viewer is aware of what the character is seeing, thus inferring what the character is thinking. For Gunning, Griffith's "moral voice" is the "proto-point-of-view/reaction shot pattern" (p. 169). He concludes his discussion of Griffith's film, A *Drunkard's Reformation* (1909): "For the first time in Griffith's filmmaking, and probably in the history of film, the psychological development of a character, primarily conveyed by editing, forms the basis of a film" (p. 169).[72]

However, I believe that it is not a character's being developed psychologically that creates the moral voice; it is the plot turning on that character's decision-making process that grounds the narrative in a bourgeois morality.[73] Moreover, this is not the initiation of character psychology in American cinema; other means to present character psychology existed—intertitles (which start around 1903), dialogue intertitles (which take off after 1910), performance by both the character and those surrounding him or her (which is available from the start), and even the representation of mental activity, such as flashbacks and dreams (which exist from at least 1903).[74] What Gunning has picked out is one method to develop a character—related to a realist aesthetic, incidentally, since it relies on an "interior" representation of character motivation. Moreover, it is not just that the editing permits a viewer to understand a character's actions, but that the character's choice has become the turning point of the plot. The recognition provides the basis for reformation. It is the case that between 1908 and 1912, films and film reviewers seem to reinforce a movement toward a cinema that stresses characterization and causal consequences based on character decision making.[75] This cinema will become the classical Hollywood cinema by 1917. Griffith's cinema is a good instance of the trend, but is only one example.

For melodramatic and realist aesthetics in middle-class fiction and drama of the period around 1900, the conventions of representing character psychology, choices based on personal knowledge, and justice as a consequence were well-established strategies of narrative form and narrational procedures. Troublesome situations had to be narrativized if moral choices were to be portrayed. People had to go bad, or nearly so, in order for them to recognize their obligations to social authority, alter their ways, and be rewarded. Narrational voices via intertitles[76] or strategies of revealing plot information might also suggest an evaluation of and commentary on those character behaviors. Another similar device was the incorporation of subplots that could function comparatively to point to optional consequences from that of the main plot-line. But most important, an ending required the "moral" plausibility that good human behavior, in spite of the amoral universe, had its own rewards from a better social order. Thus, the "total picture" theory of portraying wrongdoing (or its possibility) was so much a part of literature and drama that for cinema to end up with a regulation system that coincides with dominant systems of ideology or an aesthetics that combines melodrama and realism is not at all a surprise.

4

From Boston to Bombay

One of the most famous stories about early cinema is that on Christmas Eve 1908, Mayor George B. McClellan of New York City revoked the licenses of the city's nickelodeons, closing down moving pictures, ostensibly on behalf of the public's welfare. The event generated a coalition of exhibitors, and then producers, with a group of civic organizations that previewed and evaluated films. This organized but voluntary self-regulation through the National Board of Censorship functioned in many places as a sufficient guarantee of a film's adherence to dominant standards in the representation of troublesome images. Thus, the board was moderately successful in staving off excessive official censorship or a stricter regulation of images until scandals in the early 1920s required the industry to create a new regulatory agency to monitor its image-making.[1]

This story, as significant as it is to the history of U.S. filmmaking, should *not*, however, be a major focal point in understanding the regulation of images. Prior to the institution of the Board of Censorship, the film industry and its reviewers were already articulating rules for narrating troublesome behavior. The film industry was adopting routine early twentieth-century conventions of image regulation even as it instituted the board. In a *diagnosis approach* to regulation of images, the board represents a symptom and practice articulating and producing ideologies, not an interference.

It is still useful, however, to reconsider the creation of the National Board of Censorship in order to observe the conflict among middle-class individuals over the direction of reform and regulation in image-making.[2] As I have indicated above, while I am arguing that it is the middle class that puts woman and sexuality on the agenda for public discussion (as much as any class does), the middle class was divided in its support. In reviewing the creation of the National Board we can see why a given position from the middle class is the one made "official" (and hence productive) by the industry and can recognize the continued resistance of a minority middle-class position through the present day.

My focus here is primarily on economic and political rationales for the behavior of the movie industry in permitting one method of regulation to order its activities. In subsequent chapters I will raise other dynamics in the process of regulating representations. Regarding the method, it seems important to me that every audience member (except perhaps the smallest child) knew that some things were prohibited on the screen because their local officials or the Board of Censorship said no to that representation. Furthermore, since the set of rules was widely publicized in order to authorize the legitimacy of movies as mainstream entertainment, everyone knew what the rules were. The "do's and don't's" (as they were called in the 1920s) were hardly implicit social knowledge. A moviegoer might even have read in a fan magazine about what had to be cut out of a picture in order for the film to be screened in the neighborhood theater. Hence, as Foucault points out, what is at stake in the discourses of sexuality (or any such discourse that is so regulated) is who holds the power to determine what can be viewed and the manner in which that viewing can occur. Society in general would not tolerate regulation if regulation did not offer something in compensation for the presumed loss of pleasure and freedom that results from denying spectators certain images.

The type of regulation that the industry adopted, supported by progressive reformers rather than moral reformers, was one subtended by a total-picture theory of storytelling. Such a regulatory arrangement was extremely profitable for the film industry and productive for the larger culture, permitting many voices to discuss sexuality and gender characteristics of the New Woman and the Bad Woman. Hence, the playing out of political contentions in New York City (which was behind the events surrounding McClellan's closing of the theaters) permitted a liberal middle-class regulation of sexuality to win out over a more conservative middle-class position—or at least, a regulation that provided space for talking about diverse practices and possibilities while not offending too many of its more sensitive customers. This could occur in part because the American film industry eventually was on the winning side of the cultural shift toward a consumer society, an urban and global market, and institutional authorization for behavior from social scientific experts (rather than religious ones).

Banned in Chicago

From the point of view of a business firm, the economic rationale for permitting the regulation of product derives from the obvious point that monopoly practices will secure higher returns than cutthroat competition. Quite simply, if every company in an industry acts as if it were one big firm and cooperates, the companies can set prices so that each one takes home monopoly profits. By the turn of the century, American businesses were well aware of how to create monopolies in fact or in principle, and had even utilized the discourse of efficiency to justify massive vertical and horizontal mergers of major firms in the railroad and oil industries between 1898 and 1904. Additionally, the practices of having price leaders raise rates and using trade associations to provide protection for tacit collusion were common. Furthermore, if a product could *appear* to be a monopoly through advertising strategies, then price-setting profits might also result from consumers choosing that product rather than one made by someone else. Advertising was crucial in constructing these apparent product monopolies.

To make informal cooperation work, however, every member of the industry has to agree on what would count as generic products for which prices could be set and what would count as acceptable means for differentiation so that no one had an unreasonable advantage in securing apparent product monopolies. Unfortunately, from the perspective of business firms, informal agreements for monopolizing an industry, unlike mergers, can easily fall apart when one or a few firms decide to break ranks and speculate on short- or long-term advantages of competing in the market terrain of supply and demand. Firms that believe they can secure a larger niche in the market or even drive out former partners in an informal collusion may gamble that they can offer something that people will choose over other products available. This happens only when the firms are willing to test their strength against other firms, and often merely securing monopoly profits is sufficient reward. Breaking ranks is not always worth the risk.

As an innovation of the big business of Thomas Edison's research and development laboratory, American film production had plenty of precedents for how to behave so that it could make monopoly profits. Movie manufacturers knew that mass production of films demanded a routine production system that would necessitate to some degree standardizing the product. Yet they also recognized that the appearance of special value in a product was potentially profitable. Product differentiation—claiming that something in the movie was special and different—fueled competition among manufacturers. However, if product differentiation moved into areas that resulted in *some* customers considering the difference to be wonderful while other buyers thought the variation was in bad taste or dangerous, then the industry had a decision to make. Some firms might choose to go after the segment of the market that liked the variation, perhaps dragging the rest of the manufacturers along. Or they could all agree that the loss of some of the buyers was sufficiently costly to avoid competing on those grounds. Or they could decide that they would attempt to control competition so they could satisfy in some way every potential consumer.

In principle then, a baseline formula for standardizing product governed the mass manufacture of films. This baseline is often referred to as the classical Hollywood style, with its conventions of narrative and narration. This baseline formula has other sets of conventions on top of it: the standards for each of the various genres, for example. Westerns, war stories, melodramas, musicals, screwball comedies, and so forth are more specific formulas, which at times distort to some degree the baseline formula. Specializing in some genres might be the way a firm finds its place in the market. At an even more specific level, however, are the more particular variations on which the industry has agreed to compete. In the moving picture business, these variations are usually stars, spectacle (production values), realism, authorship, and subject matter.

In the case I am examining here, subject matter and spectacle as areas for product differentiation are what are at stake. As of 1908, two major business interests existed. One was the manufacture of films and equipment; the other was exhibition. Distribution of films to the exhibitors was not well organized. Films were short, about fifteen to thirty minutes. To put together a show, exhibitors required six to eight movies. Moreover, the exhibitors usually changed their programs twice weekly. Since the business was scarcely a decade old, production supply did not meet exhibitor demand. Moreover, purchases were usually in blocks of films, for the obvious reason that no one had time to carefully preview each and every film and make a reasonable selection in relation to the audience to which the movie house catered. Basically, the exhibitors had to rely on the general reputation of the manufacturers and distributors from which they rented.

Conflicts between manufacturers and exhibitors occurred over numerous business practices, including rentals in blocks of movies and also the quality of the product. Exhibitors consistently requested that manufacturers respond to their judgments about movies and patrons. Manufacturers had no real reason not to try to meet the requests of the exhibitors, but not all exhibitors (just as not all filmgoers) had similar views about what would sell best. Furthermore, manufacturers were constrained by the stress of turning out so many movies so quickly. Later this problem would be handled through the institution of a regularized system of production, but still movie production was quite intense.

In the specific case of subject matter, exhibitors were sensitive to the preferences of their customers, and they were also concerned about the nature of
direct competition from nearby theaters. Patrons did return to favorite houses
because of the films they would likely see or who might be in attendance or
even the quality of the environment or the extras (like live small-time vaudeville acts).[3] Yet much business was of the drop-in type, so that another theater
down the street offering some new sensation could even pull regular patrons
away from their neighborhood house. Thus, exhibitors were very sensitive to
direct competition, and that competition could take an ugly turn. Many theater owners were wary of those who might choose to differentiate theaters in
ways that could harm the reputation (and profits) of the entire business, including their own shows. The actions of a few entrepreneurs could be troublesome. Some exhibitors pointed out that patrons with any objections to some
subject matter could hardly know from advance notice (since none existed)
what they might encounter once inside a theater. Since moviegoing at this
point was so much a matter of seeing pictures, rather than any one movie in
particular, patrons disappointed at one house might avoid other theaters later.
Many exhibitors saw the entire theatrical situation as impinging on their own
ability to make money.

The exhibitors, who most directly encountered consumer variances, had
much to say when manufacturers sent them product they determined to be
unfit for showing. Cooperation was potentially much more profitable, at least
for a while, for everyone in the business. Setting ground rules, including rules
for differentiation, was a better business choice than open competition. However, throughout the history of self-regulation, exhibitors would always be in
contention with the producers over the exhibitors' lack of direct control over
the characteristics of the product available to show audiences.

Cooperation in the film industry developed in two ways. One was ex-
temely internalized. As the rules for acceptable and unacceptable representations of subject matter and spectacle developed in public places such as the
trade papers, so did tactics for providing appropriate narrative motivations
and conclusions or implying but not actually depicting some topics. These
tactics were taught to screenwriters, cinematographers, directors, and all the
personnel of the production staff.

The other way to cooperate was by designating some apparently authorized
third party to regulate the competition, enforcing the internalized rules if
they were not being strictly obeyed or if sufficient public sentiment began requesting a (re)assertion of specific rules. In the instances of the regulation of
film content, the most dramatic episodes—often dramatized just to prove that

the business would not surprise its customers with bad product—occurred in 1908 to 1909, 1921 to 1922, and 1930 to 1934. (Producers have continually tested the market to determine whether social mores would allow variations from the rules, but not until after World War II, when both industrial and social conditions had sufficiently changed, did some of the more discrete sub-rules fall away. Even then, many basic guidelines still function.)[4]

Ironically, however, while the film industry reasserted in each case of lapsed behavior its intention to compete on grounds other than offensive subject matter, the authorized third party became more and more internal to the business. As I indicate, the trade association's solution in 1908–9 to a protest by conservative religious leaders was to combine a group of liberal and progressive civic organizations into the National Board of Censorship. In 1922, after religious and social criticism as well as threats of wide legal censorship, a revived industry trade association, the Motion Picture Producers and Distributors Association (MPPDA), asked a Presbyterian church elder, Republican, and former postmaster general of the United States, Will H. Hays, to head the association and set up a board of citizens to review movies. Now the self-regulation was within the trade association, not merely indirectly funded by it, as in the case after 1908–1909. In the years 1930 to 1934, Catholics and others again demanded new rules (or adherence to the old ones) about what could be shown, and Hays responded by incorporating the Catholics' codes and their representatives into the association, making response to the regulation office part of the Hollywood production system and fining MPPDA exhibitors if they showed nonapproved films.

The pattern was nearly habitual: once complaints threatened to hinder business, the various interests in the industry cooperated on both the degree of competition (how some subject matter and spectacle would be handled) and the means of regulation (authorized and institutionalized agents to monitor the competition for the sake of everyone in the business). In a discussion of the National Board of Censorship, Michael Budd describes well the economic equation: "Fixing the level of sex and violence starts to resemble fixing prices—representing it in quantities and modes that will maximize its exchange value. This means factoring the activities of censorship—and anticensorship—groups into the equation of corporate planning, into the industrial practices which produce signifying texts."[5]

As of 1908–1909, many members of the film industry did not consider appealing only to some people. They considered the United States their customer. They believed that they could find that right equation, making everyone satisfied with their product. Furthermore, some saw the world as their eventual market. As a columnist for would-be screenwriters urged, "Stick to the idea that will be good a year from now [as] it is today and that will appeal equally to the audiences in Bombay and Boston and you have a story that is likely to sell."[6] The globalization of the industry was in its formative moments.

In 1908–1909, what might be the right formula for displaying sex and violence was no more predictable than it is today. As I indicated in the previous chapters, the social transformations occurring in the United States had produced a plethora of opinions, an illogic of notions about sex, sexuality, and the New Woman. Furthermore, no hegemony existed among the classes about the causes and solutions to economic, political, and social upheaval. Tensions existed, even within classes that might have some reason for solidarity. Instead, reformist views produced varied notions about policies to master the transformation to an industrialized, urban, multicultural, and global America.

The institutions that would dominate social policymaking were in conflict, as well. As I shall show, when the movie industry was confronted by citizens requesting regulation of its product so that they would know in advance with some predictability the quality of what they might buy in the theater, several groups contended for the right to manage the regulation. The civic and moral reformers from the late 1800s vied with the progressives and social scientists of the early 1900s (and even, in the early teens, with some more radical women's rights groups). As a contemporary, but obviously not objective, observer remarked, "Reformers are of two kinds: the self-appointed ones—always rash and violent, hasty of speech, slow of judgment, wrong in conclusions; the other kind is of an engineering turn of mind, who look for the cause while only condemning the effect."[7]

The story I am about to tell, however, has one more component beyond the economic rationale and the conflict within the middle class, and that is New York City politics, which is tied to both of these factors. The reformers who went after the movies had earlier looked at corruption in city government and the social evil because of *moral* concerns tied to religious beliefs. Furthermore, these individuals would continue to be involved in pressuring the movie business to take a stricter view about what was talked about in the narratives. Their opponents were certain *progressives* who seem to have had major links with social scientific institutions, universities, and settlement work.

One final clarification: In the past decade, film historians have increasingly realized the dangers of generalizing about the history of the movies on the basis of localizing their research to New York City. This is certainly important. As I have suggested, each municipality and state could censor mov-

ies. In Chicago, the history of the regulation and censorship of motion pictures is somewhat different.[8] For one thing, the police had legal authority to
prohibit films or require changes, a charge they took to heart.

For another thing, *Moving Picture World*, which was based in New York
City, observed that on the whole Chicago seemed more conservative than
New York. I mentioned in chapter 3 that *Moving Picture World* was surprised
when *The Lonely Villa* (Biograph, 1909) was censored in Chicago. *The Hypocrites* (Bosworth, 1914) was also prohibited there, although it played almost
everywhere else. In 1913, *Moving Picture World* reported that the Committee
on Motion Pictures of the National Council of Women, New York, judged
Chicago's censoring board to be too strict in its views about what was or was
not proper. The committee reported, "Chicago is a prudish old maid." More
specifically, after spending a day viewing films banned in Chicago, the committee declared, "What in the world is the matter with these pictures! . . . It
must be very easy to shock Chicago." The president of the Chicago Woman's
City Club defended Chicago's practices, arguing that if anything the censors
may have been "too lenient."[9] Indeed, the censor in 1909 took a conservative
view, indicating that he "only issued permits for those [films] which I consider
proper for women and children to witness."[10] This comparison between New
York and Chicago would continue through the 1910s, as I shall indicate
below.

Being banned in Chicago or in Boston or Bombay was costly to the film
industry. Individual variations from town to town made production difficult.
Was the producer who had a national or international market to make multiple versions of the story for competing in different locales? Moreover,
chopped-up prints from places with stricter limits could not then be rented to
more lenient towns where competition might be intense.

No, what was necessary, as early as 1908–1909, was a *national* system of
regulation, one that would have sufficient legitimacy to stave off most legal
censorship. That is why I choose to concentrate on what happened in New
York City. The regulation system adopted there at least had some claim to a
national jurisdiction because several national trade groups agreed to abide by
and use its organization. The story of New York City's response to calls for
censorship, as local as it is in its politics, is also the tale of nationalizing one
particular type of regulation, one very productive for talking about women.

"A Public Calamity"

Almost as soon as *Moving Picture World* began reporting about the film industry, it started describing the troubles in New York City and elsewhere with individuals objecting to the subject matter of moving pictures. Without a doubt, these objections occurred from the start of films, but as of 1907 a fairly detailed record exists. For example, on 27 April 1907, an owner of a nickelodeon was "raided" by the Children's Society and fined one hundred dollars for "imperilling the morals of young boys."[11] What the representatives of the Children's Society objected to was discovering four boys under the age of fourteen watching a movie about the Thaw-White incident.[12] The Children's Society would continue to act as a major watchdog for groups calling for the reform of movies.

This April 1907 incident in New York was preceded in Chicago a month or so earlier by an article in the Chicago *Tribune*, titled "The Five Cent Theatre," which queried the effects of moving pictures on juveniles. The essay quoted a judge as saying, "Those nickelodeons indirectly or directly caused more juvenile crimes coming into this court than all other causes combined." Jane Addams would argue within the next month for regulating Chicago's movies.[13]

In April 1907, George B. McClellan was mayor of New York City, nominated by the Democratic party and operating in part through the aegis of the Tammany Hall machine. McClellan received from Chief Police Commissioner Bingham a report on moving picture conditions. Bingham noted in particular the hazards of some four hundred penny arcades showing films accessible to children, as well as of many nickelodeon theaters. Since licenses for these small amusements were issued by the mayor's office, Bingham urged their cancellation. Penny shows were especially dangerous because of the lack of adult supervision of movie viewing, and apparently some theaters were just generally borderline places for children to be near. Westerly, Rhode Island, reported in June 1907 that one of its penny arcades had "vulgar post cards" for sale near the kinetoscopes. Hence, Westerly was banning penny arcades in general. However, the New York State Senate killed a bill the same month in which children under sixteen would have been prohibited from entering penny arcades. Senator McCarren was quoted as saying, "The Lord knows that the business community is being restricted everyday by some species of crank legislation."[14]

At this time, McClellan did not immediately take up Bingham's suggestion. However, the import of the report had its intended effect anyway. On 3 June 1907, a group of New York moving picture business people filed a certificate of incorporation for the Moving Picture Exhibitors' Association

(MPEA) to protect the industry. Their specific concerns were to avert license cancellations without proper hearings and "to prevent the use of improper pictures." In other words, they desired to protect the industry by fixing the type of competition. Furthermore, the president of the MPEA requested that the New York Supreme Court enjoin McClellan from interferring with motion picture licenses or holding hearings on them. The threatened conflict seems to have abated over the summer months, although by the end of the year the MPEA had 110 members.[15]

The Children's Society continued to monitor the penny arcades and moving picture theaters, reporting that children under sixteen were commonly in the establishments, often without adult supervision. Yet, as in Chicago, other individuals in New York City found the shows to have potential benefits. *Moving Picture World* reported in October 1907 that Professor Hamilton used comedy and educational films in his East Side work at the University Settlement Society.[16]

That fall other events besides the questions of regulating subject matter were of mutual concern to the manufacturers and renters of film. In mid-November 1907, the major companies producing films and film equipment and distributors from throughout the United States met in Pittsburgh and formed for their "mutual protection" the United Film Service Protective Association (FSA). Much broader than the New York exhibitors' group, this association included national production companies such as Edison, Essanay, Kalem, Kleine, Lubin, and Vitagraph. Renters from Cleveland, Chicago, Kansas City, Detroit, and elsewhere also participated. This group would serve as the basis for the Motion Picture Patents Company (MPPC), an attempt within the next year to monopolize the industry through a patent trust. In December, Thomas Edison, the renowned Wizard from Menlo Park, counseled the industry: "In my opinion nothing is of greater importance to the Success of the motion picture interests than films of good moral tone. . . . Unless it can secure the entire respect of the amusement-loving public it will not endure."[17]

Meanwhile, in New York City, several religious leaders took on all amusement-providing industries. Canon William Sheafe Chase, of Christ Episcopal Church, had formed an organization called the Interdenominational Committee for the Suppression of the Sunday Vaudeville. Chase indicated that he was calling upon the state government to enforce a forty-seven-year-old law prohibiting amusements on Sunday. The Sunday closing law would affect vaudeville, burlesque, football games, shows at the YMCA, concerts at the Metropolitan and Manhattan opera houses, all recitals and symphonies as

well as sacred concerts, and, of course, moving pictures. Chase's group justified this as a help to members of the Actors' Alliance and labor unions so that
they could have a day of rest.[18]

The aldermen of New York City promptly voted forty-seven to eighteen to
modify the local "blue" Sunday law. Presentations that were "moral" or "sacred or educational" were permitted. Shortly thereafter, however, the police
charged numerous motion picture theaters with violating the Sunday closing
ordinance. The MPEA responded. Its lawyers requested and received from the
New York Supreme Court a Bill of Peace requiring police not to bother Sunday motion pictures as long as they were within the New York City law. This
decision did suggest, however, that the New York City ordinance might be in
conflict with the New York State penal code. In January 1908, appropriate
Sunday shows at the vaudeville theaters of Keith and Proctor and the Eden
Musée were also permitted through a temporary injunction.[19]

As I have suggested, the exhibitors who were the first-line defense in the
moral reformers' assault against moving pictures had, in turn, to pressure the
producers about the content of the movies. In February, the FSA announced
that it would eliminate all suggestive and crime pictures from its stock. Behind the move, its publicity announced, were Thomas Edison and 125 renters
from across the United States.[20]

Another gesture to support good films also came that month. The Woman's Municipal League and the People's Institute issued a report on the nickelodeons. "Cheap theaters . . . generally keep within the law," although
penny arcades were definitely a problem. "As for the penny arcade . . . we are
convinced that it is a destructive influence, almost unmitigated. The pictures
in the slot machines tend positively toward the indecent and violent; the arcade opens on the thoroughfares, with free admission, and is often the haunt
of idlers and sometimes of worse, and it is without the leavening salt of family
patronage." On the side of the nickelodeons, however, *was* that family atmosphere. "The audiences are composite in the highest degree. On the Bowery
we have seen Chinamen, Italians and Yiddish people, the young and old, often entire families, crowded side by side. Outside the vice and hopelessness of
the Bowery. But inside was the enthusiasm of an orderly three hundred
people."[21]

In supporting the nickelodeons, the People's Institute and the Woman's
Municipal League were following the patterns of progressive reformers, investigating a situation and, by a report, urging a policy of regulation. Hence,
their procedure was different from that of moral reformers such as Chase, who

counseled suppression. In May, a field investigator for the New York Committee on Settlement Work expressed the opinion that movies could be used by social workers, and a Boston report compared the advantages of movie shows over saloons as a source of entertainment for the working class.[22]

The report by the Woman's Municipal League and the People's Institute did not convince opponents of the movies. *Moving Picture World* described the concern over the cheap live vaudeville acts that some exhibitors interspersed between the films to provide variety and continuity to the show while the projectionist changed the movie reels. A Birmingham, Alabama, paper worried about the effects some of these acts had on all the "young girls and women" who made up the audiences: "They often see a good deal more than a picture and hear a good deal more than what's good for them." Thus, even if the movies were clean, the theatrical environment might be hazardous. Complaints continued about vaudeville for some time.[23]

In May 1908, the conflict over the Sunday laws returned. The New York Supreme Court ruled that police could stop an inappropriate Sunday performance. However, a recently enacted law prohibited police from taking away a theatrical license. Rather, proceedings had to be held in which proof of a violation was required before a revocation would be permitted.[24]

Another potential blow to the exhibitors was the ruling by the New York City tenement house commissioner that moving pictures could not be shown in tenements.[25] The commissioner argued that the reasons for his decision had to do with health and with building and fire safety. William Fox, president of the Greater New York Film Rental Company (one of the largest distributors of films at that time), challenged the decision. On 24 July 1908, a judge ruled that when the movie shows acquired their licenses they had also received approval of their plans at the Tenement Commission office. Thus, the commissioner could not change his mind now.[26]

Thus by the summer of 1908, a pattern seemed to be developing in the relations between the New York City mayor's office and the exhibitors. Perhaps goaded by religious and moral reform leaders, the mayor's office and its officials looked for ways to harass or even suppress moving pictures. In response, the exhibitors, joined by the producers and renters, used both legal recourse and promises to regulate the content of the films as their defense tactics. As a *Variety* reviewer put it in March 1909, " 'The up-lift of the picture business' is the ever lasting slogan of the American manufacturers. 'We see a new light; this is another era.' 'Mistakes of the past will be corrected.' "[27] In addition, social workers and some civic organizations that appeared to be progressives supported in public the benefits of films for maintaining families, providing better entertainment than saloons and penny arcades, and even educating the working class.

This pattern climaxed with the famous events in December 1908. In mid-December, Chase, backed by several societies, warned of children in theaters without adult supervision, which was clearly illegal. In particular, he described the children watching a movie about "how a farmer boy came to the city, went to the racetrack, won money and returned home to pay off the mortgage on his father's farm." He said, "What do you think of that way of elevating youth, teaching them to gamble and justifying the vile means by the picturing of a noble purpose?" Since the police could arrest a theater manager if children under sixteen were in the shows without a parent or guardian, *Moving Picture World* warned that trouble might be brewing.[28]

Indeed it was. McClellan called a public hearing, and then announced that as of midnight, 24 December 1908, the moving picture licenses in New York City would be revoked to prevent "a public calamity." The theater owners immediately requested and received an injunction.

Speculation as to what was behind McClellan's behavior was also immediate. *Moving Picture World* pointed out that while Chase and his allies were conspicuous sources behind the action, word around town also had it that the actors' union for vaudeville had been looking for ways to get rid of movies.[29] Another explanation came from the *Survey*, published in New York by the Charity Organization Society and sponsored by progressive individuals such as Jane Addams, William Guggenheim, and Jacob A. Riis. The *Survey* suggested that as moving pictures developed, particularly in the working-class and tenement areas, their regulation was difficult. Moreover, "the License Bureau which controlled them became a by-word for 'graft.' " In September 1908, an exposé of the bureau occurred, but complaints about graft still continued. Thus, the *Survey* suspected that McClellan's revocation of the moving picture licenses in December was an attempt to indicate his tough stand against corruption in the government and also a measure to shore up his public image as an honest mayor.[30] The *Survey*'s speculation is just that, but since the events of the next few years require it, considering the history of New York City politics is important.

New York City Politics

In the late 1800s, the Democratic party in New York City was directed by Tammany Hall, one of the most famous city political machines. Unlike the

Tweed syndicate, Tammany maintained its power through police protection and shakedowns of brothels, saloons, and gambling. Reformers were incensed by the corruption they attributed to working-class and ethnic brotherhoods and, as civic individuals, sought to expose the links they saw between the lower classes and city corruption. In 1878 the Society for the Prevention of Crime was organized. As mentioned in chapter 2, in 1891, Reverend Charles Parkhurst, minister of the Madison Square Presbyterian Church, became president.[31]

From his prestigious pulpit, Parkhurst began preaching. As he expressed it later, he was worried about "the strain of current temptation" for young men and how to "make it at least a little easier for a city young man to maintain himself at his best." Thus, Parkhurst looked at gambling and "the social evil," which meant that he considered his first problem to be the police. He wanted to "fight the disease and not the symptoms."[32]

A Tammany-dominated grand jury requested proof from Parkhurst. However, he could not prove his charges so he had to gather evidence. An independent grand jury was called, and the state legislature set up the Lexow Committee. Both of these groups substantiated the claims Parkhurst made. The Lexow Report of 1895 began a fifteen-year process to rid New York City of police corruption. A City Vigilance League was established to watch for abuses. At one point, Theodore Roosevelt, as police commissioner, conducted nightly sweeps of the tougher areas to demonstrate that cops were not complicit with the criminal elements.

From this point on, the elections in New York City were dominated by reform politics. For 1894–95 a reform candidate, William L. Strong, was elected mayor, and a Citizens' Union was established to continue reform activities. The 1898–99 term was contested, with the Citizen's Union candidate Seth Low (who had been president of Columbia University) losing to Tammany candidate Robert A. Van Wyck, who was reelected. Tammany's campaign slogan reputedly was "To Hell with Reform." Once in office, Van Wyck permitted the old practices to resume, with additional funds derived from a "cost-plus" system for digging the New York City subway and installing electricity.

Low did win for 1902–1903. Part of Low's victory was due not only to reaction against Tammany corruption but also to the increasing visibility of the dangers of prostitution in terms of disease. In 1900, newspapers had begun covering the pervasiveness of prostitution in New York. In particular, they went after the Raines Law, which gave hotels favored status for liquor licenses. Saloons might even exist within tenement houses. The arrangement particularly suited cadets (the period's term for pimps) and their prostitutes. In 1900, the Committee of Fifteen began its investigation, publishing two years later the report I described in chapter 2. Parkhurst and others argued that Tammany graft and protection had permitted the social evil to continue.

In determining the mayoral nomination of George B. McClellan for 1904, the New York Democratic party split. McClellan was put up by Tammany Hall and its current boss, Charles Francis Murphy. His opponent, Judge William Jay Gaynor (who became important in the events following McClellan's 1908 revocation of the motion picture licenses), was nominated by Brooklyn and its leader Hugh McLaughlin. McClellan won the party's nomination and then the election against Low (who ran as a Republican under the "Fusionist" label).

McClellan, true to the powers that put him in office, began filling government posts with Democrats, even permitting Murphy to suggest William McAdoo (assistant secretary of the navy under Grover Cleveland) for police commissioner. Apparently, McAdoo was a failure, with his reforms of the police system amounting to window dressing—for example, changing the uniforms, ridding the force of "elderly, physically incompetent, walrus-moustached, enormously fat 'flatties,' " and improving traffic regulation.[33]

According to McClellan's authorized biography, McClellan remarked, "In Brooklyn that strange and eccentric person Justice Gaynor of the Supreme Court . . . did all in his power to prevent my putting the traffic regulations into force." Gaynor argued that some of the restrictions were a "curtailment of the constitutional liberty of the individual." McClellan eventually won in the court of appeals. McClellan also considered three police problems the most difficult to tackle: liquor licenses, which promoted graft, and the prohibition on Sunday selling, which was hard to enforce; gambling; and prostitution. "Dr. Parkhurst, in his spectacular and sensational campaign during the Van Wyck administration, had succeeded in scattering prostitution all over the city."[34] This became a common complaint. Shutting down red-light districts did not stop prostitution; rather, prostitution was just more difficult to control as it dispersed throughout the city.

McClellan also began to disassociate himself from Murphy. Prior to the election for the 1906–10 term (the terms had just been lengthened to four years), McClellan began edging away from Murphy's sphere of influence. However, at the same time William Randolph Hearst chose to run from the Independence League. Murphy apparently calculated that should McClellan run opposite a Tammany candidate, the vote might split, with Hearst winning. Thus, Murphy did not block McClellan's renomination. Although

Hearst charged fraud at the polls, McClellan won. For the next term, Mc-Clellan served without Murphy's strength behind him.[35]

Given this background, McClellan's actions toward the nickelodeons make very good sense. McClellan faced reformers of the sort behind the antiprostitution and antigambling movements, such as Parkhurst,[36] as well as politicians linked to major New York papers, such as Hearst. Police graft was common and hard to control. To protect his office and administration, Mc-Clellan needed to display that he, too, refused to tolerate vice. Moving pictures were an easy place to demonstrate that will to reform. Furthermore, while the license bureau might have made some money from graft through threats of revoking licenses, the money lost in this industry, at least in 1908–9, would be minimal compared with other sources. Thus, McClellan would not be directly provoking Tammany Hall and Murphy.

I would not go so far as to suggest that McClellan's actions were so calculating. Indeed, accounts of the period suggest that much of McClellan's behavior was to be respected, particularly his attempt to distance his administration from the control of Murphy and Tammany Hall. Yet, in the overall scheme of things, using the dramatic gesture of closing all the moving picture theaters on Christmas Eve has a resonance of public relations to it. That Mc-Clellan did not react forcibly to the exhibitors' response, as I shall describe later, suggests that he was attempting to satisfy public critics rather than that he was specifically determined to suppress film in New York City.

Indeed, the motion picture exhibitors turned to their common allies: the courts and publicity. For the former, the exhibitors met on 25 December 1908, with Fox chairing the meeting. They established a defense fund, hired a law firm, and within seventy-two hours had four injunctions, one from New York State Supreme Court Justice Blackman and three from McClellan's longtime opponent and liberal interpreter of the law, Judge Gaynor. In the hearing before Blackman, the major issue revolved around whether or not the mayor's office had grounds for closing *all* of the theaters. Three arguments for the legality of McClellan's actions were made: (1) the theaters were potential fire traps, (2) theaters might violate the Sunday amusement laws, and (3) theaters might show indecent or immoral pictures. In all three cases, Blackman pointed out that McClellan had to establish guilt of individual houses and only those houses' licenses could be revoked at will.[37]

However, McClellan's act, as legally rash as it might have been, was also dramatic. New York City exhibitors could expect public sentiment in some quarters to be on McClellan's side, so a public relations countermove seemed more urgent than ever before. Even as *Moving Picture World* announced the revocation of McClellan's closing of the houses, it urged as a "temporary pal-liative" an idea circulating among the exhibitors: to have representatives from several civic groups investigate the movies and serve as an informal cen-sorship board. Even *Moving Picture World* thought that in the long run Mc-Clellan's maneuver was necessary and perhaps even beneficial in making some exhibitors clean up their acts. As one of the writers phrased it, "No gar-den is without its choking weeds and no bed of flowers will long keep its beauty and its symmetry without the aid of the trimming knife."[38]

Specifically, the concerns concentrated on the effect of films containing crime, physical or emotional violence to humans, and indecencies. In the list of what might become prohibited images, *Moving Picture World* listed the fol-lowing suggestions: (1) prisons and prison life; (2) "the portrayal of contem-porary sensational crime" and trials; (3) "anything that could in the least wound the religious sensibilities of the public"; (4) "the lingering over the details, such things as murders and executions"; (5) "the needless piling on of horrors [as in] such films as 'The Wages of Sin' and 'For His Country's Sake' "; and (6) "every comic picture which depends for its effect on the degradation or on the personal defects of any human being."[39]

Moreover, the emphasis was especially directed toward young viewers of films. In a survey of "popular feeling," *Moving Picture World* discovered from other city papers that the widespread attitude was fear about what was being suggested to the impressionable minds of children. The *Pittsburgh Post* said movies might be educational but "more often [they were] inimical to the mor-als of the young." The *Cincinnati Times-Star* thought that "if crime and inde-cency are to be exploited in these shows, they will have little enough excuse for living." Such views were repeated in papers in Brooklyn, Hoboken, Chi-cago, Scranton, and San Francisco. Yet the children's nickels were exception-ally good income for the theaters, if the moral reformers' accounts of their large attendance were correct. In the first month of 1909, Chase was lobbying for a no-one-under-sixteen law.[40]

Thus, the Moving Picture Exhibitors' Association of Greater New York announced that it would work with social institutions and settlement groups in "weeding out any moving picture theaters which cast a reflection upon the moving picture business." One of the institutions contacted was the Bureau of Social Research, whose head, Dr. Lichtenberger, indicated that he thought "moving picture shows were both instructive and entertaining and . . . there were other kinds of public entertainment which needed more the action of the moral censor." Another group was the People's Institute, the society that had in the previous year released a report expressing the potential good that movies might do (and the society that in 1914 would sponsor feminist meetings at Cooper Union). In addition, one of its prominent members was Charles Sprague Smith. Smith had been a member of the Committee of Fifteen, which as part of the anti-Tammany reform action had investigated prostitution in 1900 and urged regulation (rather than prohibition).

Thus, the MPEA of Greater New York had reason to believe that while they would be establishing themselves as having greater credibility among the population, they might not be facing the strictest or least flexible of the reform groups. Rather than turn to the moral reformers aligned with religious authorities, they went to the progressive reformers associated with social scientific legitimacy, those who kept saying movies could be instructive and entertaining.[41]

The National Board of Censorship

As I have suggested, reform activities cannot be assumed to be homogeneous. Within the middle class, a great variety of reform theories and institutional authorizations for change have existed. The MPEA of Greater New York chose the lesser of two evils, but many of the members believed that institutional controls or regulation would ultimately be better for the entire business. As they habitually put it in metaphor, they needed a gardener to pull out the weeds so the whole flower bed would be beautiful. This choice would have implications in future years, since the progressive reformers also tended to approve of the social hygiene approach to information about sexuality, as well as, in the case of the People's Institute and several of its members, having a much more radical view of women's rights and possibilities.

The daily work of the board requires more extensive analysis than is suitable here. As the research of Charles Matthew Feldman and Nancy J. Rosenbloom indicates, sorting out how the board worked and how it dealt with public reactions to its judgments is important for understanding the role it served in social struggles of the era, as well as what did and did not appear on the screen. A broad idea of what occurred during the next several years of the board's operation is useful, however, especially as the board's work was presented in the public press. I shall concentrate on the public declarations, since it is those that set the tone for encouraging talk about women, sexuality, and other issues of social concern. We do know, however, that dissent occurred among the board members. Furthermore, the board requested specific deletions of shots and scenes from pictures. Companies became expert at gauging how they could get touchy material past the board, using the narrative and narrational methods I have described. Thus, the board's practices occasionally were of a "pointillist" nature, although in public and in general they supported a "total-picture" approach to troublesome subject matter. The records of these internal practices are now part of extensive research by several individuals, including William Uricchio and Roberta Pearson, and should be important in understanding the events of this era.[42]

By early March 1909, *Moving Picture World* published the details for the Board of Censorship. The public bodies to be involved initially on its governing council included—in addition to the People's Institute—the Public Education Association, the Federation of Churches, the League for Political Education, the Ethical-Social League, and the Association of Neighborhood Workers. Smith would be the managing director and John Collier, the secretary. (In 1910, Smith passed away and was succeeded by Frederic C. Howe, husband of Marie Jenny Howe, who promoted heterodoxy in the feminist movement.)[43] Other members of the group included the superintendent of the New York City schools, a business partner of John Wanamaker, the editor of *Century Magazine*, and Mark Twain. An executive committee would be made up of three representatives from the council and two members of the MPEA of Greater New York. The board would check all films to be exhibited. Any theater that showed a film of which the board did not approve would be expelled from the MPEA and would be unable to advertise that it was an association member. Thus, like the contemporary movements for pure foods, labeling the package would be a guide to the consumer about what to expect.[44]

MPEA associations in other cities also began expressing their interest in working with the New York system.[45] As I have suggested, the U.S. film business was already at a national level. Moreover, national trade associations had been in place for over a year. Having a centralized and standard guarantee of what could be shown nearly anywhere had business advantages of predictability and less expense (no need to do local editing of pictures). New York, as I have suggested, turned out to be more lenient than other locales (such as Chicago). Thus, local and state censorships continued, but for the time being, having a single board with some prediction of tolerance and general goodwill toward moving pictures was a good business bet.

Another event also reinforced this endeavor to use the board as an alternative to legal censorship. In early 1909, most of the major film manufacturers gathered together into the Motion Picture Patents Company (MPPC), seeking to secure a legal monopoly through patent rights on the manufacture of films and film equipment. The MPPC was quickly opposed by many exhibitors, resulting in the formation of alternative motion picture manufacturing firms, although it took a couple of years for the independents to stablize as a business counterforce to the MPPC. By March 1909, the MPPC and independent firms had both agreed to submit their product to the board for approval and asked the board to consider itself a national operation.[46]

Once the producers entered the group, they took over the financial support of the board, which by 1915 was using over 120 volunteers to preview the movies. The threat of being removed from MPEA membership for exhibitors who showed unapproved films was lifted, but the normative force of cooperation generally worked. Instead of using the method of expulsion from the trade association to control behavior, the board placed the choice of product in the hands of the consumers. In the early teens the board began the Better Films National Council, which supplied a bulletin listing the best films so that consumers would have a guide to filmgoing. Product selection was the informed customer's business. In 1914, the board changed its name to the National Board of Review, responding to Collier and the institute's objections to censorship, which I will describe later. Additionally, by then the board was examining movie scenarios, giving advice in advance of shooting if asked.[47]

Simply instituting the board did not stop the complaints of moral reformers, and the trade press itself often questioned the decisions of the board. A certain public assertion of open-mindedness seems apparent from the start. After the first few weeks of operation, the board reported to the public that having reviewed 100,000 feet of film, it had requested that only 420 feet be cut.[48] Movie reviewers were surprised about what had been left in. For example, "Rush" of *Variety* described his response in October 1909 to *The Romance of a Poor Girl* (Pathé, 1909):

> The general opinion is growing apace that the M.P.P.Co.'s Censorship Committee is either an entire joke or that its members are pretty broad in their understanding of what constitutes clean and permissible entertainment. One of last Friday's releases of the Pathe Freres factories is "The Romance of a Poor Girl." The "poor girl" is a housemaid in a mansion. She is in love with a sailor and upon his departure, as is plainly indicated by the film, the master of the mansion in which she is employed, tries to force her by money, threats and cajoleries, to acceed to his wishes. When she refuses he casts her out.[49]

The review continues the story of the girl's troubles and resistances as well as a "just in the nick of time" rescue by her sailor. In the same issue, "Walt" complains about *A Change of Heart* (Biograph, 1909), directed by D. W. Griffith, calling for a halt to such questionable films. The plot, as Walt describes it, is the tale of "a combination of young 'men' who enter into a compact to ruin an innocent country girl through the medium of a mock marriage." However, the mother of the chief instigator appeals to her son, who, in remorse, repents and really marries the girl.[50]

Compare that version with Biograph's publicity. Its advertising subtitles the film "The Dangers of Evil Association." Its first lines read, " 'He that toucheth pitch shall be defiled therewith'—*Eccles. xiii, 2*. The contaminating influence of evil companions has caused more woe than any other moral agent. Here we portray an episode in the life of the son of indulgent parents. . . . Drinking is always the feature with such parties, and the head and heart benumbed by the fumes of alcohol are never normal and the being is morally weakened, ofttimes falling into a morass of irreparable ruin."[51] Couched in religious rhetoric, the manufacturer claimed to be teaching moral lessons— about associating with the right people, not spoiling children, and avoiding alcohol—and moral reformers ought to be happy.

In fact, by June 1909, the board publicly indicated that the use of supposedly troublesome material in films would be tolerated if sufficiently motivated to be included in the narrative—specifically, if the material was a realistic detail that was necessary for the plot and not exploited for its own sake (thus maintaining the doctrine of distance), if the tale had an educational lesson (at least by the ending), and if character agency was the primary causal force (rather than coincidence). In describing instances of what, in its first days at work, the board had deleted (three miles out of a total of fifty-five miles viewed), Lewis E. Palmer in the *Survey* reported:

> The board has not catalogued its objections and does not taboo every scene of crime or wrongdoing simply because it is a scene of crime or wrongdoing, but rather bases its decisions on the general effect a picture will have on an audience. Scenes of burglary and kidnapping have passed the board as well as a famous prize fight that attracted the attention of the world a few months ago; while a French falcon hunt in detail, a bull fight, four kidnapping pictures and numerous scenes of suicide crime have been thrown out entirely.[52]

Collier himself felt the necessity of explaining the board's views at that time. Declining to give a list of prohibitions, Collier was willing to articulate a general philosophy:

> We do not condemn the representation of any crime; crime for its own sake we condemn, pictures whose chief appeal is to morbid appetite we condemn, bad taste where it becomes vulgarity we condemn. We condemn anything that seems *dangerously suggestive* in its tendencies. But barring indecency,

barring ghoulishness, there is hardly any incident in life or drama that may
not be *so treated*—presented with such a purpose shown in such a
connection, as to be acceptable to a board of censorship which recognizes
this fundamental fact:

> *That motion pictures are a legitimate form of the drama, and that the motion
> picture is entitled to draw* WITH DISCRETION *on any field of human interest
> for its themes.*[53]

Collier elaborated by explaining that the board reviewers considered the films
"as far as we are able in the place of the audience," and evaluated whether
"the sum total of effect, the unified effect, is positive and harmless, or good."
Indeed, the board tended to accept stories that focused on character agency
and choice with plausible, moral endings based on that behavior (virtue had
to triumph over vice in a verisimilar if not moral universe).[54] Such plots were
sufficient for a (nonsensational) representation of evil in the middle of the
narratives.

This position takes the point of view, described in chapter 3, of a reading
theory emphasizing the total film. Collier described the possibility of "a powerful, sweeping plot [carrying] the audience rapidly over many incidents that,
if magnified out of proportion, or if represented for their own sake, would be
objectionable." Collier and the board would continue to urge this "total picture" reading theory when they argued against national censorship in 1915.
In fact, Collier explicitly disagreed with what I have called the pointillist
view—looking at the parts out of context of the whole story, a practice that
Collier associates with the activities of the Chicago Board of Censors.

As I shall describe, the situation in New York City continued to be complicated by New York City politics. On a broader scale, however, the moral
reformers did not give up once the board was formed. Throughout the United
States, individual localities and eventually the state of Ohio (in 1914) instituted official boards of censorship. Besides Chase, another major moral reformer was Reverand Wilbur Fisk Crafts, who published a report in which he
considered some 40 percent of films shown in Cleveland to be unfit for children. To prove his case, he provided statistics of the number of films that had
instances of a perilous nature: stealing (13.4 percent), murder (13.1 percent),
drunkenness (13.1 percent), indecent suggestion (8.2 percent), housebreak-
ing (7.2 percent), loose ideals of marriage (6.5 percent), domestic infidelity
(5.8 percent), and vicious mischief (5.8 percent).[55] Crafts and Chase continued through the early teens to lobby for stricter regulation of the movies.
Both Terry Ramsaye and Kevin Brownlow write that Crafts and Chase included racist argumentation within their criticisms of the films, perhaps re-

sponding to the situation in which some film exhibitors and manufacturers were first-generation immigrants from Europe and were not Protestants. Such a racism, as I have shown, was part of the discourse of the turn of the century and nothing specifically unique to attacks on movies (although, of course, not justifible just the same).[56]

In 1914 the efforts of Crafts and Chase, as well as those of other like-minded individuals, finally culminated in the introduction in the U.S. Congress of bills to create a Federal Motion Picture Commission, whose function it would be to censor all films distributed across state lines.[57] Those bills, as well as others introduced almost yearly thereafter into Congress, died or failed to achieve a majority vote. However, the warning was strong. Additionally, the following year (February 1915), the U.S. Supreme Court decided in *Mutual Film Corporation v. Industrial Commision of Ohio* that the Ohio state censorship act was legal. Declaring films to be "a business, pure and simple" (against arguments of freedom of speech), the Supreme Court validated local and state censoring laws. Once again, the film industry mobilized to prevent further erosion of its control over subject matter. In general the industry was successful until the early 1920s, although in the next few years, several states did begin legal censorship.[58]

This public interest and conflict over censorship, as I have suggested earlier, was by no means confined to moving pictures. Comstock and others had been working for obscenity laws for some time. Recall that one writer in 1915 had argued that because Comstock's name invariably brought to mind the images he wished to repress, his name should be declared obscene and thus censored.[59]

Collier and the (by now) National Board of Review made it clear that they did not support censorship. In a series of articles in the *Survey*, Collier repudiated theatrical censorship in the name of dramatic rights to free speech. In the series, Collier compares types of narrative situations that might require self-regulation with those situations that he thinks are justifiable in terms of drama and moral lessons. In a set of three specific instances, Collier defends the representation of murder, rape, and vice as "justified through [their] relation to a significant plot" and, in one case, "because of its tragic-moral ending." Scantily dressed women were acceptable if motivated, but "vulgarity"—showing body parts for the sake of titillation or basing humor on a fantasy of sexual gratification—was not. The board did publish by 1915 a twenty-three-page booklet setting out its guidelines for use by film manufacturers and any interested citizen. Here is a sample: "Section 39. 'As a general rule it is preferable to have retribution come through the hands of authorized officers of the law, rather than through revenge or other unlawful or extra-legal means.' "[60]

To reinforce his position, Collier repeatedly contrasted the board's work with the activities of the Chicago board. "But the Chicago board takes the viewpoint of the child more exclusively than does the national board, and in considering films, is in the habit of judging each scene out of reference to the general plot. . . . The Chicago board is more sensitive—more prudish—than the national board in sundry matters" (p. 12). Collier pointed out that Chicago censors seemed to assume that audiences were either incapable of placing events into the context of an overall narrative or that their minds would easily wander from the story, into forbidden paths. Thus, Collier called the Chicago board's standards "crude, inflexible, naive."[61]

Collier, although writing about moving pictures, was explicitly against what he considered to be the threat of theatrical censorship in general. "Readers of The Survey, with . . . the Sanger case and the federal censorship of mails, will detect still wider meaning—shall we say, menace?—in the movement."[62] Collier concluded his series with a ringing call against censorship. Although he did believe that self-regulation was advisable, "censorship is impracticable and dangerous because the means involved are too crude for the ends sought; are indeed largely unrelated to the ends sought; and because the indirect damage of censorship infinitely exceeds the direct good which may be accomplished." Theater, "while truly an agent of preventive morality . . . is just as truly an agent of challenge, of conflict, even of revolution." "The theater is an institution for the development of new world-views; such development is possibly the supreme contribution of our present age of human history. To no censor . . . dare we commit the censorship of this process of spiritual revolution."[63]

Collier and the board's stand on censorship constituted (and still does) one position in a contested terrain of debate about the transformation of American culture. The views Collier expressed include an assumption that the regulation of images should not necessarily appeal to the least common denominator. In his series, Collier stressed that the board's public position was not unanimously held by its membership but represented a majority view. Furthermore, regulation was being accomplished for an entire population of diverse individuals, not just some children or people of crude minds. Collier's appeals were for permitting variety among the representations and tolerance for other views, even urging that some reform and revolutionary forces might emerge from dramatic materials.

This general ideological stance, as I have suggested, has basically dominated against sentiments for stricter types of regulation. The appearance of liberalism should not, however, result in dismissing the validity of the concerns of the moral reformers. In a time of debate about how individuals read texts, often privileged are views and data that imply that people do not read movies as a total picture, that, in fact, they are quite capable of resisting implied moral or social lessons. Thus, while some people may choose to take an anticensorship position, they need to recognize as well that they may agree in part with those holding the view that images are exceptionally powerful and that minds can do a lot of unexpected things with them. At any rate, the debates over reading theories and regulation are likely to continue, often echoing the arguments voiced nearly a century ago.

New York City Politics—Continued

The National Board of Censorship helped to some degree to subdue the difficulties for exhibitors in New York City, although some aldermen and clergy gave indications that the fight would continue. However, New York City politics also assisted the exhibitors when they ended up supporting the winning administration in the next mayoral election.

In 1909, Judge Gaynor chose to run for New York City mayor for the 1910–13 term. Urged to campaign by a group of reformers but eventually nominated by the Democrats (including Tammany Hall), thus losing the reformers' support, Gaynor was still considered sufficiently independent from Tammany and its boss, Murphy, to be a respectable choice. Gaynor was also, however, perceived to have scant regard for some kinds of reformers, especially people such as Parkhurst, for whom he explicitly had little respect. Furthermore, in an open letter in May 1909, he had called upon McClellan to fire Police Commissioner Bingham for holding a suspect without charging him. McClellan agreed with Gaynor and dismissed Bingham, who had up until then been considered a moderately acceptable commissioner.[64]

Against Gaynor were two other reformers: William Randolph Hearst and Otto T. Bannard, a Republican who also ran on the Fusionist ticket, which had the support of many anti-Tammany people. Against Hearst, Pulitzer, of the *World*, backed Gaynor. This election, like the earlier ones, again invoked charges of Tammany's association with corruption, including especially prostitution. As I discuss further in chapter 5, from 1907 on, the prostitution and social hygiene concern had been elevated from a worry about individual problems of morality and then health to a conspiracy plot of an international scope. The prevailing view of white slavery involved national, even foreign, connections planning to kidnap and trick innocent women and force them into prostitution.

In this election, accusations became particularly dirty. In June 1909, *McClure's Magazine* published an article by George Kibbe Turner, "Tammany's Control of New York by Professional Criminals," in which Turner accused Tammany of safeguarding prostitution. Then in the November issue, he followed with "The Daughters of the Poor: A Plain Story of the Development of New York City as a Leading Center of the White Slave Trade of the World, under Tammany Hall." Gaynor and Murphy immediately responded, pointing out that, during the events described, Republicans were in office. Furthermore, this accusation was a blatantly political act, timed as it was just before the election. Murphy called it "a grossly exaggerated partisan campaign story published on the word of a hired slander in the columns of a muckraking and filth-throwing magazine reputed some months ago to be on the verge of insolvency, and desperately turning in every direction for something which would attract circulation and readers to it." Gaynor, more calmly, stressed that Turner was a "racist" and a "racial bigot": "He does not scruple to lay the evils he mentions to the Jews as a Race."[65]

As I shall discuss in chapter 5, Turner's complaints led to a grand jury investigation of vice in New York City in early 1910. However, Gaynor's attributions of racism are apt. Turner initiated his tale with charges that Jews in the Polish ghetto were among the first to transport women internationally for prostitution. More specifically, around 1885, "Austrian, Russian, and Hungarian Jews began to come into New York. Among these immigrants were a large number of criminals, who soon found that they could develop an extremely profitable business in the sale of women in New York." Supposedly, Tammany Hall cooperated, even exploiting the situation to its own advantage.[66]

Gaynor himself also charged a prior administration with corruption. Seven days before the election, he reminded the city that McClellan's revocation of the moving picture licenses was "a very harsh and wrongful act." Moreover, he implied that protection money was demanded of Coney Island shows.[67] Some of the moving picture people did not have to be persuaded. Already, the MPEA and Vitagraph (a member of the MPPC) had come out in support of Gaynor "because of his sane decisions in motion picture cases" and his "liberal ideas regarding Sunday closing and personal liberty." Moreover, Gaynor's stance against graft was welcomed: "The picture men can now go on their way rejoicing that a large part of their receipts need not be turned over to grafters holding over their heads a threat to close up their places on some imaginary violation of municipal regulations if the money is not paid." Vitagraph even released "poses of Judge Gaynor." Political sentiment was not uniform among the manufacturers, however. Kalem supported Bannard, also producing movies showing him.[68]

Gaynor won the election, perhaps because Hearst took votes away from Bannard. During the next few years, Gaynor's administration pursued a liberal and tolerant attitude toward moving pictures, although Gaynor, of necessity, introduced legislation to improve the business.

One of Gaynor's first encounters with movies, however, was to insist, as he had when a judge, that the subject matter of movies should not be tightly regulated. When the Jeffries-Johnson fight picture was ready for exhibition in the summer of 1910, Gaynor refused to prohibit its screening because no law existed to justify closing it down. The *New York Evening Journal* (Hearst's paper) attacked his decision. The *Journal* then went on in the following month to begin a general offensive on moving pictures, including printing articles about murders, crimes, and suicides purportedly caused by people watching movies. Finally, it was revealed in *Moving Picture World* that an individual who had started the Anti-Immoral Moving Picture Association to promote censorship of the films had done so at the instigation of "a well-known dishonorable New York daily" as a way to discredit Gaynor. Shortly thereafter, the Presbyterian Ministerial Association repudiated the individual and his goals.[69]

Although he was a friend to moving picture exhibitors, Gaynor was also aware of the possibilities for graft in licensing and inspection, as well as the fire, health, and safety hazards of poorly constructed facilities. Moving pictures had until then been governed by a series of laws, not at all coherent or plain. In December 1910, one year after the start of his administration, Gaynor assigned his commissioner of accounts, Raymond B. Fosdick, to report on moving pictures in the city. By March 1911, Fosdick supplied his findings. Only the penal code specifically dealt with film, and that required that children under sixteen needed a parent or guardian to attend films. Licenses were of two types. If the theater had a stage, it was a "theater or concert" license (annual fee of $500), revocable only by the Supreme Court. Without a stage, the business secured a "common show" license ($25 per year), which could be canceled by the mayor. Additionally, seven New York City departments had statutes relating to the physical conditions of the theaters. If the theater had a capacity of over 300 people, it had to conform to certain building codes. Fosdick calculated that of the 740 operating theaters, 290 houses had theater licenses. Furthermore, about 600 houses had a capacity of fewer than 300 people. Fosdick thought many theaters were unsafe and urged a committee to discuss improvements.[70]

Gaynor formed this committee in May 1911. *Moving Picture World* considered the committee to be friendly. Collier was one of the members. By November 1911, a proposed ordinance was completed, and exhibitors were not pleased with some of its contents. Among the proposals were regulation of content through administrative action rather than statutory means, better building codes, and the prohibition of vaudeville in theaters with fewer than 600 seats. The reason for the last recommendation was the committee's view that "cheap vaudeville [was] inherently poor, almost impossible to control, and socially objectionable."[71]

The specific set of recommendations became known as the Folks Ordinance, but it lingered on the city council's agenda. Meanwhile, those who wished to censor movies managed to convince Alderman Courtlandt Nicoll to sponsor such an ordinance in April 1912. Neither ordinance moved anywhere during 1912. By the end of the year, one amendment had been made to the Folks proposal: the Dowling amendment would have placed all films under the supervision of the board of education. The ordinance passed the council in late December.[72]

Gaynor promptly vetoed it. In his letter to the board of aldermen, Gaynor wrote:

> It has hitherto been the understanding in this country that no censorship can be established by law to decide in advance what may or may not be lawfully printed or published. Ours is a government of free speech and a free press. That is the cornerstone of free government. . . . The truth is that the good, moral people who go to these moving picture shows, and very often bring their children with them, would not tolerate the exhibition of obscene or immoral pictures there. A place in which such pictures were exhibited would soon be without sufficient patrons to support it.

Gaynor also equated the idea of precensoring films with the system used by Russians, a connection exhibitors would later make to stress that censorship was un-American.[73]

It took until the summer of 1913 for Gaynor to succeed in getting the Folks Ordinance, minus the censorship clause, passed by the city aldermen, but he did. Shortly thereafter, he spoke at the third national convention of motion picture exhibitors to the delighted response of those present. As passed, the ordinance defined moving picture theaters as those auditoriums with fewer than 600 seats. These houses would be licensed by the mayor's Bureau of Licenses. Minimal building and fire codes were established. Theaters with fewer than 300 seats but with live entertainment would have to meet the standards for over-300-seat theaters when they reapplied for their licenses.[74]

Gaynor began a campaign for reelection in the fall of 1913, but he died suddenly in September 1913. The winner of the election was John Purroy Mitchel, whom the film industry expected to be fair-minded about movies. Indeed, as I have indicated above, the battleground for censorship was already shifting to the national front.

In December 1912, Alice Guy Blaché, president of the Solax film company and the only woman in the film industry in a top management position, expounded at length on her views about censorship. Blaché had the legitimacy of speaking as a woman on the topic, an authority she exploited. She turned to the focal issue of the effects of films on young people by telling a story about working-class children visiting the Metropolitan Museum of Art, where they saw nude statues. The teacher "made plain to them the difference between vulgar nakedness and nude art." Such an education, Blaché believed, was important for these and any class of child. Blaché furthermore condemned the "old maids" and "male tea-drinkers" who would take from the movies the opportunity to teach moral and social lessons through "the triangular plot and stories of real life." No, "by shutting our eyes against the evils that exist in this world, we will not succeed in eliminating those evils. They exist and will exist, and the more we talk about them, the more they are discussed, the more apt are we to correct them. Hypocrites and the 'I am holier than thou' element are not the kind who help society."[75]

Blaché, many members of the film industry, the National Board of Review, Mayor Gaynor, and influential people of the middle-class professions and society agreed that talking about bad things was the better solution to reforming society. No one absolutely rejected regulation of films, assuming that some representations were, indeed, vulgar or salacious and not art. What they did not want was a strict censorship that prohibited narratives and narrative material dealing with crime and sexuality, because, as Blaché put it, the more the problems were discussed, the better chance of solving them.

Such a position about censorship and motion picture content was not completely altruistic. As I have indicated, economic rationales existed to encourage cooperation on what would be regulated and how. In the People's Institute—and John Collier in particular, as well as Judge William Gaynor—New York City manufacturers found willing partners in their hope to expand attendance at films. Sanctifying the movies by the prestige of important civic organizations and insuring the quality of the product to be consumed had a progressive air about it. The industry was publicly authorized by important people and groups to make films that would be both instructive and entertaining. For the young film industry, self-regulation was a useful strategy for product competition as it sought customers from Boston to Bombay. It was also useful for a social formation that wanted to talk about sexuality and social transformations, which was the larger reason for what occurred.

5

The White Slave

The laxity in sex matters in this and other countries cannot be said to be due to the broadening of women's views. The women who have entered upon the life of civic and social enlargement are not those who "go astray." The sexually loose women are not the so-called advanced women. They are the parasite women, the indulged women, the women who do not think.[1]

In "Sex O'Clock in America" (1913), the author is advocating that when thinking about women the readers should not confuse the Advanced Woman with the Gone-Astray Woman. A good deal of talk is being generated to distinguish the two and explain the latter. In the next three chapters I shall discuss three cases from the early teens of such a regulation of the characterizations of the Advanced or New Woman and her opposite, the Gone-Astray or Bad Woman. These cases exemplify the three types of women the author of "Sex O'Clock in America" warns against (although, of course, all sorts of other bad women existed during the era). The first case is *Traffic in Souls*, in which Little Sister is the woman who does not think. *A Fool There Was* portrays the dangers of the parasite woman, and *The Cheat* is the tale of Edith Hardy, the indulged woman. These films have been chosen because they are well known and have been considered previously as examples of the representation of women during this era.

The three films also illustrate three possibilities for ideological activity through narrative regulation.[2] I have indicated earlier that each of these films not only describes the threat or failures of the Bad Woman, but also provides prescriptive or reformist visions for the New Woman. More than one message per film exists to speak to and with the many women in the audiences for these films. Recall that in the early 1900s women were peering into the kinetoscopes and that one commentator on *The Unwritten Law* (Lubin, 1907) indicated that over two-thirds of the audience consisted of women, who were intensely interested in the action. Images that disrupt the norms, the Bad Woman in these cases, display the boundaries and frazzled edges of current norms, and, thus, a Bad Woman sets an agenda for change. A Bad Woman does work in excess of her actual social importance, but she exists in order to provide a lesson in narrative about her alternative.

These narratives, however, are not content with illustrating only the Bad Woman, since that representation would not necessarily suffice to meet the compromise guidelines established among the groups contending for the right to regulate public culture. Showing only crime (here as it relates to sexuality) might not ensure the reading that the progressive reformers argued would justify their permission to display such activity. Adding subplots or even examples of the New (good) Woman could through repetition reinforce the social and moral lesson. All three films illustrate this. In *Traffic in Souls*, Mary Barton (the elder sister) is instrumental in saving her sister because she *did* think. Her intelligent behavior is, moreover, put to the use and submission of patriarchy as she turns to her father and her fiancé (who is a policeman!) for assistance in rescuing Little Sister from her follies. In *A Fool There Was*, the younger sister acts as the alternative voice to Kate Schuyler's Victorian idealism. In this film, Kate remains faithful to the tenets of the previous generation, against the advice of her younger sister, and the conclusion displays the failure of those former ideals to restore the family when it is confronted by the onslaught of sexual passion. Where a new social order triumphs in *Traffic in Souls*, the older one fails in *A Fool There Was*.

The third case, *The Cheat*, is the most prescient of what would become a preferred method for narrating. Rather than split the New Woman and the Woman Gone Astray into two entities, creating an older-styled melodramatic opposition of characters in which one or the other wins or loses, having a character transform herself from a Bad Woman to a Good Woman has great moral and social force (and is more in tune with the new melodramatic-realist aesthetics). Preferably, this Bad Woman cannot have more than teetered on the brink of impure behavior, but in any event her recognition of the right way to act saves her and her family. Thus, internal regulation (in continuity with Protestant religion as well as the new self-help ethos) is favored over external regulation (prohibition and punishment for transgressions), and the audience can have a happy ending.

Thus, I am suggesting two points about criticism of these films. One is to consider the productivity of trying to regulate an image. The films will display the value of desire by the New Woman while also trying to regulate that desire to the right degree and the right object, providing both negative and positive images of what the (utopian) New Woman should be. I want to emphasize that because diverse opinions existed about what the New Woman should be, the films (and literature and drama) do not produce the same images—thus, the productivity of the regulation.

A second critical operation that I am advocating is the avoidance of allocating to a single character a reified ideological definition: "Advanced" or "Gone Astray," for instance. In an analysis of the ideological functionings of regulated texts, keeping distinct the ideological images ("New," "Bad") and the characters who operate in a narrativized fiction is necessary in accounting for the transformations and incoherency of a text.[3]

In both these critical points, I am stressing regulation as an imperfect activity—imperfect at least from the point of view of a theory of containment. In *Sexual Dissidence,* Jonathan Dollimore argues against thinking of dominant ideologies as all-powerful and of resistances as merely false consciousnesses, acts that only confirm the authorities of dominant systems. Rather he insists on a more local and partial analysis of the effects of resistances. In particular, Dollimore counsels seeking "the part played by contradiction and dislocation in the mutually reactive process of transgression and its control." Although I would be inclined to modify how "mutual" this relation is, Dollimore aptly sets out an agenda for cultural analysis:

> So the critique of ideology identifies the contingency of the social (it could always be otherwise), and its potential instability (ruling groups doubly contested from without and within), but does not underestimate the difficulty of change (existing social arrangements are powerfully invested and are not easily made otherwise).[4]

In the regulation of Woman at the turn of the century, it would be remiss, I believe, to conclude that in all instances the possibilities for women were contained in ways perfectly felicitous for patriarchy, imperialism, monopoly capitalism, and consumer culture—which in any case did not have a "mind" of its own to know or predict what might suit it best. Contradictions, dislocations—anomolies—exist in these films as traces of the cultural il-logics at work. The sociological and psychological imperatives to maintain or transgress the boundaries of contemporary norms produce a discoherent text (Dollimore's valuable term), but a text having sources in the society that produces and consumes it. These discoherencies thus open the doors to a variety of interpretations and places from which to struggle for the meaning of Woman (and Man). As Annette Kuhn describes this, "Cinema took part in producing and circulating certain forms of knowledge of the socio-sexual, and consequently in that proliferation of discourses on sexuality which is said to mark this period."[5] This proliferation of discourses while regulated was not capable of being perfectly contained, if for the simple reason that the power structure itself (bourgois middle-class America) was divided on some of the matters.

People in 1911 realized that viewers mentally filled in gaps in stories and could do this for supposedly taboo scenes. Thus, within two years of the institution of the Board of Censorship, counselors to budding screenwriters could give all sorts of formulas about how to handle sensitive material. Richard V. Spencer writes that because the Board of Censors would taboo certain subjects, producers would

> refuse to consider scenarios dealing with brutal or wilful murder, highway robbery, suicide, kidnapping, theft, or kindred crimes, though at times some of the above are suggested, but the crime itself rarely shown on the screen. . . . Other classes of scenarios tabooed are those containing scenes of an immoral or suggestive nature, inconsistent melodramas, heavy tragedies (except in rare instances), trick pictures, risque farces, and most costume plays, unless the plot is clean cut and original.[6]

I am not quite sure what was wrong with "costume plays," but other ways existed for a writer to get around these boundaries on representation. The stories might be told through framing the tale with a moralizing voice of narration in the intertitle prose.[7] They might also use character agency to determine causal events. Conclusions were *consequences*, not merely of causality, but also of personal decisions. Epes Winthrop Sargent explained, "Stories of murders, thefts, abduction and all crimes are not wanted unless the moral is strong and rightly placed."[8]

Although the films I am about to analyze have much to say about sexuality, they were generally accorded a positive reception because they did abide by the rules, which were not that tough in retrospect, although they were complicit with dominant middle-class ideologies. Even though some controversy occurred around *Traffic in Souls,* it was more directed toward related films that failed to obey sufficiently these guidelines. These three films, then, while outstanding examples of the regulation of female sexuality and women's identities, are also representative of the contradictory and ambiguous production of cultural meanings for the generation of sex o'clock in America.

"Authentic" and "Authorized"

In "The Repeal of Reticence" published in March 1914, Agnes Repplier lamented all the talk going on about sex. She remarked that this talk was legitimated because it claimed to be " 'original,' 'authentic,' 'authorized.' "[9]

Repplier was actually specifically referring to *Traffic in Souls* (released by Universal in November 1913). In particular she was discussing the film's advertising, which claimed that the movie was a dramatization of a report by John D. Rockefeller Jr. about the conditions of vice in New York City. Using the warrant of some authority's approval for a touchy subject was an old literary and dramatic device that filmmakers had readily adopted. Yet, as other scholars and even Rockefeller himself noted, this was false advertising: Rockefeller said the use of his name was " 'unauthorized' for *Traffic in Souls.*" Rockefeller did permit his name to be used in support of the theatrical production of *Damaged Goods*, which opened earlier in the year: "I endorse the proposed production of Brieux's play, 'Damaged Goods.' The evils springing from prostitution cannot be understood until frank discussion of them has been made possible. Worthily presented in a spirit of sincerity, this powerful drama will assist in breaking down the harmful reserve which stands in the way of popular enlightenment."[10]

If *Traffic in Souls* did not have Rockefeller's approval, perhaps it was in part because the film *contradicts* what groups connected with Rockefeller had concluded about the business of prostitution. The false advertising had its effect, at any rate. Business was quite good, with New York exhibitors taking in five thousand dollars in the first week and twenty-eight New York theaters showing the film during the initial month's run.[11]

Traffic in Souls did strong business in New York and most of the rest of the United States (the Board of Censorship passed the film with some discussion but eventually only five minor alterations), but it was banned in Chicago. As the *Moving Picture World* reviewer, George Blaisdell, anticipated:

> It is a big subject—one that has been given grave consideration by many thoughtful men and women. These divide naturally into two groups—one favoring battling with the evil, or, as the more advanced would phrase it, the evils of the evil, in the old-time secret way; the other would come into the open and fight a condition as ancient as the beginnings of history with modern weapons—and the chief of these publicity. To those who hold the latter of these opinions, "Traffic in Souls" will be warmly welcomed. The picture is bound to arouse bitter antagonism. Surely its friends, and among these are the members of the National Board of Censorship, are entitled to ask that the production be seen before it is condemned.[12]

Blaisdell indicates that publicity about the social evil is the choice of one segment of society, including the members of the Board of Censorship. Chicago censors, as I have noted, tended to take the other view.

The film thus both traces and provokes a set of controversies about the truth of aspects of the social evil as represented in film. Was *Traffic in Souls* a docudrama or an out-and-out fiction? Who or what authorized its talk? Was the talk helpful in the fight against "the evils of the evil" or actually some kind of deviant behavior in itself?

As I discussed in chapter 2, around 1906, something of a transformation in the discourse about prostitution began. Among other things, the social hygiene movement started, and normally reticent individuals chose to discuss the health dangers of the "conspiracy of silence" for the family. Roosevelt and others began talking about "race suicide," connecting a decline in child birth-rates among one group of Americans with threats to Anglo-Saxon heritage. Moreover, George Kibbe Turner asserted that women were being forced into prostitution (an old story) and, furthermore, that a conspiracy connected with specific ethnic minorities operated an international "white slavery" syndicate. Thus, not only were "white" women being forced into this evil, but, in addition the perpetrators were non-Anglo and likely even foreigners! To interpret the cultural meanings of parts of *Traffic in Souls*, knowing the claims and counterclaims about white slavery is useful.[13]

Turner's essay in *McClure's Magazine* in 1907 was only the start of the foray into uncovering the white slavery conspiracy. Clifford G. Roe, an Illinois assistant state attorney, inaugurated that year prosecutions for the crime, and the following year, the U.S. district attorney in Illinois opened white-slave trials. Also in 1908, President Roosevelt proclaimed U.S. adherence to an international white slavery treaty, formulated six years earlier in Paris, to tighten immigration laws permitting the prosecution of panders. Numerous articles appeared in respectable journals such as *Harper's Weekly* and *Collier's* about white slavery. Turner produced the two articles for *McClure's* in 1909 that accused New York City's Tammany administrations of involvement in protecting a trade in women.[14]

As a result of Turner's charges and the general climate, in January 1910 a judge of the Court of General Sessions in New York City charged a grand jury to investigate allegations of white slavery existing in the city. Appointed foreman of the jury was Rockefeller. In June 1910, Rockefeller's jury reported that *no* "organized conspiracy" of traffic in women existed, although perhaps informal networks of communication operated among individuals who knew each other. Fifty-four indictments were presented, some involving lower-level policemen, but Tammany Hall was basically exonerated. Affected by this work, Rockefeller orchestrated a committee of three individuals (himself, Jacob Schiff, and Paul Warburg) and hired Roe of Illinois fame to study immigrant women and the danger they faced as potential victims of unscrupulous people. He also sought means for rehabilitation of fallen women, taking the stance that women who had been prostitutes might return to become profitable members of society. In 1913, he incorporated the Bureau of Social Hygiene to scientifically study women "delinquents";[15] he also commissioned studies of European police systems and methods to handle prostitution. Two of the books were *Prostitution in Europe* by Abraham Flexner and *Commercialized Prostitution in New York City* by Katherine Davis and George J. Kneeland. Kneeland had worked in 1900 for the New York City Committee of Fifteen (which had also included Schiff as a member). A third volume was produced by Raymond B. Fosdick, who had worked previously for Gaynor and was the individual who produced the Gaynor administration's liberal report on New York moving picture theater regulation. Ultimately, Rockefeller's allies connected prostitution primarily to men's greed and women's attraction and submission to men.[16]

Rockefeller's work, however, was not necessarily the dominant or the most sensational view of prostitution and white slavery. Beyond the first moves against white slavery, including Roosevelt's proclamation of adherence to an international white slavery treaty, was the passage by the U.S. Congress in June 1910 of the Mann Act, which permitted prosecution of anyone transporting women across state lines for illicit purposes. Additionally, since the white slavery scare was not confined to New York (*McClure's* subscribers were nationwide), other cities also began their own investigations of white slavery. Between 1909 and 1914 at least twenty-two white slave docunovels were published, some moderately titillating but all rationalized as cautionary tales based on reality.

The result of all this investigative work, talk, and legal regulation was a hodgepodge of theories, opinions, and "true stories" about white slavery. Turner's initial portrait claimed that Chicago had ten thousand prostitutes and a yearly profit of twenty million dollars. He located four areas to battle: criminal hotels, houses of ill fame, cheap dance halls and saloons, and men, "largely Russian Jews." The women most likely to be ruined were "especially the low-paid employees of department stores and factories."[17]

Other such versions of white slavery include Ernest A. Bell's *Fighting the Traffic in Young Girls; or, War on the White Slave Trade* (1910). The subtitle for Bell's exposé begins, "A complete and detailed account of the shameless traffic in young girls, the methods by which procurers and panders lure innocent young girls away from home and sell them to keepers of dives." Bell admitted that not all the traffickers in the international market were French; some were Jews, Italians, Sicilians, Greeks, and even English Americans. His major advice was unlikely to be heeded. He told young women not to be lured to the big city where they could slip; "the danger begins the moment a girl leaves the protection of Home and Mother." Dangerous places included restaurants (where wine and liquors were sold), amusement parks, dance halls (which were "truly the ante-room to hell itself"), large department stores (if the woman worked behind the counters and thus came into contact with customers), ice cream parlors and fruit stores (since they were "run by foreigners"), and, not surprisingly, the five-cent movie theaters (where children could come and go without guardians). Bell and his associates did advocate public discussion, and his book even prints pictures of children affected by gonorrhea and syphilis transmitted from infected parents.[18]

Roe also produced his version of the troubles in his 1910 *Panders and Their White Slaves* and his 1911 *The Great War on White Slavery*. In *Panders and Their White Slaves*, Roe takes the docunovel approach, using short "true" stories to illustrate the proposition he is arguing: this "systematic traffic and sale of girls" was not in "the realm of romance rather than of that of actuality." The first story was of Agnes, who went to a dance where her lemonade was drugged, and then awakened in a house of shame. There she was held to pay off her supposed debts and whipped when she tried to send a message out. Agnes was lucky; she finally managed to contact her parents, who rescued her.[19]

As Bell indicated, one of the major concerns of this strand of discussion about white slavery was the lack of safety in particular public places. Those who believed that a white slavery conspiracy existed tended to exaggerate the number of places and the size of the dangers. One of the most famous examples of this as it relates to moving pictures was the article in *Moving Picture World* in March 1910, " 'Recruiting Stations of Vice,' " published when Rockefeller's jury was still in session. The article reported the publication in the New York *Evening World* of a statement by Rev. Anna Shaw (well-known "in the ranks of progress"), who said: "There should be a police woman at the entrance of every moving picture show and another inside. These places are the recruiting stations of vice. In Chicago recently twenty-three young girls in one month were lured from a moving picture show and shipped to Texas for immoral purposes on the representation that they were being engaged for a theatrical spectacle. This could never have happened had two police women been stationed there."[20]

Not everyone agreed with the conclusions of individuals who believed in the white slavery conspiracy. Beyond Rockefeller's associates, the *Survey* (published by the Charity Organization and including on its board of directors Jane Addams, Jacob Riis, and William Guggenheim) indicated in 1909 some skepticism about the melodramatic, innocent-victim, bondage motifs so apparent in parts of the storytelling. Turning to the preliminary report of a U.S. Immigration Commission study of white slavery, the *Survey* informed its readers that "dive-keepers and procurers" might work together "but not, the commission holds, to such an extent as to warrant belief in the great 'vice trust' discovered by recent magazine writers. . . . Innocent women form only 'a small percentage,' but procurers are on the watch everywhere to decoy un-attended immigrant girls, and girls who live here, into disreputable houses where they are held against their will." The traffic is mostly in "the importa-tion of women who had become immoral before they left their own coun-tries."[21]

Obviously some parts of the story might be authentic, but versions from the U.S. government and social science research occasionally suggested less victimization of the women and more cooperation on their part. In fact, as vice commissions in the various cities began issuing reports after 1911, a great variety of causes were deduced as reasons for women being prostitutes. As I discussed in chapter 2, religious explanations by this point were not favored; social science was replacing institutionalized morality as the authority for de-scribing social problems and proposing regulatory solutions (often through state legislation). The Chicago Vice Commission report in 1911 was one of the first of these reports. It specified the following as the causes for prostitu-tion: (1) "bad home conditions and lack of recreational privileges"; (2) "lack of adequate protection for young immigrant girls upon their arrival in this country"; (3) "the temptation of underpaid young girls and of children"; and (4) "the prejudice which often almost forces Negro girls through lack of other employment to serve as domestics in disreputable houses." An individual member of the commission also included in his report additional causes in-cluding "the pursuit of pleasure," "subnormality, rendering the victim suscep-tible to temptation or to exploitation," and "lack of education in sex physi-ology and hygiene." This writer also mentioned (in the only such case that I have discovered) that the "wrong done to young girls and even to little chil-dren are with awful frequency charged to their own fathers, brothers, uncles, or cousins." Beyond prohibiting prostitution (because it "is pregnant with dis-ease" and because prohibition is necessary to save the race and "honor to womanhood"), the Chicago Vice Commission counseled as remedies (in this order): "Wise teaching of sex hygiene in the schools . . . as a means of child protection in the future"; leniency and help for first-time offenders; governmental support for incoming immigrants; and medical certification of health before marriage.[22]

Furthermore, although public places might be dangerous, they were not inherently the cause of the problem. For example, O. Edward Janney (M.D.), spokesperson for the National Vigilance Committee, warned against condemning moving pictures, "which under proper restrictions may be an important and valuable educational and recreative factor." What the theaters and families needed to do was to regulate the situation a bit more, brightening the rooms so they were not pitch dark and being sure children were under parental supervision.[23] Education about these dangers was the appropriate public response.

This concern over the wandering of women in public places reinforced the metaphor of "going astray." The Vice Commission of Minneapolis reported in 1911:

> One of the most disturbing phases of the present situation in Minneapolis, and an alarming social symptom, is the large number of young girls in the streets at night in the downtown sections, and in the business districts of the outlying sections. They may be found in numbers loitering about the fruit stores, drug stores and other popular locations, haunting hotel lobbies, crowding into the dance halls, theaters, and other amusement resorts; also in the saloon restaurants and the chop suey places and parading the streets and touring about in automobiles with men.
>
> It would not be fair to charge that all or a large proportion of these girls are prostitutes. It is perfectly plain, however, that many of those who are not, are on the direct road.[24]

This direct road (past the chop suey places) is what these guardians thought was the direction being taken by young women who were not thinking about the dangers involved in haunting the public sphere and consuming commercialized entertainments. A Massachusetts Vice Commission research report indicated that 51 percent of the prostitutes studied were mentally defective. If women did not (or could not) think, they were also not yet cognizant of some of their own passions. Working in department stores was dangerous because the clerks "become aware of needs that they did not know they had." As the *Nation* put it in 1913, echoing sentiments expressed earlier by Jane Addams, if white slavery was a "sin," so was the wage scale provided by the "whole industrial system," which did not permit sufficient gratification of these women's desires for a better living standard.[25]

No, many of the commissions dismissed the more lurid portions of the

white slavery conspiracy. The Vice Commission of Philadelphia reported in
1913 that it saw little evidence of white slavery in the narrow sense—
"namely girls held in actual physical subjection, forced by locks and bolts, by
cuffs and blows, to lead a life of prostitution." That did not mean, however,
that a more subtle subjugation did not exist or that pimps did not physically
abuse the women who worked for them.[26]

If the public documentations surrounding white slavery were heterogeneous in attributing causality (women were victims of evil people; women
were victims of lack of intelligence or larger social structures), the docunovels
duplicate that range of views. I have already mentioned that in Roe's *Panders
and Their White Slaves*, Agnes was a case of the first version of causality: human individuals did evil things to other people. According to Laura Hapke,
the figure of the prostitute very seldom appears in fiction in the 1800s, but at
the turn of the century among writings by men authors, the prostitute is represented as "a woman constantly threatened by entrapment, economic exploitation, and her own naiveté and vulnerability." Hapke believes that this
representation is a defense against thinking that the women had knowledge of
their situation or, even worse, partial or full agency and responsibility for it.[27]
Such a view would confront images of women as innately pious, pure, submissive, and domestic. The bondage representation might also be a subtle psychological opportunity for sadomasochistic fantasies by both men and women
readers.

Some of the white slavery stories reproduced such a vision of the woman as
innocent victim. (All the pieces claim to be based on real-life stories that
were to serve as powerful warnings to their readers.) Others, however, treated
the woman as "gone astray." In either case, the woman could be saved; the
difference was in how she was to be rehabilitated—whether she was to be
merely freed from her house of bondage or reeducated to dominant social
norms.

Examples of the first view—the prostitute as victim—include Roe's *Panders and Their White Slaves* and his *Horrors of the White Slave Trade* (1911),
which had thirty-two half-tones "portraying this terrible slavery." Roe received legitimacy for his stories from B. S. Steadwell, who was president of
the American Purity Federation. The first story was of Mildred, who eloped to
Chicago with a gentleman who brought her to the house of shame. She escaped by yelling at a passing parade. Hazel's husband sold her into slavery
from which she escaped. Fannie was induced to come to the big city and
found herself in a brothel, not a hotel. Mabel went to the theater, became
drunk, discovered she was pregnant, and, disgraced, ran away to Chicago

where she worked as a clerk in a store until a man took her on as a kept woman.[28] These stories suggest a naiveté by the women and the unscrupulous behavior of evil men in relation to that "weakness." This might be said to be the religious, individual-agency theory of white slave as victim. It could, however, work with the social hygiene thesis that women needed to be informed about the public sphere and threats to their personal integrity.

However, another set of stories places more of the agency and the responsibility in a larger context of family and social structures, becoming a social-structure theory of victimization. In either case, the white slave is still perceived to be a victim, not an agent of her situation. Thus, denial of sexual passion in a woman is maintained almost totally (except when seen as the reason a woman might fall prey to a man's advances). Depending upon the theory of causality for the victimization, the solutions differ: religious reaffirmation, socialization, improved economic status, and so forth. Thus, the debates of the twentieth century around individual agency versus social-structure causality permeate these discourses.

The social-structure theory of the white slave often blamed the family as the most immediate environmental context; accordingly, Reginald Wright Kauffman's two books can be viewed as alternatives to Roe's. Kauffman published both *The House of Bondage* and *The Girl That Goes Wrong* in 1911. *The House of Bondage* was the novel-length tale of Mary Denbigh, an urban high-school girl of a Pennsylvania German mother and a Welsh father. The family was religious and stern, but when the mother was too strict, Mary began to rebel. Moreover, her family had withheld information about intimacies or the wider life in which Mary lived. Stopped on the street one day, Mary agreed to meet Max Crossman at the picture show. There he promised to take her to New York City, and he would marry her. Although the rest of the story falls into the melodrama of Mary being drugged in a restaurant and waking the next morning in the brothel, the blame is explicitly laid to larger social structures and attitudes. The novel's narration implies that a more tolerant and receptive household environment could have reduced the generational conflict. Moreover, had Mary *more knowledge* of the public sphere she might have recognized the dangers surrounding her when she ventured into it.

The novel itself actually is quite interesting and important beyond the story of Mary, since it introduces a subplot about Tammany Hall, reproducing in a dislocated way the additional thesis that prostitution existed because of political corruption. A Tammany man, Dyker, was courting Marion Lennox, settlement house worker and daughter of Joshua Lennox, a political reformer. Dyker helped provide protection for the brothel in which Mary lived, but he also aided Mary's escape. A third subplot was the romance of Hermann Hoffman and Katie Flanagan, who encountered sexual harassment while working at a department store. The ending was tragic; Mary took revenge on Max by having sex with him although she had a venereal disease. She tried to go home but was rejected, and she was finally left wandering the streets, unable to commit suicide and even unwanted at the brothel.

The Girl That Goes Wrong by Kauffman is, like Roe's anthology, a set of stories about typical instances of how women became prostitutes. His stories were originally printed in the popular journal Leslie's Weekly. "The Girl That Was Bad" and "The Girl That Wanted Ermine" tell of spoiled children whose parents were to blame. "The Girl That Studied Art" gave in while an art student in Paris (that dangerous European locale seems important). "The Girl That Wasn't Told" and "The Father That Was Careful" blamed parents for failing to give their daughters adequate knowledge of the world. Other stories continue these themes. The Survey reviewed The Girl That Goes Wrong, strongly recommending it: it had "not the faintest tinge of a morbid interest and a secret satisfaction on the part of the author at being in touch with such things." Yet at the end of the review, the critic hesitated. Perhaps the effect on the readers would not be quite what the author intended.[29]

If Repplier worried about films such as Traffic in Souls portraying the reasons women went astray, she and others like her could not be sure what people might actually think about the enlightening and educational stories with which they were now being bombarded. Moreover, even if the tales were told as cautionary lessons, legitimated by various institutions claiming power to discuss these matters, what was authentic and authorized was not clear. Were the true stories in McClure's Magazine about international white slavery rings drugging and tricking women into prostitution a more adequate version of the world in this day of urbanization and globalization? Or were the vice commission and social science reports more authentic, with their attribution of causality to insufficient public education, economic structures, and consumer desires? Or was Kauffman's blame of parental shortcomings the way to see through the social evil? Authentic and authorized, yes, but which one? Into this play of narratives came the white slave movies, including Traffic in Souls.

Three Houses in the Big City

Traffic in Souls was filmed during 1913, rather far along in the furor over the white slavery conspiracy trend. It was, however, something of a sensation in its successful New York and national release (including the ban in Chicago).[30] Yet its success was also a provocation for additional stories along the same line, not all of which obeyed the rules well established for telling such troublesome tales. The fallout over the film's competitors and imitators might have furthered the decline in public approval of the more sensationalized versions of the narrative, although other circumstances, such as new scandals, likely contributed to a more general waning of interest. The movie business itself would take the line that more lurid white slavery stories were unfit for general public consumption.

Traffic in Souls was not the first movie to discuss white slavery. As I have indicated in chapter 3, prostitutes had appeared in short films such as A Rose of the Tenderloin (Edison, 1909). The Past Forgiven (Solax, May 1913) took up after a white slave had been saved: "The heroine of this picture has been a white slave, but has been rescued by a Salvation lassie and sent to a ranch where a cowboy has married her." The crisis occurred when the cowboy discovered her past, but a reconciliation was achieved. The reviewer commented, "The photography is clear, though the subject cannot be called fresh."[31] In this review, "white slave" seems almost a generic substitute for prostitute. Moreover, the theme of forgiving and redeeming fallen women seems old to the reviewer. Drugging people's drinks seems frightfully common. This occurs in How They Do Things on the Bowery (Edison, 1902), The Unwritten Law (Lubin, 1907) (when White is seducing Nesbitt), and The Musketeers of Pig Alley (Biograph, 1912). Directed by D. W. Griffith, the plot of Musketeers has the heroine saved from such a trick, motivating her debt to a local underworld boss.[32]

A few white slave movies were made in Denmark in 1907 and later.[33] Griffith directed a white slave rescue narrative in the 1908 Biograph film, The Fatal Hour. In this film, a woman who is walking in the countryside with a suitor is set up by him to be kidnapped by a Chinaman. A woman friend who suspects the circumstances to have been engineered by the suitor flirts with him and then drugs his drink. When the suitor passes out, the woman searches his pockets, finds valuable information, and calls the police, who rescue the potential victim from the brothel. A further twist occurs when the adventuresome woman who acted as the detective is also kidnapped by the gang and tied up in front of a device that will shoot her when the clock strikes noon. She is, as is part of the Griffith formula, saved in the nick of time. This film plays out the woman-as-victim thesis for prostitution. The Fight against Evil (Rex, released 14 September 1913) seems closer to the standard range of white slave narratives that imply human agency as the cause for prostitution. "A story with an intended moral, some of which is very obvious. It tells of a working girl who is led to the white slave market by a man whom she called in from the street when her mother died. . . . It contains a good lesson for unsophisticated girls and also for parents." In *The Temptation of June* (IMP, released 3 November 1913), June resisted the advances of a rich man in the "great metropolis," much to the approval of the reviewer.[34] Both of these films seem to stress individual responsibility and knowledge as important for the causality of the events, as opposed to Griffith's *The Fatal Hour*.

Released almost at the same time as *Traffic in Souls* was Biograph's *By Man's Law* (November 1913): "A two-reel number, following in the wake of numerous theatrical productions dealing with the white slave traffic. The story is strong and well pictured; it shows how the oil trust grinds down a family of independent producers, so that the girl eventually is forced to look for work on the street. She is followed by white slavers and dies at the close of the picture. This is rather sordid and pessimistic in type and cannot be called a pleasant picture. At the same time it is well constructed and powerful in the emotions it excites."[35]

Directed by W. Christy Cabanne, *By Man's Law* also featured a strike by workers, and class conflict operated as a consequence of the disparity between the rich and the laborers. The film emphasized the hypocrisy of the oil magnate who, when approached by a woman working for the Society for the Prevention of Vice, gave her a check as "a chance to turn public opinion." "His son consents to join the Reformer's Society," as well. Yet the effect of the magnate's charity act was that oil went up two cents. Additionally, upon the death of the workers' sister, who had become a white slave, one of the brothers kidnapped the daughter of the oil magnate and, showing her the body of his dead sister, nearly killed the magnate's daughter. Unlike *The Fight against Evil* and *The Temptation of June*, *By Man's Law* follows the social-structure theory of white slavery, specifically connecting the cause for prostitution to economic circumstances (a favorite theme at the Biograph studio). The woman was not tricked into her situation, although she was economically forced into prostitution in order to feed herself and her family. Thus, at the time of the making of *Traffic in Souls*, films exemplifying a full range of explanations for prostitution had been produced and exhibited: *The Fatal Hour* (woman as victim of evil people); *The Fight against Evil* and *The Temptation of June* (woman as human agent); and *By Man's Law* (woman as victim of social structures).

Traffic in Souls was released sometime around 24 November 1913. As a six-reel production, it was much more spectacular in its opening than *By Man's Law* (a two-reeler), receiving premiere status at Weber's Theater in New York City with admission at twenty-five cents. Accounts of its production suggest that

the owner of the manufacturing and distributing firm, Carl Laemmle, may not
have been directly aware of its making (not surprising, given the size of the
business at that point), but a picture of that scope would have been common
knowledge to all of the people working around the studio. It certainly was
known to Laemmle by the time of its release.[36]

The film is unusual for American movie production in several ways. First
of all, although six reels means a running time of about seventy minutes, that
length of film was over twice the typical length for most feature (multiple-
reel) films in 1913. About half of an evening's program of movies was often
still at only the one-reel, twelve-minute length. Second, the individuals who
produced the film had not been working on extended-length films prior to
this one. Hence, they had little experience in the formal problems of stretching a narrative across seventy minutes. The director, George Loane Tucker,
however, was a devotee of Broadway theater, and longer films were occasionally being produced by this time.

In retrospect, the film is remarkably prescient of what would by the late
teens become standard classical Hollywood narrative and narrational practices. It quickly establishes its major characters through visual iconography
and editing procedures; it sets out plot information early, motivating coinci-
dences that might otherwise be considered implausible if introduced late in
the plot; it develops multiple plot lines, including an appropriate heterosexual
romance among the young people in the story, and interweaves the plot lines
so that the crosscutting is not merely for suspense but also plot progression
and thematics; it provides (apparent) coherence and closure through retribution for the guilty and rewards for the innocent—here, as in most romances,
in the form of a heterosexual coupling of the policeman hero and the major
woman protagonist. In all of this it conforms to the rules of regulating subject
matter and spectacle that were being codified within the film industry. Specifically, it emphasizes individual character agency as the primary causal force,
with events a consequence of that agency.[37]

The story opens in the house of the Bartons.[38] The first intertitle introduces Mary Barton, "the head of the family." She eats breakfast and clears
away the dishes. "Her Sister," however, sits on her bed, slowly stretching.
Mary calls to Sister, who responds just as slowly as before. "Her Father, The
Invalid Inventor," completes this family. Father sits bundled in a wheelchair,
facing a contraption on the table. Kissing him lightly, Mary heads out the
door while Sister is still dressing. Mary's fiancé, officer Burke, happens to be at
a nearby check-in station. Seeing each other, Mary stops to chat. They join
hands, he leans to kiss her, but she turns and looks back toward a window

washer. An exchange between Burke and the young man permits, when the young man turns his head away, the romantic kiss. Through cutting to a shot of the man turning his head and then cutting back just at the end of the action, the film discreetly conveys the event while maintaining the couple's privacy. Clever editing on the action lets the viewer fill in the missing imagery and propriety is asserted as a governing rule for this film.

These opening two scenes have done much work. Beyond asserting that the narration will be circumspect in its treatment of sexual passion, *Traffic in Souls* has established Mary and Sister as opposites. Mary is energetic, efficient, and dutiful. Both Mary and Sister work at Smyrner's candy store as clerks. Sister is lazy, and when late to work, tries to sneak in. She ignores the reprimand of her boss. If Mary respects her relation with her father and her fiancé, Sister has yet to learn the value of paying attention to social regulations imparted by male superiors. Moreover, Mary is already being rewarded for her submission, for she has a solid, amorous heterosexual romance with none other than a pleasant member of the police force. Sister, as the film will show, has not yet figured out who might be a good candidate for her coupling.

The Bartons are only one family in the tale. The film crosscuts to another household: the Trubus home. The introductory title to William Trubus forewarns in an odd way Trubus's secret identity. Yet on a first viewing of the film, spectators who did not already know the story might think that the appellation implied his social status, and it does. "The Man Higher Up" will become an ironic term. In an upper-class sitting room, Trubus opens his mail and finds a letter indicating pleasure in anticipating his speech at the Union Institute. His wife undoes the morning paper and reads that a Citizens League has been formed with William Trubus as its head; its function will be "to clean the city of the infamous traffic in souls." A third Trubus enters, the daughter, Alice. The paper also (conveniently) announces the rumor of Alice's impending engagement to Bobby Kopfman, "the greatest society catch of the season."

The working class and the upper class. Now the underclass: "They who traffic in souls." The first shot of the scene introducing this set of characters is of a woman in fancy night clothes who hits another woman. Our madam counts her cash and then reluctantly turns it over to her cadet. A young woman attempts to sneak out of the house, but the cadet grabs her and stops the escape. Then he and the madam leave. On the way through the streets, the cadet points into the candy store, where he indicates that he has found another good prospect. They arrive at the office building of "the man who finances the social outlaws. The Go-Between."

Figure 5.1. *Traffic in Souls*. Mary needs to counsel Sister.

Meanwhile, Trubus leaves his home and arrives at the same building, walk-ing past the floor where the social outlaws work and upstairs to the offices of the International Purity and Reform League and then his private inner office. There Trubus dons a headset and begins watching what is transcribed on a recording system linked to a dictograph in the office of the social outlaws.

At this point, three lines of action begin to interweave. In one, the nar-ration imparts the information that the ultimate boss of the traffic in souls is none other than Trubus, who—in grand narrative irony—uses as his front his position as director of an international reform movement fighting the social evil. In a second plot line, policeman Burke, as an officer of the law, observes a country woman being led by a suspicious character into a house. Upon in-vestigation, Burke bursts into the brothel, freeing her and two Swedish im-migrant sisters whom the narration has shown also being tricked into entering the place.

Meanwhile, in the third line of action, Sister flirts with the cadet. Looking on, Mary is quite upset with this and counsels Sister about her behavior (fig-ure 5.1). At the end of the day, however, Sister ignores Mary's cautions. When the cadet arrives, she leaves with him. To trick anyone following them (including Mary and Burke, who look on), the cadet enters a cab on one side

Figure 5.2. *Traffic in Souls*. The Cadet drugs Sister's drink.

and then exits the other side to catch a second taxi in which the couple de-part. What was Sister thinking when such a maneuver took place? Or was she thinking at all?

Just as in earlier scenes with the country girl and the two Swedish immi-grant women, the film recapitulates the docudramas of the white slavery nar-ratives. Sister is taken to a café and dines with the cadet, who passes a note to a confederate asking for a safe cab. Then he drugs her drink (figure 5.2) while she dances with another of his allies. Sister, feeling woozy, is led to the cab and driven to the brothel. Wakened by water splashed in her face, Sister dis-covers she is imprisoned in a house of shame. At the close of the lines of ac-tion, in a powerful tour de force, the film crosscuts among three families and "homes" at the end of the day. Mary prays (figure 5.3). The Trubuses gather to say goodnight (figure 5.4). Little Sister is a new member of the brothel's house, her virtue threatened (figure 5.5).

The plot to this point might seem incredibly regressive in its representa-tions of women—their intelligence, place, and obligations—and, in a final analysis, *Traffic in Souls* should be understood as being readable in its time as having such features. It does place women in a subordinate role to men, coun-seling women to act appropriately to preserve the family. It also attributes causality for prostitution and white slavery to evil people and individual

Figure 5.3. *Traffic in Souls*. Mary prays Sister will be safe.

agency. However, *Traffic in Souls* also provides a new regulation for the Good Woman that is not a repetition of the old Victorian features of piety, purity, submissiveness, and domesticity. At least three contextual and textual circumstances cause me to caution against assuming that this movie has *only* one cultural meaning, that *Traffic in Souls* merely repeats middle-class, patriarchal values, cautioning women to stay out of the public sphere and at home where they cannot be threatened. That would be a very narrow reading of the film's contradictions and dislocations in representing women as cultural transfer points in debates about a changing America.

The Illogics of the "Traffic in Souls"

Up to this point, *Traffic in Souls* might be viewed as taking the stance that a conspiracy of white slavers existed, roaming the streets of the big city looking for thoughtless country girls, immigrant women, and store clerks all too ready to go out for a night on the town. However, as I noted, the head of the white slave network is represented as an apparently lawful individual. Furthermore, Trubus is a civil leader promoting purity and reform and has high social status and power. This suggestion that those investigating white slave trade are hypocrites, worthy of suspicion,[39] has an even more complicated angle. In a

Figure 5.4. *Traffic in Souls*. The Trubuses end their day.

trade paper review of *Traffic in Souls*, the *Variety* critic writes, "Professedly based on data gathered by the Rockefeller white slave researchers, there's a laugh on the Rockefeller investigators in the play in the personality of one of the white slavers, a physical counterpart of John D. himself so striking as to make the observer sit up and wonder whether the granger of Pocantico Hills really came down to pose for the Universal." The Man Higher Up, Trubus, *looks like Rockefeller.*[40]

What does this joke mean? I think at least for spectators who read the text that way it provided a bit of rather chaotic resistance to the Rockefellers as symbols of social and legal power, who were generally disliked anyway. Moreover, the movies, muckraking literature, and melodramatic and realist texts of the era also often challenged robber barons, whose activities, as I have indicated earlier, were condemned by many middle-class reformers, including the progressives. The challenge is not just a joke on Rockefeller as an individual, however. Such a reading of the film also becomes a rebuttal to the assertions of Rockefeller and his experts about white slavery and the causes for prostitution. The Rockefeller grand jury report had concluded that some lower-level cops were corrupt, that no international white slavery conspiracy existed (only informal networks at a local level), and that larger social structures

Figure 5.5. *Traffic in Souls*. Little Sister is at the house of bondage.

(economic dependency, women's subjugation by men) were primarily respon-sible for prostitution.

The film denies the first allegation and rewrites the second two points. In particular, officer Burke in earlier scenes and in the final rescue is the hero who prevents the entrapment of several women; he is not complicit in the system nor are any of his comrades. In fact, the average man as the hero be-comes something of a class criticism of the Rockefeller report. Second, *Traffic in Souls* dislocates the term *international* from the white slave narrative and recombines it with the front—the International Purity and Reform League—that Trubus uses to make his money. Furthermore, he is the man higher up in a large economic structure that is forcing women into prostitution. Thus, in a possible reading of the film, it might be said that an international conspiracy to enslave women *does* exist and that the gigantic, vertically integrated eco-nomic system run by Trubus-Rockefeller is what is behind that enslavement. Thus, the conspiracy exists in a social structure—monopoly capitalism.

Such a convoluted and conservatively radical reading of the film is likely stretching what would be a more probable interpretation by any specific au-dience member in 1913, although something of that possibility does fit quite comfortably within the dynamics of the discourses by some women's movement leaders. Recall that their explanation of the plight of prostitutes was indeed an economic analogy between literal and figurative slavery to men as a result of the lack of power by women to control their own economic status. Women who had to rely on men to certify their identity were just the sorts of people progressively radical feminists were out to liberate in their work for equality.[41] Thus, connecting Rockefeller (or any upper-class individual) to the cause of prostitution could produce a variety of cultural meanings for the film within its historical context.

A second set of contextual and textual circumstances promotes another possible interpretation of the complex of terms that does not challenge the individual-agency (evil-people) version of the causes of white slavery in so strong a way as the Rockefeller–social structure thesis does, but that also does not reduce the film to a mere repetition of the good woman as the Victorian ideal. The film suggests another explanation for prostitution, at least by *white* women (and it *is* "white slavery").[42] This cause is their naiveté or ignorance (rather than any economic need or, even worse, their sexual desire). *Traffic in Souls* displays a lot of talk about the dangers of not thinking. It does not portray the victims-to-be as out of place or wrong for being in the public sphere. Mary Barton is shown to be quite normal as a working girl. Just being a clerk in a candy store was not sufficient to warrant the charge of promiscuity. No, rather the error by Sister was her individual behavior once in that public sphere. One might say something of the same thing for the country girl and the two Swedish sisters. The country girl does all the things that women even today are warned against doing when they come to the big city. She wanders around looking lost; she takes the advice of someone she does not know (rather than asking a policeman for directions); she does not watch whether anyone is following her. The Swedish sisters also are too trustworthy, relying on the assumption that strangers are always nice people. The film does not chastise women for entering the public streets or working in heterosocial situations. It *does* suggest that they must keep their wits about them. This position is quite within the norms being advocated for the New Woman in modern America: good women are *thinking* women.

This second aspect to the film is reinforced by the third set of circumstances that I wish to emphasize. Mary Barton is the individual who can be most directly credited with saving her own Sister. She keeps her head in a difficult situation and, acting as a detective, she literally follows the thread connecting the International Purity and Reform League to the headquarters of the white slavers. How does this happen?

Figure 5.6. *Traffic in Souls*. Mary follows the wire to the outlaws' office.

The next morning Sister has not returned home (nor has she given in to the demands of her captors). Earlier in the film Mrs. Trubus (who knows nothing of her husband's business) has visited the candy store and talked with Mary, one of her favorites. When Mary comes to work, her employer fires her because a newspaper story suggests that candy stores are a place for white slavers to find victims, and the boss is unhappy about the publicity. As Mary leaves the store, Mrs. Trubus finds Mary to be the solution to another previously motivated problem. Mrs. Trubus has just contributed to the firing of Mr. Trubus's secretary because she had entered his office and found the secretary kissing the man the audience knows is the Go-Between. Mary can work for Mr. Trubus.

This coincidence is as fortuitous for the narrative as is the next one. Mary has been at work for only a matter of minutes when Mr. Trubus accidently spills ink across his desk. He calls her in to help clean up, then goes into the outer office to chair a weekly meeting of reformers. This leaves Mary in the private office, where she discovers the headphones. Picking them up, Mary "recognizes the voice of the man who took her sister away." The headphones are connected by a wire, and Mary follows that wire across the room and out the window (figure 5.6). Down the fire escape, she continues until she arrives outside the outlaws' office and even sees the man who enticed Sister to go out with him. "She realizes her employer and his secretary must be in league with the infamous traffickers."

Mary immediately responds with intelligence and calm. She acts as though nothing has happened when Trubus returns to his office, and she quietly calls Burke, to whom she tells the information at lunch. Mary's activities from the beginning of the drama until this point have been certified as the right way for a modern woman to behave. She may be a working woman in a heterosocial sphere, but her reward for her behavior is a tidy home in which she is "the head of the family." This oddly placed prose characterization, which is the very first intertitle of the movie, seems a powerful discourse about the potential of women in the twentieth century. She preserves the family (eventually Sister will be saved) as she lovingly cares for her (unpowerful) father. She does this by working industriously. Mary is also permitted a normal sexual passion: she wanted the kiss from Burke, but she requested a propriety about the display of physical contact. Most important, though, Mary is capable of following her own intuitions when she is confronted by empirical evidence. Mary knows how to think and act upon sense data and her reflections.

This vision of a good woman is not the Victorian image of the pious, pure, submissive, and domestic woman. Mary is these things, yes, but in a new guise as a self-reliant, natural, caring, and public woman. The terms are shifting. In part they do so because Sister as the Bad Woman, or at least the woman about to go astray, has been typified as self-centered, slothful, shallow, and thoughtless. Mary has the right, from her behavior, to be given the title of "head of the family," for she will likely reproduce with Burke the next version of the ideal marriage, in which companionship counts for much in the (utopian) arrangement. Mary and officer Burke, the New Woman and the Law, *work together* to rescue the woman in trouble.

By no means is Mary an oddity as a thinking woman in this early cinema. Despite some residual images of the Victorian woman (especially in some of D. W. Griffith's movies), many early films cast women as detectives and active individuals, aiding boyfriends and husbands who are in need of their support. Griffith also portrayed such intelligent women, as in *The Fatal Hour*. A 1906 film is another, earlier instance of this. In *Foul Play* (Vitagraph), a false friend leaves evidence that covers up his manipulation of company funds to play the stock market, making the husband appear to be guilty instead. A trial convicts the husband. The distraught wife, after praying with her children, disguises herself, follows the friend, has lunch with him and drugs *his* drink, then gathers papers that prove *he* is really the criminal. The husband is freed and the family reunited. By the early teens, as Ben Singer has noted, serial stories were predominantly constructed around a heroine. Although often helped out by her boyfriend, the serial queen investigated wrongdoings, became involved in physical danger, but escaped through her active intelligence and physical abilities. *The Perils of Pauline* (Eclectic Films, 1914) were short detective stories told episode by episode.[43]

To viewers of *Traffic in Souls,* this woman-centered solution, in which a female takes initiative and uses her brains, must surely have contradicted for audiences the more passive imagery associated with the women victims (the country girl, the Swedish immigrants, Little Sister). However, although Mary does discover the causal connection, she needs help in bringing the outlaws to justice. This help comes not from Burke but from her wheelchair-bound father. Although not physically powerful and not the "head of the family," Dad is useful anyway. He invents amazing contraptions. Most recently, he has achieved a way "for intensifying sound waves and recording dictagraph sounds on a phonographic record"! Is it a mere coincidence that the real inventor of the phonograph and dictaphone is also the individual credited by Americans with inventing the moving pictures—Thomas Edison? Father does not look like Edison, but Dad supplies the machinery to put the criminals away.[44]

As a docudrama about white slavery, *Traffic in Souls* was asserting itself to be part of the pervasive social discourse about the social evil, its causes and effects, and its remedies. Although the filmmakers are certainly not claiming this movie to be an authentic visual recording of the situation in the mode of a newsreel, they are justifying having regulated it so that it meets with at least the permissible range of views about the social evil. The narrative has supplied a process through which a newly configured family can emerge, one that gives credit to the source of the family's power: an ability to verify criminality (via recording devices such as movies) and a right to capture and punish the guilty.

The son-to-be takes up the father's functions by helping Mary hide the recording devices in Trubus's office. The next morning, at the risk of Trubus catching her, Mary operates the machinery (she is capable of handling this invention), and with the evidence secured rushes to the police station. Burke has located the brothel where Sister is being held. So together, the police force, Burke, and Mary drive to the house. The film returns to its tripart crosscutting between the police outside the house timing the surprise raid, Little

Figure 5.7. *Traffic in Souls*. Little Sister is about to be whipped.

Sister "near the breaking point" (she is about to be whipped into submission; see figure 5.7), and the Trubus family (Alice and her fiancé's family are arranging the engagement details). Sister is rescued in the nick of time.

The narrative is not complete, however, without the capture of the Man Higher Up. The police arrive at the Trubus household and inform him that "the invention of the father of the girl you sought to ruin will convict you" because "your conversations are on these records in your own voices." The Kopfmans storm out. Taken to jail, Trubus is demoted to the status of the many villains awaiting trail. Yet the final blow of plausible poetic justice must be delivered. Trubus is released on bail and returns to his house. Mrs. Trubus dies (perhaps to be read as a suicide) and thus "escapes her husband's shame"; his daughter rejects him because, as Alice says, "You've killed my mother." In trying to make money from a public house of bondage, in deriving profits from the subjugation of women, Trubus has destroyed his own private home. The family cannot exist on the basis of deceit and inequalities. The film ends with a shot of Trubus prostrate next to the body of his dead wife, in contrast to the united family of scientist and small businessman father Barton, law officer Burke, head of the family Mary, and rescued Little Sister.

If Edison and the movies can provide verification of criminality that might be admissable in court, men are also still the enforcers of the law's judgment.

Thus, the equity between the sexes is not total. Officer Burke is given the narrative climax, in which he chases the slavers across the rooftops, finally shooting the head pimp. Women such as Mary may have been permitted to participate in the detection of crime, but they must still watch the men serve as the agents in administering the law's verdict.

Traffic in Souls is thus a contradictory film with several possible strands of meaning contending for an individual audience member's attention. Perhaps the film was hedging its bets, but more likely it was displaying the contradictions in the middle-class discourse about women, families, prostitution, justice, and big business, a discourse in which both an individual-agency theory and a social-structure explanation for the cause of prostitution were voiced. Women are sometimes passive victims and sometimes active agents in their own destinies. In fact, a pointed moral is to watch out when in the dangerous big city or even in the more intimate candy store. Women are not condemned for existing or functioning in the public sphere, but they are encouraged to be dutiful, respectful, properly passionate, and thoughtful. In an equal relation, women can work with men to bring criminals to justice. Such messages within the regulation of women's subordination to men (as daughters, workers, and wives) were still powerful antidotes to older prescriptions of remaining innocently in the home.

Traffic in Souls met with a reasonably good public reception, perhaps because it provided a variety of cultural meanings from which individual audience members might recognize their own positions in the discussions or even take heart through the utopian representation of Mary as detective and intelligent head of the family, Burke as a good working cop, and Trubus as a criminal brought to justice.

As I indicated earlier, *Traffic in Souls* did very good business at the box office.[45] In general, as well, entertainment critics praised it. Blaisdell, in *Moving Picture World*, took the moralizing and propagandizing tone: "If such exhibition serve to quicken the official or public conscience in lethargic communities; if it help to preserve to society any one of the 'fifty thousand girls who disappear every year'; if it tend to make more difficult the vocation of unspeakable traders, then indeed will there have been substantial excuse for the making of this melodrama of today." "F," in the New York *Dramatic Mirror*, also thought it a good lesson: "It is a film for children above the age of fifteen to see."[46]

The *Outlook*, a moderate journal of the era, also sanctioned the film's exhibition because of its lessons and adherence to narrational protocols. After opening its essay on the prevalance of discussion about sex ("many seem to think that the present generation has been the first to discover the existence of sex"), the *Outlook* concludes that *Traffic in Souls,* while not perfect, was acceptable: "It is too much to say that there were not objectionable features in these films. They were false in some particulars of fact, and out of proportion in the presentation of others. Yet there can be little doubt that, no matter from what motives observers came to witness their production, they could hardly leave the theater save with a heightened disgust for the horrors necessarily attendant upon the continued existence of the social evil." In fact, the writers thought the movie might be presented to freshman college classes, or "with suitable interpretation," to seniors in high school. A young man might be less inclined after seeing the film to "link his body and soul to such an infamous system."[47] The *Outlook* did receive letters disagreeing with some of its conclusions. One point was that the conditions represented in the movie did not apply to small towns, only the new urban scene. Moreover, the film might prematurely interest adolescents in mature male activities. Finally, *Traffic in Souls* might be all right, but it was also only one of the white slave films currently showing.

Indeed, another movie, released within a few weeks of *Traffic in Souls,* did produce a much different reaction. Eventually, a jury of twelve New York men judged it obscene. In one sense, it is surprising that this would be the case. *The Inside of the White Slave Traffic* was produced by the Social Research Film Corporation and endorsed in the intertitles by, among others, three U.S. justices, Fredrick Howe (husband of Marie Jenny Howe and head of the People's Institute), Charlotte Perkins Gilman, and Carrie Chapman Catt. The film promised that it was "a pictorial report of the life and habits of those engaged or associated in The White Slave Traffic. Their ramifications and system employed—as they are in truth and fact, without any exaggeration or fictional indulgence."

The film has a strong documentary quality; its sets are definitely not the studio decors of *Traffic in Souls.* It also eschews the sensationalism of melodrama. No massive fights or chases of the sort that Burke initiated occur. In fact, the film is more a chronology than a narrative. Individual scenes of events connected to prostitution are not always linked into any kind of personalized drama, although the scenes do propose to follow the chains of white slavery for one woman, Annie. Some generic events happen: the classic drink-drugging scene, as well as a faked marriage. The traffic is also represented as national; girls are sent from one city to another in the trade. *The Inside of the White Slave Traffic* does not allocate causality for prostitution to anything, perhaps relying on public knowledge of the white slave events to carry the spectator through the scenes. (The prints I viewed lacked many expository intertitles, which, if they existed in the original film, probably created more explanations.) Given the women's-rights and feminist beliefs of the film's sponsors, the filmmakers likely assumed that spectators could understand from available public talk that general social structures (such as the dependency of women upon men for their economic well-being) were the larger causes for the events being pictured.

This film was authorized, but perhaps it was *too* authentic, falling beyond a realist aesthetic and into naturalism. Both Robert Allen and Kevin Brownlow make the point that, as a documentary, *The Inside of the White Slave Traffic* was exceptionally graphic, showing actual prostitutes soliciting on New York City and El Paso (Texas) streets.[48] Even the liberal Board of Censorship cautioned against showing the activities of streetwalking or the insides of brothels, although the film did not sensationalize these events in ways it might have.

Also important in explaining the judgment of obscenity, I think, is that the melodramatic aesthetic (used to good effect by *Traffic in Souls*) permitted by its very conventions and as part of its traditional narration a strong moral tone and a narrative retribution for the evil villains. A documentary, however, is not supposed to tamper with reality, and *The Inside of the White Slave Traffic* ends without such an explicit prescription against doing wrong. The movie concludes with the death of Annie, who is one of the victims, buried as an outcast in a potter's field.[49] Thus, melodrama helped *Traffic in Souls* present its material in ways acceptable to the general public. The protocols for narrativizing troublesome material called for a total-picture theory of film viewing to justify the introduction of individual scenes of suspect nature, but *The Inside of the White Slave Traffic* failed to do a sufficient job in creating plot outcomes that were the consequences of individual characters' agency, since it seems to have assumed a social-structure explanation for white slavery and thus no one in the film recognizes an error and reforms.

The social-structure causal theory did not correspond with the dominant focus on individuated characters and personal agency as the reason for events. A social-structure theory of causality would not be part of what would become the classical Hollywood cinema, which included within its norms the ideological attribution of causality to individual agency. Thus, not only was the film too graphic, it lacked proper ideological representations of humans and plausible closure as a consequence of those individuals' behavior. *The Inside of the White Slave Traffic* could too easily be used by viewers in ways other than as a social or moral lesson. Melodrama was better for containing the troublesome pictures.

The Inside of the White Slave Traffic was scandalous enough to provoke legal action in New York City despite the administration's general tolerance of movies. A city judge declared the film obscene, and its producers requested a jury trial. That judgment was quickly made in March 1914, with the producer found guilty but with a recommendation for mercy added. *Moving Picture World* and the film exhibitors and producers had already moved to withdraw support from any further white slave films in the larger interests of the industry. By January 1914 *Moving Picture World* had banned from its pages any advertising for such films.[50] The genre would continue underground for many years, but it had already provoked an even stronger enemy—ridicule. Kay Sloan indicates that by 1914 parodies such as *Traffickers in Soles* and *Damaged: No Goods* were being produced.

Traffic in Souls illustrates the bad woman who does not think. She is a danger for the social stability of the family. Yet *Traffic in Souls* also advocates a New Woman who is capable of heading the family, thinking and acting on her observations, and working with the men around her in the heterosocial public sphere. The consequences of the New Woman would be the united family in which passion would be private. The white slave is a consequence of not thinking; the New Woman would be rewarded for using her head.

6

The Vamp

In Lea Jacobs's valuable study about censorship during the 1930s, she quotes an industry spokesperson: "The important thing is to leave the audience with the definite conclusion that immorality is not justifiable, that society is not wrong in demanding certain standards of its women, and that the guilty woman, through realization of her error, does not tempt other women in the audience to follow her course."[1] The predecessors to the fallen woman genre that Jacobs discusses include the vamp cycle, typified by A Fool There Was, a film released in January 1915 by the William Fox company. Based on Rudyard Kipling's poem, "The Vampire," A Fool There Was certainly met with part of the 1930s industry spokesperson's goals. An audience departing from the film undoubtedly could see the dangers in some women's behaviors.

Yet whether the audience was likewise warned against imitating the vamp is uncertain, for, as Jacobs notes, a "Cinderella" motif also accompanied some of these narratives. Fallen women might have fallen morally, but they might also have risen financially, carried to a higher monetary status through their alliance with their lover. Jacobs argues that one of the aims of the post-1934 censors was to lessen the narrative disjunctions between the pleasures of the successful rise and the requisite punishment required by the censors' view that error must meet its reprisal, a rule continuing from the period that I have been examining. However, had the 1930s censors regulated the 1915 A Fool There Was, the movie might never have been released—for the vamp pays no penalty for her crimes. The vamp was a woman gone astray, a parasite woman who could feed off the solid stock of America, destroying the vital future it should have. Yet, it is not obvious of whom the film's audience was to be the most critical. A Fool There Was might be said to be more in a fallen man genre, the lure of sexuality debilitating and ruining a prominent civic leader and father, wreaking destruction on the family unit. The character of the vamp seems almost to be merely a foil for an extensive examination of the power of sex, women's rights in this new age, and the crumbling belief in the assertion that some nineteenth-century notions of the family's behavior were still pertinent for twentieth-century America.

Thus, A Fool There Was displays some surprising distances between the regulation of bad women from around 1915 through the 1920s and their regulation during a portion of the depression era. While in certain ways the movie forecasts issues in the Cinderella story that Jacobs describes as problematical to that generation of moral guardians, A Fool There Was also illustrates that a range of values about who was at fault and what were appropriate solutions was circulating in 1915. Furthermore, discussion of these sexual topics was by then acceptable for public entertainment.

Despite the representations of adultery, degeneration, and "abnormal" female behavior, the reviewers for A Fool There Was saw the movie, if a bit much for the juvenile crowd, as suitable for the mass adult population assumed to be present in the theaters. It was not a scandalous confrontation to norms or experiences that mainstream America knew. Perhaps in part this was because the filmmakers established a high art aura to the production, since the movie's sources for adaptation included not only Kipling's extremely popular poem but also a recent Broadway play by Porter Emerson Browne.[2] Thus, A Fool There Was claimed to address issues suitable for a cultivated, even sophisticated, audience. This address seems to have worked without much trouble. For example, the reviewer for the Motion Picture News declared the film "powerfully absorbing in all its parts." Margaret L. MacDonald, for Moving Picture World, called it "splendid," with " 'sin' [having] been presented in its most revolting aspect."[3] "D," for the New York Dramatic Mirror, described the significance of the plot:

> The people are of to-day, with the interests of modern business and social
> life; but the veneer amounts to nothing when shot through by the lightning
> bolt of sex. The Vampire is a neurotic woman gone mad. She has enough
> sex attraction to supply a town full of normally pleasing women, and she
> uses it with prodigal freedom.[4]

Thus, the film seems to have raised issues considered acceptable for discussion. What is at stake, then, is what the cultural meanings were for its viewers. For one thing, the vampire's victims seem more to be blamed than she, for they are represented as the fools. Men's responses to the lure of sexual opportunities in this age of erotic possibilities thus need examination. If society must account for the gone-astray woman, it must also consider the effect such a woman has on men, particularly ones already married, as was the case with John Schuyler in A Fool There Was. For if the goal of a modern marriage is lifelong companionship and sharing, how should society react when adultery by the husband occurs? Moreover, as part of this, how does one explain the victimizing woman? The white slave might be simply a woman who does not think, but the vamp had intelligence and will in her pursuit of men upon which to prey. What, if anything, could counter her?

The Vampire's Threat

Rudyard Kipling's poem "The Vampire" begins with the stanza:

> A fool there was and he made his prayer
> (Even as you and I)
> To a rag and a bone and a hank of hair,
> (We called her the woman who did not care),
> But the fool he called her his lady fair—
> (Even as you and I!)[5]

As Peter Gay writes, "the fear of woman has taken many forms in history," including the archetypal figures of Delilah, Cleopatra, Carmen, Salome, and the Beautiful Woman without Mercy.[6] Kipling's vampire seems to fit in this long tradition, for what is most important to Kipling is her incomprehension of the effects of her behavior: "(And now we know that she never knew why) / And did not understand!" This representation of a heartless woman flies in the face of much nineteenth-century prescription about the essentially moral woman, but it illustrates well the variable meaning of "woman" as a "transfer point" for debating changing social formations. Nineteenth-century women could also be satanic sirens, luring men to crash on the shoals of sexual pleasure. While I am quite willing to read the representation of the seductress in psychoanalytical terms applicable across a number of generations of Western civilization, in this instance I want to focus on the specific cultural meanings this vampire has for this period. Thus, granted that the vampire can be considered a projection of male fear or hatred of women, what else does the vampire connote? What happens when a stereotypical Other is placed into a social fantasy?

The female seductress had several forms in the late eighteen hundreds. She was Kipling's vampire, a woman of ambiguous origin and impenetrable motives. She was also the gold digger. As Robert Allen remarks, women had occasionally been represented as leading men to their ruin, but the gold digger was quite different from the middle-class woman who might "fall" into sin. The gold digger was working class and thus had "little if any 'reputation' to lose."[7] Her motivation was that of the Cinderella myth—the fantasy of a rise in class with the concomitant rewards in an improved standard of living. She was a woman who lived off the man with whom she was attached. Ironically, of course, if the woman is a wife and of the same social status as the man, such a representation did not apply. Rather, for the gold digger to be perceived as the parasite, it required her to be calculating, intelligent, and willful rather than the object of a man's choice for elevation.

In both cases—the vampire and the gold digger—what most scholars (such as Gay) assume is that minimally these bad women implied a threat to contemporary representations of masculinity. Lewis A. Erenberg writes that "the pleasure-loving woman would also destroy male identity. For those who adhered to the nineteenth-century conception of masculinity contained in the self-made man, passionate women would lead men away from self-control toward a life of sensual expressiveness. Men's concentration would be broken, their money lost, and their business affairs ruined."[8]

Moreover, beyond the implicit threat to masculinity was the explicit (and perhaps worse) threat to the surface features of identity: economic and social classes were at stake. If "man" was known by his income status and social allies, alterations in those indicators said something about his strength, his manhood. As Sumiko Higashi argues, particularly about the film A Fool There Was, the virtuous wife who "posed no sexual threat" actually served to "[protect] man from his own excesses."[9] The vamp was dangerous because she could destroy not only a man's discipline and will by feeding off him, she could deprive him of his home, financial security, and social status.

This double danger of the seductress is well articulated in Kipling's poem, which dwells on the fool's loss of physical goods: "A fool there was and his goods he spent." Moreover, however, this loss is transformed into a metaphor: "The fool was stripped to his foolish hide." Although Kipling does not pursue this analogy within the poem itself, he must in part have been drawing on another common representation: the woman as the more deadly of some species. Motifs of the supernatural or diabolical are sometimes used to explain how a woman could have such unnatural power over the man. The vampire or spider image of sucking away the man's blood was a powerful metaphor for the threat she represented.

Numerous films during the period ruminate upon the fallen man theme. Often a man's self-control deteriorates as a consequence of drink. But the cause could also be the bad woman who diverts him from the proper path. A Fool There Was was not the first attempt to film these seductive women. For example, D. W. Griffith exploits Victorian sentimentality in The Mothering Heart (Biograph, 1913). A young woman (played by Lillian Gish) marries her suitor, but as he succeeds in business, he wants to enjoy the good life of the cosmopolitan scene. He drags his wife to one of the new fancy restaurants that have Apache dancers to entertain the diners, but his wife is awkward and out of place. There the husband realizes "the Idle Woman" at another table seems interested in him. Coincidence and desire permit his pursuit. The wife leaves the husband, and soon so does the idle woman who attaches herself to a "new light." (These women always discard their victims when the men run out of money.)

The film might end in the simple lesson that responding indiscriminately to sexual passion has no rewards but numerous losses (and that new commercial leisure places are dangerous). However, Griffith employs a traditional nineteenth-century device to reconcile the couple. Their baby becomes ill, and the husband arrives just as the child dies. Although angry, the wife recognizes the "child" in her husband, and forgives him, producing a "happy" ending. This device of the child, pure and virtuous, leading to an adult's salvation was common and was used elsewhere in the 1800s, such as in the Little Eva subplot in *Uncle Tom's Cabin*. Thus, Griffith was drawing on a long-standing tradition about the healing powers of the innocent.

The fallen man plot obviously needs more exploration, but the more immediate precedents to *A Fool There Was* seem to repeat the general pattern of the establishment of a secure home and family; the intervention of sexuality, which diverts the man from his family ways; his (at least financial if not social) degeneration; and then either some kind of reformation and rescue or a punishment. If the man is rescued, the source of that salvation is often through the virtue of a pious woman or child in conjunction with some sort of self-revelation. In this case, the implications of the conclusion are some type of reestablishment of the unity and integrity of the family. In the case of punishment, the loss may simply be the destruction of the family. In this sense, the subplot of the Trubus household in *A Traffic in Souls* exemplifies the fallen man plot, for Trubus, who is tainted by his criminal association with sex for hire, loses his social standing and his wife and daughter.

At least one of the earlier two film versions of "The Vampire" neatly fits the dramatic plot of rescue and reintegration into the family.[10] In 1913 Kalem released *The Vampire*. A recent sensation was the "Vampire Dance" performed by Bert French and Alice Eis, and Kalem framed its tale around the dance to feature it as the redeeming catalyst that saves the fallen man. The framing story is about Harold, who tires of rural life and decides to go to the big city to make his fortune while promising to return to his girlfriend Helen. He is successful, but one evening while at a fancy restaurant he is picked up by a woman who, according to one reviewer, is "dressed in close fitting silver silk." Some time passes, and later he sees the vampire dance "which represents in a strangely graphic way a vampire coming out of the woods to destroy a young artist." Struck by the implications of the dance's story, Harry begins his regeneration, rejects the "woman of the white lights," and returns to Helen. A promoter for the film argues that "it is a feature so surcharged with realism that the beholder chafes under a sense of helplessness at being unable to render aid to the doomed victim." The reviewer seems to agree: on the whole it was "human and convincing."[11] The reformation and reunification action, however, do not occur in Kipling's poem or in the immediate predecessor to A Fool There Was. Kipling leaves the fool in his misery. Porter Emerson Browne, in the novelization of A Fool There Was (1909), does, as well.

Fox's version of A Fool There Was remains generally faithful to the fallen man genre, but it alters the characterizations of the vamp's behavior to fit more into a twisted version of the gold-digger approach to the seductress. In doing this, it also psychologizes the vamp, producing a film more in line with the dominant ideology that behavior had rational sources and could be changed if an appropriate object lesson was available. A Fool There Was supplied character agency as the cause of the bad woman's actions rather than attributing the source of the events to the metaphysical (villains sin).

As far as I am aware, prior to this version of A Fool There Was the vampire had usually been represented in the traditional image of the heartless woman. Explanations beyond that implied the supernatural and the diabolical. Browne's novel deviates by giving her a personal motivation: she is the illegitimate daughter of a French aristocrat and a common woman who dies at the child's birth. The aristocrat names the woman "Rien" (nothing) to indicate his lack of care about these events. Years later when the aristocrat returns, Rien walks toward him, and as he backs up at the sight of her, he falls off a cliff. She says, "Bien" (good). Rien reappears as "the Woman" "darkly beautiful, tall, lithe, sinuous." Her effect on men is described as "hypnotic."[12] Thus, Browne's motivation for the vamp's heartlessness seems much more psychological and personal compared with Kipling's and others' representations of the woman without mercy. What is at stake for Browne's bad woman is some type of revenge.

The Fox version, like the Browne story, also avoids either causal ambiguity or the innuendo of the supernatural. As an instance of what I am arguing is the increasing stress on human behavior as causal motivation, A Fool There Was locates the vamp's behavior in psychological terms. The film is even sub-

Figure 6.1. A *Fool There Was*. Kate ignores the vamp.

titled "A Psychological Drama." The vamp pursues John Schuyler, the fool-to-be, because she desires to rise in social status.

This motivation is forcefully set up in the first scene of the film. In a classic instance of exposition, *A Fool There Was* begins with John and Kate Schuyler introduced as a happy, well-to-do couple. Kate's sister Elinor, their friend Tom, and the Schuyler's daughter round out the family. Into the fair afternoon by the ocean where John has been captaining his yacht comes the vamp. She is already of the nature to destroy men (her current victim accompanies her), and her cruelty is illustrated by her smelling but then crushing some lovely roses. She wears a close-fitting gown, rather gaudy in style, and certainly at odds with the frocks Kate and Elinor have on. The vamp observes Kate, Elinor, and the child. Moving up to them so as to create the opportunity for conversation, she says hello to the child, but Kate ignores her and takes the child off to the side (figure 6.1). The vamp declares: "Some day you will regret that."

Indeed, upon reading in the paper the next day that John Schuyler has been asked to be a presidential envoy to England, the vamp casts aside her current beau. Luckily for the vamp, Kate is unable to join John on his trip because Elinor has a serious car accident (she falls out of a car's back seat

Figure 6.2. A *Fool There Was*. The vamp and John while away the days.

when she is waving goodbye and the car starts suddenly). Besides, John will only be gone a month. The film constructs a pathetic fallacy: a lightning storm unsettles Kate, who worries, "Storm and darkness! Is it an omen?" But John's friend, Tom, reassures her all will be well. Of course, all does not turn out as Tom predicts, and even he should have taken heed when the vamp's rejected lover shoots himself on the deck of the boat just before departure. Tom again unwisely assures Kate: it was just "some ship noise," he reports.

The vamp seduces John in Europe, replete with images of idleness and decadence (figure 6.2). There, she also introduces him to drink, reinforcing his collapse with a physical decline due to alcohol. Continuing the artiness already established through the foreshadowing of John and Kate's fate, the filmmakers use costuming and makeup to create visual metaphors. As John declines, his hair turns white; his body becomes frail. Likening the events to a spider sucking her victim until it dies, *A Fool There Was* is rather obvious in its symbolism of the parasitical spirit of the vamp.

Part of the vamp's revenge and motivation fails, however, and she seems quite angry that her scheme is not successful. While she is Schuyler's companion, she is not accepted as a member of his social group. Her attempt to secure status mobility through the liaison fails. Instead, John falls, rejected by his former friends. When the wife of one of his associates discovers he is with the vamp, she refuses to stay at the same hotel. That revelation makes it into the "Town Tattler" column, in which John is described as having "fatuously fallen under the spell of a certain notorious woman of the vampire species." Upon John and the vamp's return to the United States, his friends and business associates desert him one by one, and he is reduced to drinking alone by the fire. Eventually, Schuyler is stripped to his foolish hide, and, as the intertitles quote the Kipling poem, "So some of him lived, but most of him died." In the final scene, the vamp tosses flowers over him, and will plainly leave him altogether.

Schuyler becomes an object lesson in the fallen man genre. Kipling warns repeatedly in his poem that Schuyler's foolishness could be ours ("Even as You and I"), and obviously the point of the story, well observed by the censors and the reviewers, is that pursuit of sexual pleasures to the neglect of the family unit leads to loss of social status, financial well-being, and even humanity. John Schuyler's degeneration is physical as well as social. His punishment is the loss of family and friends, even the loss of the woman whose sexuality held him so strongly. A *Fool There Was* also implies, however, that the vamp's threat is not merely a personal one directed toward one man's masculinity. John's failure produces the destruction of the home as Kate and his child lose him to the overwhelming power of the sexual drive. Bad fortune derives from immoderate and unsanctioned behavior, and John's decline is a melodramatic lesson about the necessity for self-control in consumption. Evil in the form of the "devil" temptress triumphs, and the weak-willed must pay.

If this were all that the film suggested, it might be quite in line with Victorian norms about bad women, even if the film motivates the vamp's behavior as a drive to improve her social status. However, A *Fool There Was* provides two other sides to the story—the points of view of Kate Schuyler and her sister Elinor. These views become a dialogue about a woman's responsibility in this situation. This dialogue, moreover, asserts the failure of older ways to handle the problem of sexuality. It is in the subplots that the film widens its cultural meanings and talk about "woman" in the twentieth century.

Sexual Intemperance in the Age of the Repeal of Reticence

To me, the curiosity of this film is its insistence on rejecting nineteenth-century solutions to the situation of adultery. In at least two ways, A *Fool There Was* suggests that norms of wifely virture, childhood innocence, and everlasting faithfulness in a doomed marriage are no longer sure values. As I shall detail, Kate Schuyler may be said to represent the traditional Victorian woman; Elinor articulates the New Woman's position. Although the film does not permit Elinor's proposals to be tested, it does repudiate Kate's approach to the wayward husband. However, even the introduction of Elinor's thoughts about what her sister should do seem strikingly significant for broadening discussions about marriages and families in the modern era. Elinor advocates divorce.

When John returns to the United States at the vamp's insistence, they take up residence in his townhouse. Already Elinor has attacked Tom and John's secretary for trying to shelter Kate from the truth about why John has dallied in Europe for so much longer than the original month he was to be there. When Elinor sees the article in the "Town Tattler" about the "millionaire reformer" now under a vampire's spell, she confronts them: "You men shield each other's shameful sins. But were it a woman at fault, how quick you'd be to expose and condemn her."

Elinor forcefully articulates the complaint on most advanced women's lips that the double standard no longer would be tolerated. She stands in judgment upon the men who in their paternalism think they know best. Twice previously Tom has unwisely advised Kate to ignore warnings that had she heeded them, might have altered the outcome of events: once, when the storm seemed an omen; and again, when the noise on the ship might have been linked to the vamp and her danger revealed to John prior to his departure.

Elinor does not stop, however, at her accusation that men are quick to label women "bad" but slow to charge their brothers with sexual excesses. She breaks the information to Kate. Then, after an afternoon drive in which the Schuylers' child sees her father with the vamp, Elinor proceeds to take even more dramatic action. She arranges a meeting with Kate, Tom, their lawyer, and herself: "Kate, I sent for our lawyer; you must tell him all, and be divorced!"

Having a character in a movie in 1915 advocate divorce has a cultural significance of quite a different nature than it would today. Although I shall discuss the changing expectations of marriage in chapter 7, here I want to speak about the shock that divorce presented to transforming America. Between 1880 and 1916, the rate of divorces increased dramatically. In 1880, one divorce occurred for every twenty-one marriages; in 1916, the figure was one in every nine.[13]

This change did not go unnoticed or undebated. As Elaine Tyler May indicates, multiple pieces of legislation restricting the dissolution of marriages were enacted after the 1880s. In 1892, groups such as the New England Divorce Reform League (founded in 1881) helped introduce a constitutional amendment to require federal regulation of marriages and divorces. In 1895, South Carolina banned divorce. Teddy Roosevelt was not only concerned about men's physical culture and race suicide, but in 1906 he also declared that marriage was sacred. If one were driven to divorce, at least no remarriage should occur. Divorce had multiple moral and social aspects, for those against it saw it as capable of, according to William L. O'Neill, destroying "the family, which was the foundation of society and civilization." Moreover, women were to blame; they were just spoiled. O'Neill recounts one "progressive" woman's antidivorce views: "Even adultery was no excuse for giving up the fight . . . because men were instinctively promiscuous and their lapses from grace had to be tolerated for the sake of the greater good."[14]

Other people did not agree, arguing that the possibility of divorce might actually strengthen the family. In *What Eight Million Women Want* (1910), Rheta Childe Dorr reasoned that while divorce might seem to threaten the family, it was not good for children and wives to experience misery and disease. Marriage might mean more if it was no longer an institution of lifetime submission for the wife. By the late 1880s and 1890s, radical thinkers advocated short-term contract marriages or even dissolving the institution of marriage as a whole. By the early 1900s, some social scientists provided statistics that indicated divorce encouraged "a new kind of marriage marked by higher spiritual standards and greater freedom." In 1908, all seven sessions of the annual meeting of the American Sociological Society were focused on the "problem of the family," the code vocabulary for divorce, with a dominant opinion growing in favor of it in the appropriate circumstances. The *Outlook* in 1910 began moderating its antidivorce voice, suggesting that in some cases it might be a better solution than continuing an unhappy relationship. Even some liberal ministers interpreted the Bible to read divorce as possibly acceptable.[15]

Elinor's suggestion, then, had an aura of new thought to it. Her position was an advanced one. However, in the debate at the table, Kate turns to Tom and asks what he thinks. Tom replies, "Your promise was 'till death do us part.' Stick, Kate, stick!" Kate takes Tom's advice, not Elinor's. This turning point in the plot has a certain ambiguity about it. Since many audience members likely knew the tragic ending implied in Kipling's poem and represented in Browne's play and novel, the rest of the film must have seemed a pathetic fulfillment of the fate of John and Kate Schuyler.[16] However, for those audience members who did not know that John was doomed or who held out hope that the adaptation would not be faithful to its sources, the film might have evoked suspense. Would Kate be able to save her marriage? Would sticking by her man be the right choice?

The rest of the film deals with Kate's responses to John's infidelity. Six months pass, and word comes to Kate that John has deteriorated further. Additionally, the vamp has left him. Kate determines that she will go to him. Word reaches the vamp, who arrives just as Kate is hugging John, about to take him back. The vamp enters, calls to him, kisses him, and he crumbles at her knees. Kate leaves.

Kate tries a second and more desperate means to bring John around. As I indicated, the function of children in some Victorian melodramas was to serve as a means for salvation. Throughout A Fool There Was, Kate and John's daughter has been characterized in almost cloying terms, but on the whole the reviewers perceived her as the only bright relief in the otherwise morbid story. The child, referred to in one intertitle as "Innocence," reinforces the pathos of the tale from the narration's point of view. She knows her father is in town but cannot understand why he does not come home. One scene shows her praying, "And bless mamma and, dear God, p-please s-send m-my p-papa home to m-me!" One can only begin to imagine how this scene affected women and men in the movie audiences. Kate Schuyler decides, "As a last appeal I will take his child to him!" Kate and daughter arrive, but once again the vamp's sexual lure overwhelms John, and he remains with her (figure 6.3). The strongest weapon in the Victorian arsenal—innocence—fails when confronted by sex appeal.

Crosscutting with the final scene of John lying near death and the vamp strewing flowers over him is a scene at the Schuyler's country home where the story started. The first scene displayed the integrated family of "captain" John, Kate, Elinor, Tom, and daughter. The final scene of the Schuylers splits John from the rest of the group. However, even Kate has disappeared from the home. On the hillside remains only Tom, Elinor, the child, and her doll.

As I suggested, Elinor seems to stand in judgment of both the Victorian double standard and the nineteenth-century norm of remaining faithful to the marriage vows no matter what. That Elinor prevails within the picture of the new family while both the vampire and Kate are absent implies much to me. What precisely it indicated to its audience of 1915 is less clear, since none of the reviewers remark particularly about the sister's outspoken points of view. Yet the absence of comment could also suggest the increasing acceptance of divorce as a solution to a disintegrating marriage. Scholars of the family in this era indicate that organized opposition to divorce disappeared

Figure 6.3. A *Fool There Was*. Even the child cannot succeed.

after 1917, although, of course, many individuals still hold the opinion that it is contrary to their personal values.

The sensation of A *Fool There Was* derived mostly from the major plot line: the vamp's seduction and John's deterioration. The reviewers were much less interested in any debates about divorce than they were, like John, mesmerized by the power of the bad woman to destroy the strength of a leading citizen. The vampire role was played by Theda Bara, who made her reputation as a rising star in the movie industry through her portrayal of this bad woman. Much has been written about Bara's career as a consequence of this film. Although early studio publicity foregrounded her past as exotic and aristocratic, by 1916 she was stressing a distinction between her on-screen roles as a "professional temptress" and her "true" self as "deeply religious" and good-hearted. By 1921, her mother was describing Bara as a fanciful but average child who might fib now and then but quickly repented. It was all good to act the bad woman but not really to be one. Still the role made her an audience favorite. In a poll of readers conducted in 1916, Bara ranked as the fifth most popular female star after Clara Kimball Young, Anita Stewart, Virginia Norden, and Mary Pickford, and ahead of many others, such as Pearl White, Lillian Gish, Mabel Normand, and Blanche Sweet.[17]

Bara also became quite adept at analyzing her favorite role for those fascinated by a woman's ability to so captivate a man as to ruin him. In interviews, she would explain what she believed were the features of the vampire. In one 1915 article in the *Peoria Journal*, she was quoted as declaring: "Seriously, I do not know what gives certain women a strange, witchlike power over men. One thing I know. A vampire cannot be fat. There never was and never will be a fat vampire! I think most vampires are dark women, though some have blood-red hair and green snake-like eyes. Elinor Glyn is a good specimen of this type physically."[18] Vampires also could not love. To love would be to lose one's powers. It was love or be loved.

What was the vampire's motive? According to Bara,

> Believe me, for every woman vampire, there are ten men of the same type— men who take everything from women—love, devotion, beauty, youth, and give nothing in return! V stands for Vampire and it stands for Vengeance, too. The vampire that I play is the vengeance of my sex upon its exploiters. You see, . . . I have the face of a vampire, perhaps, but the heart of a "feministe."[19]

Bara's declaration of taking on the task of playing characters revenging her sex probably had opponents as well as advocates, but her ability to declare that in some way her bad woman was justified while remaining a favorite star for several more years is important in considering the cultural meanings of *A Fool There Was*. Obviously many viewers in some ways sympathized with, or even advocated discourses in accord with, whatever they saw the vamp as meaning, although others found her behavior abhorrent. Bara recounts instances of women slashing posters of her and sending her letters expressing their anger about women who attracted the men they loved.

A Fool There Was has its conservative discourse: it is easily read as a traditional fallen man film in which the victim is appropriately punished for his behavior. Thus, it fits into the requirement by the National Board of Censors that improper character behavior meet its just reward. However, at least two other discourses complicate the matter. One is the advocacy by Kate's sister for abandoning a double standard and for divorce as the solution in this case of blatant and continued loss of self-control, which prevented the father from taking proper care of his family. Such an advocacy does not contradict the norms of the family as an integrated unit headed by the man, but it does redefine what marriage might be about. Now it is not "until death do us part," but only as long as each member of the marriage provides certain assets to the union. At this point it is not even emotional offerings that Elinor expects. This advocacy seems so acceptable and obvious that its normative status underlines the pathos of Kate's and the daughter's appeals. The choice "to stick" becomes almost absurd in light of what was left for their marriage had John returned home. Still Kate's choice must surely have had its adherents. Christian charity and pity might provoke sympathy for Kate's burden from many in the audience, as well as a recognition of her as victim of John's behavior. What is also, of course, traditional is the sense that Kate will receive her reward in heaven, if not here on earth.

Additionally, the reviewers never queried the bad woman's end. No one asked that the censors punish her. Perhaps because the focus was on John Schuyler's foolishness, the reviewers assumed that the vamp deserved whatever she succeeded in obtaining. Then, too, she did not get what she wanted most, at least in this film. Social mobility did not come with money and her alliance with Schuyler. Hence, the vamp only accomplished the destruction of a man.

Post-movie interest in Bara as bad woman also suggests that Americans wanted to know what accounted for the hypnotic effects of sexual pleasure. Even if this bad woman had gone astray, she seemed much more intriguing than the Victorian Kate. If the bad woman ought to be setting an agenda about what was at stake in the changes the social formation was experiencing, this bad woman complicated the task since she did not provoke the enmity of the entire audience. In some ways, she was able to assert control over her own life as she destroyed her victim's self-will. Yet although some bad women had such control over their lives, it was only partial, for these bad women still needed to be attached to a man for their social meaning. As a parasite they managed in the symbiotic relationship to control their hosts, but they were not permitted to range free. Such bad women provided alternatives to the dutiful Victorian woman, who also found herself in a similarly dependent but also submissive role. Of course, however, this vampire woman was finally of the devil. She might be observed but never fully emulated. No, the better model was yet to be found.

A *Fool There Was*, like *Traffic in Souls*, needs to be understood as providing a range of discourses in which its audiences might find moments with which they could identify and even in which they could fantasize the film's agreement with their points of view, or that introduced them to talk about the new ideas of sexual passion, men's frailty in relation to that sexuality, women's potential power, and women's continued negotiation of their identities in relation to the men to whom they were attached. In this film, the bad woman was the parasite woman. As fascinating as she might be, the film also produces an alternative voice: that of Elinor, who advocates the elimination of a double standard and a marriage not restricted by the mores of intolerable tolerance on the part of just one of the partners. Had she been permitted to say more, Elinor would have spoken, as many women were speaking at the time, the belief that neither the husband nor the wife should exist in dependency upon the other. The advanced woman (utopian vision though it might be), from Elinor's point of view, would have entered into a partnership of equal standards and rewards, where neither individual would feed off the other. Elinor as an advanced woman represents another "transfer point" in the talk about new values. The film itself stands as a typical example of how regulation worked. By psychologizing the characters and creating appropriate ends that adhered to social and moral ethics based on the characters' choices, bad women and sexuality could be studied. It could even become an artful spectacle, as the film created visual metaphors of the vampire as spider. The function of the narrative voice coming from the position of Kipling's poem further made the story a morality tale. Hence, a whole array of narrational techniques permitted the representation of a bad woman, adultery, and scandal.

7

The Butterfly

One of the dangers of the modern urban culture was the disappearance of traditional methods of knowing social status and the presumed moralities associated with that status. Indeed, it is hardly surprising that the governing aims of the new progressive social scientists included a special concentration on the causes for deviance and crime. If the small village knew who was kin to whom and who was good or bad, individuals who chose to associate with particular people at least had foreknowledge of the situation into which they were placing themselves.

That was not the case once society was more extended and mobile. In *The Theory of the Leisure Class* (1899), Thorstein Veblen attempts to account for the conspicuous waste that his culture was expending on consumer items. He argues that these goods, especially clothing, were acting as a symbolic system communicating the social standing of the owner. The method of recognizing status that had been provided by social knowledge of the members of a small close-knit group was transferred to cultural signs that individuals were free to read or ignore. Regulation that was once imposed from external and widely communicated systems of meaning was now a matter of an individual's regulating himself or herself in relation to a rather complex and variable system of social theories, views of human responsibility, and conceptions of the universe—its origin and end.

Moreover, Veblen further articulates the significance of this new language system to gender differences as experienced in modern marriages. He writes:

> Propriety requires respectable women to abstain more consistently from
> useful effort and to make more of a show of leisure than the men of the
> same social classes. It grates painfully on our nerves to contemplate the
> necessity of any well-bred woman's earning a livelihood by useful work. It is
> not "women's sphere." Her sphere is within the household, which she should
> "beautify," and of which she should be the "chief ornament."[1]

For example, the status of the household and the husband's financial success

are announced in how expensive and fashionable are the garments that the
wife wears or how beautiful she might be perceived to be. These gestures suggest that she and her family belong to the leisure class, whose members need
not work. Articulating the status of her family through her spending habits
was her job.

Several conflicting meanings are thus at stake in the adornment of a
woman in this age. One is what dress signifies about a wife and her husband's
status. Another is what clothing implies about how well the woman does in
complying with the new consumer culture. To dress poorly not only means
that a woman is in a lower economic and social rank but also, if she should be
able to afford better, that she is failing in her chief duty as consuming wife for
a successful businessman.

Of course, traditional Puritan ethics about productive and restrained behavior were contradicted by the new norms of leisure and display. Moreover,
it would have been foolish to act in such a way as to destroy the very message
one wanted to send. Spending too much money could lead to financial ruin.
Spending on the wrong things could endanger the home. A consumption well
regulated in degree and object orientation was necessary for the maintenance
of the household unit. The new public woman was all very good, but she
could go astray through any extravagance in relation to the real status of her
place in the social hierarchy. Signs were to be faithful to their referents.

Elaine Tyler May, in her analysis of marriage and divorce in this era, writes
that views about what was anticipated or desired by the husband and wife
were changing to support a regulated consumer culture. Some conflicts came
from the failure of the new notion of "romantic love" as the basis for marriage
to maintain itself in light of the realities of everyday life.[2] Yet another conflict
was dissension over the expenditure of family incomes. This balancing act—
spend to display social status but spend within reason and on the appropriate
objects—required counsel to the young bride. Certainly the old economic
partnership image of marriage needed transforming in order to rescue the institution of marriage in the wake of the rising divorce rate. What would re-
place the earlier rationales and roles for coupling in this era of conspicuous
consumption and leisure?

Veblen's ironic view of the duties of the trophy wife is unmistakable. He,
like other critics of women's servitude to men, perceived marriages built on
inequitable economic exchanges and roles for the two people as producing
extremely limited roles for women. In the deal implied in such a marriage
contract, "women sought men who could support them instead of men they
admired and loved; men sought women who would be good housekeeper-

mothers, or if they desired prestige, they looked for a housekeeper-mother with social distinction. In both cases . . . the woman was restricted to being the 'homemaker' and the 'social butterfly.' "[3] Critics such as Veblen increasingly advocated family structures that were based on values other than economic ones.

Certainly the new consumer culture in which women continued to operate as a signifier of social status did nothing to alter the terms of the deal. *Good Housekeeping* analyzed the conflicts in its 1914 essay "The New Marriage." It pointed out that gone were the days in which

> each home was a self-sustaining, self-sufficient unit. . . . According to social experts, fully three-quarters of woman's traditional share of the work of the world has gone out of the home, and it is still considered unwomanly by many good and worthy people for woman to follow her job. . . .
> . . . The modern wife is seldom a productive helpmate. In many cases she is not even a reproductive one. She is a consumer, a helpmate in helping him spend what he earns.[4]

Moreover, since the wife has little to do besides be attractive it is hardly surprising that either she or her husband strays. *"If we train our girls to cultivate the one art of charming men, we must not be surprised if, after a certain amount of stress and strain, they seem inclined to resume the practice of the only trade that they have been allowed to learn."*[5] The author encourages as a solution the goals advocated by the "new-woman movement" in which the woman follows the traditional woman's best characteristics: she produces. "Woman's sphere is not the house. It never was. Woman's sphere is the home. It will always be. If three-quarters of the home has left the house, woman is going to direct three-quarters of her energies upon things outside the house." Once the new woman is given her own social status through her own efforts, then, a new "companionate" marriage will take hold.

One type of woman-gone-astray, then, was not one who consumed or operated outside the house but the woman who in venturing forth publicly to do her consuming work behaved in ways that endangered the home. A woman was not de facto bad for being in the public sphere. She was bad when she assumed that the marriage contract was a mere monetary one in which she was to flit about as the social butterfly, going from flower to flower. She was bad when her meaning was limited to being an ornament. Worse yet was when she could not adjust her consumption to her income, her desire to her position. Overconsumption was as threatening to the home as inadequate consumption in this modern era.

The film *The Cheat* articulates this view of one social butterfly, Edith Hardy. While I will argue that the film resolves itself in a fashion quite within the regulation mode, it does have several moments in which it advocates talking about the contradictions faced by the modern wife. A woman counseled to remain quiet finally ignores that advice and in doing so saves her marriage. The film itself displays the dangers of a marriage based on separating the roles of husband and wife, man and woman, so rigidly. It also provides an example of the best type of plot development in narrating social problems since it does not delegate the good and the bad to individual characters but produces a transformational arc in characterizing Edith and her discoveries about sexuality and marriage. Such a narrative strategy would become a favorite in the classical Hollywood ideology. It was a strategy fully compatible with the regulatory system set in place through the Board of Review, which emphasized individuals learning lessons rather than broad restructuring of economic and social systems. It is a good case of regulating woman and her sexuality.

"The Social Butterfly with the Singed Wings"

In discussing the 1980s, Fredric Jameson argues that pleasure is linked with the "mindless consumer" who is gendered as "she." Jameson connects this notion to the 1950s: specifically, "Philip Wylie's 'Momism,' . . . and the psychoanalytical terror of a consuming Mom, who not only presided possessively over all the new post-war products but also threatened to eat *you* up as well: a consumption fantasy with teeth in it, according to all the archaic textbooks."[6] Jameson's observation ties in with the metaphor, which I discussed in chapter 6, of the vampire as a spider sucking out the lifeblood of John Schuyler. Yet women could emasculate men not only through physical sexuality; they could also do it through emptying the family's pocketbook.

This narrative exists as a cliché by 1912. A description for a Solax movie, *The Prodigal Wife* (1912), reads: "The old story of the indulgent husband and the spendthrift wife in a new setting. At length, when the financial crash is pending, she has a dream before the fireplace, which brings her to her senses, and thus trouble is averted. Such pictures get uncomfortably close to real life and for this reason exert a good influence."[7]

I find the title of the movie significant. The wife has gone astray, undoubtedly out in the department stores as she wandered fascinated by the exotic goods she could see, touch, and smell. That her desire led her there was due to the modern global economy and culture of consumption. Thankfully, the moral to the parable upon which the title draws is that once the sinner re-

Figure 7.1. *The Cheat*. The butterfly is introduced.

pents of her excesses she will be welcomed back to the patriarch's arms. A tidy
little sermon to the venturesome but uncontrolled woman!

Edith Hardy in *The Cheat* is immediately positioned in the film to take up
the stereotype of the beautiful but flighty wife. Played by Fannie Ward, Edith
is introduced in the titles as "The Butterfly" (figure 7.1), the narrational
voice suggesting some distance from her behavior and repeating discursive
metaphors circulating in the culture. Her husband, Richard Hardy (Jack
Dean), has already been described as a "New York Stock Broker." The opening situation provides a narrative containment of those spectacle images. The
first scene begins with Edith dressing. She takes a phone call from her husband, who is examining a handful of bills, including one for a black evening
gown, a chiffon evening gown, and a point lace negligee. Richard makes a
request that will set up the dramatic conflict: "Can't you economize 'til my
investments pay? It won't be for long." Richard is articulating what will be a
common norm for behavior among the middle class. One ought to defer gratification until able to afford it. That is, taking pleasure is perfectly acceptable
as long as the means to pay for that pleasure are available.

Edith responds as the third of the three types of gone-astray women. While
she does not seem to think very much, she also is not exactly the parasite.
Rather she is indulged. Edith whines, "If you want me to give up my friends

and social position—well—I won't." Edith has a right to the status in which she lives since she is the legal partner of Richard. Furthermore, as is established shortly, Edith still retains the semblance of the middle-class female civic reformer. She is the treasurer for the Red Cross, which has raised ten thousand dollars for the European war. When Richard confronts her again, Edith justifies her purchases of gowns as necessary for the affairs sponsored by the Red Cross. Thus, Edith in this case seems the spoiled child who cannot adjust her expectations to the short-term wait required by the reality of her husband's rather reasonable request. Furthermore, she is clearly conceiving of herself as a conspicious consumer. Her status and identity is contingent upon herself as a spectacle through the new and fashionable gowns she wears.

Moreover, however, Edith is characterized as a liar who uses her allure to achieve her goals. After hanging up on Richard, she is picked up by Hishura Tori (played by Sessue Hayakawa).[8] She is clearly angry, and dutifully and solicitiously, Tori inquires what is wrong. Edith responds: "The same old story—My husband objects to my extravagance—and you." Now, nothing in the first scene specifically indicates that Richard to this point has other than complete trust in Edith's behavior, although he has a short-term problem with her consumption patterns.[9] Yet as the film progresses, it is evident that Edith at least connects her indulgences in clothing with her acquisition of the attention of the "ivory king to whom the Long Island smart-set is paying social tribute"—as the film introduced Tori. Thus, Edith associates her sexuality with her consumption behavior. Ultimately, of course, Tori, who seems merely a pawn in Edith's maneuvers, turns out to have much more power for influencing the game than she imagines.

The movie, however, does not place all the blame squarely on Edith. She may be a prevaricator—of the small white lie sort—but her expectations of being indulged are justified by the ways she has been treated by her husband. A short scene provides the opportunity for another angle on the couple's relationship. After Edith hangs up on Richard's call in the first scene and tells her fib to Tori, the other side of the picture is revealed. Busy at his desk, Richard declines joining his co-workers who are headed out to golf. One fellow articulates common advice for modern husbands: "Dick, you're working too hard over this deal—Don't forget you have a wife." Richard counters, "It's for my wife I'm doing it." The negligent husband, in his own way a gone-astray man, is in some part being chastised in advance for the tragedy about to happen. Richard not only has not been available to attend to his wife as he ought, but he seems to accept or even encourage her consumption behavior. He is making money just so she can spend it. The narrational voice via the other character's comment provides an indication that Richard may be as much to blame as Edith is, for this is not the image of the new ideal, the companionate marriage.

The triangle is thus established when the wife's interests turn excessively outside her home because of her lack of control and her husband's lack of attention. The ornamental and desiring wife, the inattentive and indulging husband, and the all-too-interested outsider provide the mix for trouble. Two events set up the complication that is Edith's initial difficulty. First of all, Richard is unable to pay for another new gown, providing a barrier to Edith's goals. Secondly, Edith makes a very bad mistake. To achieve her desires, she tries to enter Richard's realm. A friend of Richard's confides to Edith that he thinks Richard's deal will fall through. Richard should be investing in United Copper. Edith calculates. What if she were to put the ten thousand dollars she holds for the Red Cross into United Copper herself? With the earnings, she could pay for her gowns. This act is doubly egregious. Not only does Edith try to act as a man (doing business), but, furthermore, she trusts the wrong man. Her alliances should always be with her husband. This act, however, also foreshadows her more serious violation of alliances.

The speculation into United Copper fails. Thus, not only has Edith failed to get money for her gowns, she has also lost the Red Cross fund. Again, instead of turning to her husband, in part because she overhears him telling a friend that he could not raise a dollar "to save my life," Edith goes even further astray. She reaches outside her traditional social circle to newcomer Tori.

Scholars examining this film have rightly stressed the racism and nativism of *The Cheat*.[10] As I discussed in chapter 1, a foreign culture implied alternative sexual practices. *The Cheat* emphasizes this through its narration. Tori's behavior, while at first merely pleasant, has already been characterized as odd. A rather eerie scene has occurred in which Tori, showing off his home, has displayed to Edith that he brands every item he owns with his seal. "That means it belongs to me," he declares. This duplicates in the diegesis how the film introduced Tori in the opening credits: Tori was immediately characterized by that behavioral gesture, a good instance of externalizing character in melodramatic aesthetics.

Moreover, Tori takes advantage of Edith, displaying a violation of the rules for social conduct. When she hears of the failure of United Copper, she is still in Tori's study. She faints; Tori turns out the light, carries her to the side, and kisses her. She wakes, but does not know of Tori's kiss. Then she overhears her husband indicate his inability to have access to any funds. Tori volunteers to fund her as Edith imagines her disgrace. The film represents her thoughts: a vision of her exposure is superimposed in the right-hand corner of the image, "Society Woman steals Red Cross fund." The deal is clearly struck. In an intertitle Tori queries, "Do you agree?" Edith nods. As she departs, another intertitle provides the deadline, "Tomorrow."

Eventually, the narration of the film will declare "East is East and West is West and never the Twain shall meet." However, at this point, the possibility of such a congress occurring is a strategy by which audiences can begin shifting the blame away from Edith and toward the Oriental. What Edith has promised, even though audiences might be sympathetic with her plight, is adultery. Her control of her situation is certainly out of bounds, having derived from her earlier excesses. She may be a victim of larger social forces toward conspicuous consumption, but so far she has not been choosing the lesser of two evils, and so her behavior cannot be rewarded. However, the plot has been constructed so that the explanation for her behavior at least is not a direct desire for the Oriental man, but a consequence of excessive desire for material objects, an improper entry into the business of Wall Street, and the inappropriate taking advantage of Edith's errors. Ironically, of course, what Edith is enacting is the paradigm of the American marriage contract in its most vulgar sense. The crudeness of the exchange upon which marriages may be made is becoming visible. In fact, East and West might, indeed, meet on this point. Marriages have been business exchanges. The two cultures are not that different in their views about women, a scary possibility from which the narrative will never fully recover.

Edith's potential adultery as an assault on sensibilities is thus diverted by the motivations and race of the man with whom Edith has engaged herself. As an Oriental, Tori is burdened both diegetically and intertextually by features implying some abnormality in his desire for the American woman. Just as African-American males were assumed to have insatiable interests in Anglo women (as exemplified in The Birth of a Nation), likewise Asian men threatened the sanctity of the culture. Recall my discussions in chapter 2 of middle-class fears of "racial hybrids" and "ethnic horrors." The first protests against Chinese immigrants had occurred in California in the 1870s. By 1882, exclusionary laws against Chinese had been passed in Congress. After 1900, Japanese were also attacked. In February 1905, the San Francisco Chronicle published several inflammatory articles, including one titled, "Japanese a Menace to American Women."[11]

Thus, by casting the possible partner in the relation as an Oriental, the dynamics of the potential sexual intercourse alter significantly. Had Edith made her deal with another Anglo male of her own social class, no sympathy for her plight might have been generated among the audience. Rampant racism changes and confuses the range of cultural meanings. Edith might be perceived by many as caught in Tori's clutches when he takes advantage of her mistake. This clever narrational strategy represses the direction of causality being laid to Edith's agency and feeds into seduction fantasies. According to Frank Luther Mott, several bestsellers in the 1800s employed this plot. In *The Awful Disclosures of Maria Monk* (1836), a woman is forced to be a "black nun," available to the priests who visited the convent through underground tunnels. Another such tale was *Wife No. 19; or, The Story of a Life in Bondage* (1876), purportedly the revelations of one of Brigham Young's wives.[12]

By the turn of the century, however, some stories were not only describing illicit sexuality by women but condoning, if not totally pardoning, these affairs. A famous and widely read one was Elinor Glyn's *Three Weeks*, published in 1907. This novel goes beyond sympathetic looks at the working woman forced into prostitution such as existed in contemporaneous stories told by the male authors of *Sister Carrie* and *Susan Lenox*. *Three Weeks* does distance its events by placing the action in another continent (decadent Europe—so useful for justifying the story without suggesting that Americans would do such things) and in another class (the aristocracy).

While on a trip to the continent, Britisher Paul Verdayne finds himself attracted to a mysterious woman who eventually arranges a meeting with him. The woman seduces Paul, and they begin a torrid affair. This plot sounds a good deal like the classic *A Fool There Was*. However, while the seductress turns out to be a woman using a man for her own ends, the ends are quite different from the vampire's. This woman is a queen who desires an heir that cannot be provided by her husband, a vicious king. Her liaison with Paul is motivated as justified for the continuation of her family and because of her husband's cruelty. As *Three Weeks* concludes, the queen is killed by the king, although a child does result from the affair with Paul. "And so, as ever, the woman paid the price," concludes the novel.[13] An impression exists that talk about the double standard and the shifting dynamics of women's consciousness about their situation makes punishing the wayward woman a cliché more and more recognized as such and less and less tolerated as acceptable. The novel appears to have been adapted for the screen in 1914, and our Flapper of 1915 had thought the original "pretty dull."[14]

Thus, *The Cheat* utilizes several methods to back away from making Edith such a gone-astray woman that she cannot be redeemed at the end of the film. By casting the partner-to-be as an Oriental who takes advantage of Edith's errors, racist feelings might be mobilized and illogical attributions of the cau-

Figure 7.2. *The Cheat*. Edith has been branded.

sality of the events laid to Tori's motivations. Moreover, Edith's behavior is narrativized as necessary and not as free choice once the investment fails. Thus, if her ends are justified, the activity might be forgiven. Her promise is couched as a debt to save her and her husband's reputation, not an act to dishonor her marriage contract. Thus her sexual act would not be directly related to any desire for the man.

Had Edith been forced to enact the exchange, *The Cheat* would have been a very radical, and likely censored, movie. However, a coincidence in the plot seems to save Edith. Her husband's investments pay off overnight; he had been promising it would not be a long wait. Edith secures a check for ten thousand dollars to return the borrowed money to Tori. Tori, however, is not interested in the money. "You cannot buy me off," he declares. Edith makes the classic move when threatened in such a manner; she volunteers that she will kill herself first. Tori hands her a gun and then moves to kiss her. In a struggle, he tears at her and then brands her to indicate his ownership (figure 7.2). Finally, she shoots not herself but him.

As Tori slides down the door, Richard arrives. He had followed his wife when she tried secretly to slip out of their house. As his wife flees, Richard enters the house. He takes the blame when the servants and later the police arrive. Edith has returned home unaware of Richard's difficulties. The next morning, the notoriety Edith had sought to avoid has now happened. The newspaper headlines read "Shooting in the Smart Set. Richard Hardy arrested. Young Stockbroker shoots [Japanese Ivory King]. Motive a Mystery."

This second turning point in the plot is also the preparation for Edith's redemption. Rather than take her usual way out and lie, Edith confesses to Richard that she shot Tori. Why was she in Tori's rooms? Again, the full truth is revealed: "I lost the Fund money—[Tori] knew it and offered help—if I would pay the price." By talking, Edith has begun the reparations necessary to reestablish and even alter the marriage's relationship. However, the talking is also much linked with Foucault's argument that speaking of sexuality has been the modern era's replacement for religious confession. Admitting and investigating desire is itself a means of mastery and control. As I have argued, for the middle class talk was becoming vital to protect the class from infringements upon its boundaries and to regulate the behavior of the New Woman and the New Man.

For the regulation of this bad woman, Edith's talk is an important forward step. For the first time in the movie, she takes responsiblity for her actions and her desires. And for the first time in the movie, she and her husband kiss without a deception operating between them. However, for lessons to be clear, repetition is handy. Furthermore, other strands to the narrative are still to be connected. Thus, her husband admonishes Edith, "I *forbid* you to speak." Richard Hardy will stand trial.

Both Tori and Richard tacitly agree to maintain the fiction that Richard shot Tori. In Tori's case, revealing that Edith was in his rooms and shot him would scarcely do his reputation any good; in Richard's view, he is also protecting his family's name. Richard refuses to give any motive for his behavior beyond stating that he was trying to disarm Tori. That silence becomes crucial, for the jury finds Richard guilty. Edith, however, rushes forward, crying, "I shot [Tori] and this is my defense." Edith bares her shoulder revealing the brand (figure 7.3). The court's audience rushes toward Tori, and as the police move to protect him from the mob, the judge puts aside the verdict, declaring Richard to be a free man. The final shot shows Edith and Richard walking out of the courtroom supporting one another.

Edith's agency is demonstrated yet again in her rejection of the rule of patriarchically imposed silence. As some scholars have argued, Edith has to reveal the objectification of the woman as a unit of exchange in sexual relations to permit this unification of the family, but I believe that the plot is not so unilaterally repressive in its cultural meanings. For the audience of the period, Edith's choice to talk is a significant one given the period's obsession with the

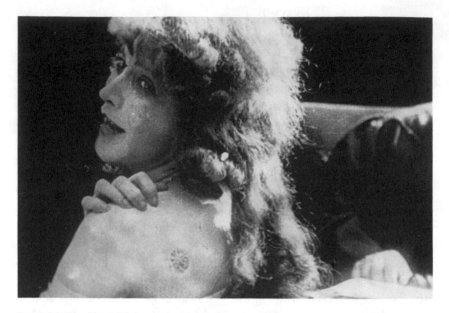

Figure 7.3. *The Cheat*. Edith reveals the brand.

double standard and the repeal of reticence. Moreover, her choice to talk re-
deems her, since she is now taking charge of her own behavior. Regulation is
now coming from internal discourses about a woman's social and personal responsibility for her and her family's life instead of from the exercise of external regulations (sin, guilt). Edith may have nearly been a bad woman; now
she is becoming a New Woman who expects to control her gratification in
relation to her desires so that she can escape the plight of being owned by
someone other than herself. Being an indulged woman has its price—which is
just not worth it. Edith exemplifies the changing images of a good woman's
behavior. She is to follow her own intuitions, becoming an intelligent, independent, mildly aggressive, and appropriately moderate desiring woman. The
ideology of character rather than economic or social structure as cause and
effect for events is played out in *The Cheat*.

The Cheat received various praises and criticisms. W. Stephen Bush in
Moving Picture World called Edith the "social butterfly with the singed wings"
and described the performance as "masterly" and the film as having "extraor-
dinary merit." His reading of Edith's final declaration is worth noting, since it
interprets the sources of Edith's choice as having several possible causes: "The
trembling wife is no longer able to restrain herself. Her passion rising superior
to all the form and severity of the court procedure, she leaps upon the witness

stand, a fearful and unconquerable resolve in her eyes."[15] This will and passion overwhelms the law that has been operating with reserve. Whether Edith's behavior is from her typical lack of control or from a fresh and "unconquerable resolve" is left ambiguous in Bush's remarks.

Variety's reviewer recognized the racism in *The Cheat's* narrative structure. "Fred" writes, "For without the third point of the eternal triangle having been one of an alien race, the role of Edith Hardy in this picture would have been one of the most unsympathetic that has ever been screened and therefore would have been useless as a vehicle for any of [the Lasky company's] women stars."[16] "Fred" also thought that the husband deserved what he experienced and that the courtroom scene was a sop to California racism against the Japanese. What is so apparent to a critic in 1995 was just as obvious to one in 1915. The *New York Times* also agreed that *The Cheat* may have been inappropriately pandering to certain sensibilities of the audiences: "Is there any more excuse for this sensational trash than for the old-fashioned melodrama in which half the characters were killed off at the end of the play?"[17]

That reviewer's remarks are telling, since the fight of good and evil is a hallmark of the melodramas with which *The Cheat* is being associated. One significant difference does seem to exist for me, however. In the melodramas to which the *New York Times* reviewer refers, good and evil were allocated to specific characters. In *The Cheat*, the potential for evil migrates from Edith Hardy, the social butterfly, to Hishura Tori, the racial outsider. Edith may have started to go astray by lying, by refusing to control the degree and orientations of her desire, by trying to enter the business world of the stock market, and by seeking financial rewards from an alliance with a male other than her husband. However, she is capable of recognizing, even if it is forced upon her, the ultimate degradation of her position if she fails to alter her behavior and the direction of her desire. The family is reunited, but it is through the woman's agency and humiliating confession regarding her own activites in the age of consumer culture.

Thus, unlike *Traffic in Souls* and *A Fool There Was*, the narrativization of *The Cheat* employs a transformational arc for its main character. This still provides the possibility of representing the New Woman versus the bad woman. However, rather than two women representing oppositional behaviors, one woman experiences a conversion, which permits the tale to conclude with an appropriate ending. That conclusion is the simple declaration that hope to be redeemed is held out for any woman who has gone astray. Understanding her behavior and her desires and then self-regulating them will prevent the New Woman from going bad. She needs to think, to be self-sufficent when necessary, and to take responsibility for her behavior based on what is proper for the social welfare of her family. Otherwise her home will disappear.

As moralistic and conservative in terms of family values as this movie may seem, it still encourages the view that women have their own potential for controlling their lives. Indeed, in a consumer culture, they may need to be very well trained in doing this—by movies or other media. Talk about consumption was part of the twentieth century.

Other Butterflies

Edith Hardy was only one type of social butterfly about whom talk and regulation were needed. *Good Housekeeping* had located several characteristics of the "modern wife." She "is seldom a productive helpmate. In many cases she is not even a reproductive one. She is a consumer, a helpmate in helping him spend what he earns." Although Edith Hardy was one of these modern wives, the focus of the plot of *The Cheat* does not address another angle to the new marriage, one which deeply distressed some individuals. As I discussed in chapter 2, many middle-class families were choosing to limit the number of their children in order to improve their standard of living. However, once woman is thought of not as just a producer but primarily as a consumer, the meanings of her sexuality and desire change. This alteration requires regulation for the sake of the modern economy.

While voluntary motherhood fit into the new life of consumerism and leisure, voluntary motherhood also had its opponents. Theodore Roosevelt strongly counseled against it because of its threat to a continuation of the Anglo-Saxon heritage. Moreover, the restrictive Comstock Act was particularly addressed to prevent women from making active and informed choices in the matter. The Comstock Act was legislation against obscenity, but one of its chief focuses was on birth control literature.

The battle over talk about birth control escalated during the early 1910s. The primary individual in this fight in the United States was Margaret Sanger, who arrived with her husband in New York City in 1910. By 1912, she was writing about female sexuality in the New York *Call*, a socialist paper, and thus violating the Comstock Law. In 1914, she published *The Woman Rebel*, covering many topics, including female reproductive rights, and followed that with *Family Limitation*. The threat of up to forty-five years in prison for violating obscenity laws forced Sanger to travel to Europe. Others, including Emma Goldman, began speaking publicly about this issue. Sanger returned in 1915 and goaded the federal prosecutor's office to pursue the case against her. It backed down. In 1916, Sanger opened a birth control clinic.[18]

In her analysis of films of this era, Annette Kuhn remarks that *Where Are My Children?* (Lois Weber, 1916) is a good instance of the Hollywood industry's regulation of women through narrative structures and concluding social lessons. She rightly connects *Where Are My Children?* to its racist origins of fears of race suicide, and she describes how it provides a sermon from which women could take counsel. Kuhn assumes, however, that concerns about race suicide in the United States were less troublesome by 1916 than they were in Britain. Thus, she explains the ability of the film to be shown in the United States as attributable to less dissonance in the middle class about these issues than existed in Britain because of the suffragette movement.[19]

Given the continued struggle today in the United States over birth control rights, it would scarcely seem that some kind of acceptance or homogeneity of views about birth control existed in 1916. Instead, it might be better to understand the toleration of *Where Are My Children?* as due to the *lack* of uniformity in the middle class during the transition period to a consumer culture. As I have stressed throughout this book, to view the middle class of the 1910s as homogeneous is to miss the conflicts over determining meanings for the new age. The middle class was much more divided about utopian goals as residual and emergent practices competed for dominance. Even then, the emphasis on public and secular sources for expertise produced a variety of discourses, as people were increasingly urged to talk about social ills in the belief that discussion would produce solutions. Eugenics argued that the right people ought to have the babies. The racism and classism in that notion were unexamined.

Although *Where Are My Children?* has been considered as a film bold for its discussion of birth control and abortion, the film is also quite conflictual in its systems of representation. The movie begins with the obligatory "we-are-showing-this-for-your-own-good" disclaimer, even by then a clichéd procedure for escaping official censorship. It then presents a very confusing double plot. On the one hand, Richard Walton is a district attorney who defends the transmission of birth control information because he believes that uncontrolled birthing among the poor is a primary cause of crime. A series of shots detail the products of overpopulation in the working class—sick children, couples fighting, "suicides."

On the other hand, Richard's wife wishes to prevent any births that might interfere with her leisure life. As an intertitle charges after she has an abortion, "One of the 'unwanted ones' returns [to heaven], and a social butterfly is again ready for house parties." Eventually, an abortion patient of the doctor who aided Mrs. Walton dies. Walton tries and convicts the doctor for murder, but in gathering evidence, he learns of his wife's and her friends' behavior. Walton returns home to confront these socialites: "I have just learned why so many of you have no children. I should bring *you* to trial for manslaughter, but I shall content myself with asking you to leave my house!" He labels his wife "a murderess." The punishment meted out to Mr. and Mrs. Walton is barrenness and loneliness in their old age.

This film is remarkable in changing course midway through the film. While birth control for the poor is recommended, abortion for the rich is vilified. No sense of this altering of agendas seems to occur. Does Walton ever recognize that he is using one standard for the poor, another for his social class? Or was the distinction between timing and means of preventing the birth of children readily available for distinguishing the two acts and arguments from one another?

In fact, some of the middle class was quite willing to talk openly about these issues in movies. Other portions of the middle class were not of the opinion that birth control and abortion had its place in the theaters. Yet the film passed the Board of Review, with restrictions, and most local censor boards, and it played to large groups of people in carefully selected sites. The authorization for its acceptance was also provided through the publicity that the well-known woman director, Lois Weber, produced the film.[20]

"Social butterflies" was a period term attached to women who had gone astray from the regulated consumption that society and the U.S. economy encouraged by the 1910s. Desiring material objects was promoted, but spending needed to be balanced with a family's real status and ability to pay. Desiring and being desired were acceptable provided that that behavior remained within the sanctioned bounds of a marriage. Excesses in desire or improprieties in object direction could disrupt the family. In such a case, a bad (desiring) woman could redeem herself. She needed to regulate her behavior to correspond to the means available to her. Likewise, the husband should not permit himself to indulge a potentially wayward wife. He should also be attentive so that she did not seek to practice her skills as ornamentation on other men. Thus, the two individuals could find support in each other, rejecting the exotic and foreign. Agency was in the individual's realm, and the woman and her sexuality would participate in the new marriage.

Conclusion

The Cheat does not quite get us to *Open All Night*. Ten years intervene between the two movies—in the form of economic, social, and cultural change, including World War I, Cecil B. DeMille's sex comedies of the late teens, and the Valentino movies. However, *The Cheat, A Fool There Was, Traffic in Souls,* and many other pictures from the early teens are indications that the American middle class was interested in investigating the nature of woman and woman's behavior. The films also illustrate the limits of such thinking. None of the films went so far as to advocate, as some freethinkers of the period did, trial marriages or even free love. None of the films proposed open marriages or sex outside of marriage. They did acknowledge the power of sexuality to drive individuals' actions. They were also well aware of how sexual interests could confuse young women or foolish wives and husbands. Passion in a heterosexual relation was not only commonly assumed, but also, in the new companionate marriages, was to be actively cultivated as the means for establishing the couple's bond.

Yet in this transitional period into an industrialized, urban, multicultural, global, and consumer society, the struggle over what the New Woman would mean was not just a question of gender debates. A New Woman was necessary for the new order. Women were necessary for the heterosocialized labor market; women were needed as consumers in the exotic department stores; women were important in the expansion of consumption into the realm of pleasure and leisure. Thus the debates over the meaning of woman and her actions are also about constructing new social arrangements to correlate with changing economic conditions. The old binary oppositions of public sphere and private sphere were falling apart, and commentators were quick to point out their fallacious and harmful effects.

Yet the society had real worries about the movement of women into the public sphere and into a culture of cultivating desires. The concern over prostitution is over how urban romances are to be conducted, how women are to protect themselves when their families are at a distance, and how one is to work in a heterosocial environment. The worry over men's adultery is about how to cope with foreign influences and whether a woman ought to move on with her life, perhaps as a single parent. The problem with abundant goods is how to avoid overspending or becoming too much the ornament that the marriage contract implies.

None of the bad women in the films was truly evil, as they might have been in an era of villains within a moral universe. The milder two cases of bad women were women who did not think and were overindulged. They were easily cured of their errors when their virtue was threatened. The more diffi- cult case was the vamp who was permitted the unusual procedure for "women without mercy" of being allowed to have some common-sense motivation for her behavior. The vamp was being humanized into the gold digger and away from the archaic threatening woman, although that monstrous feminine fig- ure would return in other guises in movies such as *Fatal Attraction*. The vamp was explained as wanting social mobility. The narrative did not, however, re- ward that goal, since her means were so heartless. The role of the parasitic woman was an unacceptable one. Bad women in these narratives functioned as cautions to support normative behavior. To do this, the older arbitrary good-versus-bad melodrama gave way to a characterization involving human agency, implying the potential for behavior transformation. Other aspects of melodrama aesthetics remained, and it is hardly surprising that all three of these films utilized rather clichéd conflicts, externalized characterizations, contrasting subplots, and at times a heavy-handed narration to convey regu- latory lessons. Films about women and families continue to function within revisions of those aesthetics through today.

From a more progressive and potentially resistant perspective, another new aspect to the representation of woman is what is implied as normative behav- ior for the New Woman. She should think. Moreover, she should think for herself, relying on her own intuitions and not those of the men around her. She should take charge of her life. She might even need to violate older ta- boos, such as the prohibitions against divorce or talking about social prob- lems. While others have noticed that the New Woman participated in the culture of consumption, I have tried to suggest that specific features charac- terized her activities: balance and reasonableness, self-awareness, and appro- priate object choices. Yet those limits provide new behavioral opportunities. Self-consciousness and self-will could lead a woman in the right path, and these desirable features gave new imperatives to self-examination, self-help, and perhaps personal empowerment.

Old systems of kinship in small towns and rural societies had their ways of constructing social and moral norms through religion and public rituals. These systems relied on a closer communication system. Such unity was disappearing, as were the traditional means of regulating behavior among women and men. New methods were required, including the modern mass media, which could be used as a contemporary communicator of moral fables, even authorized by invoking the socially responsible status of institutions such as the Board of Censorship/Review.

The complexity of storytelling and the differences of opinion about the changes, however, produced a diversity of views about what new practices were best. While these films were talking about women and sexuality, they were saying multiple things, sometimes illogical within the narrative but not within the cultural context. Spectators could derive several messages from the films. While a pointillist theory of movie-viewing might be a bit extreme in its regard of the power of images, a whole-picture theory may also have given too much credence to a spectator's willingness to follow complicitly with the main plot and resolution. These films provided cultural meanings rather than a single lesson. They were, moreover, a very good place to talk, parceled off into the sphere of entertainment as they were. The reviews of these films illustrate this variety of opinion.

The function of this book has been to reconsider the question of the representation of women and the regulation of women's sexuality during the turn of the century in the medium of cinema. I have wanted to underline that the middle class did not repress these topics. Rather, the middle class in all its diversity was fascinated with the question, Who was the New Woman and what did she want? To know who that woman was would also involve describing the new bad woman. The middle class did want to regulate the representations of woman and her desires, but since no uniformity existed in the explanations for a woman going astray, the representations and their utopian implications are only mildly similar. Woman as a sign could be appropriated and reinscribed in all sorts of contexts. Some representations—such as many of the idealized women in D. W. Griffith's films—could be quite old-fashioned, imitating the dated Victorian images of the pious and domestic woman. I have not examined those images. The ones that I have considered are representations leading toward the Flapper and the "It" Girl of the 1920s. The next decades would continue the investigation as the social formation struggled over the transfer point of woman to define her in terms valuable to modern society and its economic directions. Some of the trajectories of these representations must be linked to economic and political conditions (such as the effect of the 1930s depression or World War II's impact on women's occupational choices); other aspects derive from psychological, social, and cultural contexts.

A lot of this talk about the New Woman came from women expressing their hopes and expectations. I have concentrated on contemporaneous fiction written by women rather than men. I have also used films that had at least some element of women's authorship. *The Cheat*'s coscreenwriter was Jeanie Macpherson, who was a successful writer in Hollywood through the 1920s; *Where Are My Children?* was cowritten and codirected by Lois Weber.

Mencken said of the 1915 Flapper that "the age she lives in is one of knowledge." Moreover, "she has been taught how to take care of herself." By the 1920s, a woman's sexuality was generally regarded as positive. *Current Opinion* queried about sex o'clock in America, "Is this overemphasis of sex a symptom of a new moral awakening . . . ? Is it merely the concomitant of the movement for the liberation of woman from the shackles of convention that will disappear when society has readjusted itself to the New Woman and New Man?" It does not yet appear that that is the case.

"Fun, One Cent" by John Sloan illustrates one of the most important points for this book. Women were seeing images and hearing much new talk about who they were or should or might be. The very heterogeneity of that talk cannot be dismissed. Even though women might be objectified into objects for the male's gaze, women watching women as objects of that gaze must have been empowered in at least some local ways. Who a woman is was by no means settled. Moreover, "Fun, One Cent" also pictures women talking and laughing with one another as they take turns looking at girls in their nightgowns. While in some measure we can recover some of the possible meanings they shared, much still will remain mysterious for us. Yet the facts persist that women were traveling in the public sphere, through the books and into the theaters, where representations of their possibilities—both good and bad—were everywhere. The movies participated in that complicated middle-class revolution of representing a repeal of reticence, and women were involved in leading the way.

Notes

Preface

1. Relayed to me by Susan Dalton.

2. Judith Butler, *Gender Trouble: Feminism and the Subversion of Identity*; Teresa de Lauretis, "Technologies of Gender"; Judith Flax, "Postmodernism and Gender Relations in Feminist Theory."

3. V. N. Volosinov, *Marxism and the Philosophy of Language*, pp. 21, 23 (italics in original).

4. Stephen Greenblatt, "The Forms of Power and the Power of Forms in the Renaissance," *Genre* 15 (1982): 2–6, passim, quoted in Frank Lentricchia, "Foucault's Legacy—The New Historicism?" p. 234.

5. Carlo Ginzburg, *The Cheese and the Worms: The Cosmos of a Sixteenth-Century Miller*, p. xiv.

6. Ginzburg is writing about a period in which it might be reasonable to suggest that two classes—a dominant and a lower—exist. Although traditional Marxists often try to maintain the conflict as between two groups (following dialectics), I shall not follow that breakdown, recognizing that although, in theory, there may be two economic classes, social classes formed out of the class struggle can proliferate. This proliferation, however, might well be argued to be an advantageous discursive structure for the dominant economic class. That is, thinking that many "lifestyles" exist can displace attention from economic exploitation.

7. Michel Foucault, *The History of Sexuality: An Introduction*, pp. 33–34.

8. Ibid., pp. 44–45. Foucault seems to imply a power-station analogy, with transformers re-energizing and transmitting power and pleasure to new, distant locations.

1: The Repeal of Reticence

1. [H. L. Mencken], "The Flapper," pp. 1–2.

2. Agnes Repplier, "The Repeal of Reticence," p. 298.

3. Ibid.

4. Ibid.

5. "Sex O'Clock in America," *Current Opinion* 55, no. 2 (August 1913): 113–14.

6. Repplier, "The Repeal of Reticence," p. 301.

7. T. J. Jackson Lears, *No Place of Grace: Antimodernism and the Transformation of American Culture*.

8. Both the shift from moralists to scientists and the transformation from a culture of production to a culture of consumption are sometimes represented as more totalizing and irrevocable than they likely actually were. As Horace Newcomb suggested to me, in certain regions such as the American South, religious authority still retains strong influence among people. Additionally, it is likely that a culture of consumption has been added onto a culture of production rather than replaced it.

183

9. Lea Jacobs, *Wages of Sin: Censorship and the Fallen Woman Film, 1928–1942*.

10. Tom Gunning, *D. W. Griffith and the Origins of American Narrative Film: The Early Years at Biograph*.

11. Janet Staiger, *Interpreting Films: Studies in the Historical Reception of American Cinema*, pp. 101–23; Tom Gunning, "The Cinema of Attractions: Early Film, Its Spectator and the Avant-Garde."

12. Perhaps because of the availability of information about New York and Chicago—both big cities—the history of early exhibition has emphasized the class distinctions among the various sites of exhibition. However, in mid- to small-sized towns and rural areas, a mixing of classes seems quite common, making suspect some of the argumentation that it was a specific class's concern about the proletariat seeing movies that produced the difficulties over representation. It is the case, as Robert C. Allen pointed out in reading a draft of this book, that the two large cities of New York and Chicago served as ports of entry for immigrants, and thus the question of cinema providing ethnic acculturation was more important in those situations. The major point to note, though, is that neither city should be taken as representative of the common pattern of the introduction of films, class interests in seeing them, or responses to the movies' subject matters.

13. Elizabeth Ewen, "City Lights: Immigrant Women and the Rise of the Movies," p. S51.

14. Lauren Rabinovitz, "Temptations of Pleasure: Nickelodeons, Amusement Parks, and the Sights of Female Sexuality," p. 78.

15. Miriam Hansen, "Adventures of Goldilocks: Spectatorship, Consumerism, and Public Life," p. 5; also see her *Babel and Babylon: Spectatorship in American Silent Film*. Hansen's use of the term *public sphere* has a very special meaning for her. In *Babel and Babylon*, she notes that describing society as divided between a public and a private sphere has a long history of use. Appealing to Jürgen Habermas's discussions (1962) and Oskar Negt and Alexander Kluge's reworking of the terms, she employs the framework they create to extend an argument made earlier by Judith Mayne ("Immigrants and Spectators"), that movie houses were an alternative public sphere for women in the teens. She notes that feminists (specifically Joan Landes) reviewing Habermas's theories believe that " 'the bourgeois public is essentially, not just contingently, masculinist, and . . . this characteristic serves to determine both its self-representation and its subsequent "structural" transformation.' . . . the masculinization of public life also involved a restriction of women's activities to the domestic space, and the concomitant alignment of the familial sphere with a new discourse of an idealized femininity" (p. 10). While no gender arrangement for public and private had to have existed, a bourgeois historical discourse created one as "essential." Hansen points out that it is not surprising that the binary terms *public and private sphere* and *masculine and feminine sphere* reflect the dominant discourse and that the opposition would begin to fray at the turn of the twentieth century. Hansen follows general terminology to make her argument about cultural and representation shifts during the period, as well as using parts of the discussion to claim a public space for women (pp. 114–19). As Hansen notes, the "public/private" opposition has a long and troubled history, but what it does provide is a representation of spaces that were perceived to exist during the time I am discussing. Thus, like the term *gender*, the notions of "public" and "private" sphere should be considered ideological representations. I shall use them in the common way they have been employed, not in the specialized meaning that Hansen creates by adopting the terminology for part of her theoretical framework.

16. Stephen Heath, *The Sexual Fix*, pp. 2–3. See Michel Foucault, *The Use of Pleasure: The History of Sexuality*; Jeffrey Weeks, *Sex, Politics, and Society*, pp. 5–16.

17. I do not mean here to imply a vulgar Marxist assertion that social and cultural behaviors are mere epiphenomena of the economic base. In part the mode of production and consumption is itself a representation (derived from the economic base of capitalism and then monopoly capitalism). Thus, the actual situation is complex, with multiple determinants producing the transformation that I am describing.

18. Peter Conn, *The Divided Mind: Ideology and Imagination in America, 1898–1917*, p. 268; Robert M. Crunden, *Ministers of Reform: The Progressives; Achievement in American Civilizations, 1889–1920*, pp. 105–6.

19. I shall indicate in chapter 3 that showing nude or scantily covered bodies in respectable sites had rules, derived in part from context, function, and form of the display. The point here is that spectators could, if they so chose, see how bodies were constructed. In either a respectable or a marginal site, viewers could also employ their own interpretative strategies to respond to those sights.

20. *Pull Down the Curtains, Suzie* (American Mutoscope and Biograph, 1904); *What Happened on Twenty-Third Street, New York City* (Edison, 1902). *Pull Down the Curtains, Suzie* is a tease about voyeurism: Suzie leaves her gentleman caller and enters her room. She removes her belt, skirt, blouse, and corset while we watch her—*and* him watching her from the sidewalk below her window. Then, just as it seems to be promising, Suzie pulls down the window shade. Other films do exist that permit individuals to see more and enjoy it. In *What Happened on Twenty-Third Street*, a woman's skirt billows up as she walks over a subway grate. For an analysis of this and other films exploring women's bodies, see Judith Mayne, "Uncovering the Female Body." I shall also discuss such films further in chapter 3.

21. For example, Robert Sklar, *Movie-Made America: A Cultural History of American Movies*.

22. Lary May, *Screening Out the Past: The Birth of Mass Culture and the Motion Picture Industry*, p. 53.

23. This is not to say, however, that the working class was aligned with the middle or upper class. Rather the forms of its domination and its resistances are diverse, not easily summed up as unified practices.

24. See, for instance, Teresa de Lauretis, "Technologies of Gender"; Judith Butler, *Gender Trouble*; and Judith Flax, "Postmodernism and Gender Relations in Feminist Theory." On issues of the representation of women in the early cinema, see Annette Michelson, "On the Eve of the Future: The Reasonable Facsimile and the Philosophical Toy"; Linda Williams, "Film Body: An Implantation of Perversions"; Ewen, "City Lights," p. S59; Sumiko Higashi, *Virgins, Vamps, and Flappers: The American Silent Movie Heroine*; Jacobs, *Wages of Sin*, p. 8; E. Ann Kaplan, *Motherhood and Representation: The Mother in Popular Culture and Melodrama*.

25. Michael Rogin, " 'The Sword Became a Flashing Vision': D. W. Griffith's *The Birth of a Nation*," p. 158. Also see Mark Thomas Connelly, *The Response to Prostitution in the Progressive Era*, in which he argues that the prostitute is a master symbol for a wide range of anxieties between the 1890s and World War I.

26. I find Hansen's work on the production of movies in this period in her *Babel and Babylon* to be generally compatible with my position, although I shall be considering films more mainstream than D. W. Griffith's *Intolerance*. However, Hansen wants to assert her readings as likely for the audiences of the time. This is somewhat suspect to me. In the readings of the films that I shall do in chapters 5, 6, and 7, I argue only for the reasonable possibilities of finding various meanings in the text—given the social and cultural contexts in which the discourses are embedded, which I describe. Hansen provides less context for her hypotheses. She also provides no other confirming evidence. Also see how her approach to real audiences contrast with mine in *Interpreting Films* (chapters 5 and 6), where I am specifically attempting to discuss actual receptions of films of the era.

27. The work of Ben Singer is an important corrective here. His discussion of the serial-queen genre in movies between 1912 and 1920 suggests more diversity to the teens' film images of women. The genre, he shows, "oscillates" between "contradictory extremes of female prowess and distress, empowerment and imperilment." Singer, "Female Power in the Serial-Queen Melodrama: The Etiology of an Anomaly," p. 93.

28. Annette Kuhn, *Cinema, Censorship, and Sexuality, 1909–1925*, pp. 2–6, 108.

29. Neither Kuhn nor I would argue that one should *not* consider the specific work of a censoring group (the work of Jacobs, for example, being valuable). However, for some questions, focusing on the wider social mechanisms regulating representations may be important for understanding how a dominant group is responding to troublesome material.

30. Butler illustrates this operation by applying it to the problem of the construction of gender. In an extended argument in *Gender Trouble*, Butler theorizes that the incest taboo is a taboo not only about what counts as male and female identity but also a taboo against homosexuality. In application, then, if a culturally dominant ideology asserts that such-and-such behavior is prohibited, then not only is the taboo creating an identity for those who might or might not possibly enact that prohibition, but "good" and "bad" behaviors are also being constructed. Butler, *Gender Trouble*, pp. 73–74.

31. Kuhn, *Cinema, Censorship, and Sexuality*, p. 128.

32. Linda Williams, *Hard Core: Power, Pleasure, and the "Frenzy of the Visible,"* p. 2.

33. Jacobs, *Wages of Sin*, p. 3

34. Judith Mayne takes this perspective in turning to the 1901 Edison film *Trapeze Disrobing Act*. Dangling from a swing hung in a theater auditorium, a woman strips from a very proper dress to her tights. This garb is still respectable within the bounds of protocols for the stage at the turn of the century. However, that the woman does this undressing in front of, and to the very obvious delight of, two men makes the terms of the relation unequal. Her work is for their pleasure. Mayne, "Uncovering the Female Body," p. 65.

35. I have checked with several scholars of early cinema about the date of the first film recording of a couple copulating. Although Ben Brewster believes that as soon as moving-image cameras existed such films must have been made, neither he, Charles Musser, Richard Abel, Kristin Thompson, nor Tom Gunning have seen or know of any from the first decade of movies. Al Di Lauro and Gerald Rabkin do assert that by 1904 production and a market for films of "fully detailed sexual activity" existed (*Dirty Movies: An Illustrated History of the Stag Film 1915–1970*, p. 46). This claim also occurs in Joseph W. Slade, "Violence in the Hard-Core Pornographic Film: A Historical Survey." While I agree that some such films were probably produced, their very lack of existence suggests how taboo it was to make such films.

36. Of course, I would not forget that a whole history of eroticism exists prior to the invention of cinema.

37. Christian Metz, *The Imaginary Signifier: Psychoanalysis and the Cinema*, p. 66. Obviously, censorship and regulation have been very successful in producing representations of violence, sexual behavior, and their synthesis, violent sexuality. Our society has experienced a great deal of pleasure, and a large economic success, in making these fundamental human responses to socialization taboo and then capitalizing on them.

38. Williams, *Hard Core*, p. 35.

39. "Sex O'Clock in America," 113–14. William Marion Reedy was writing in the St. Louis *Mirror*.

40. I want to stress that what is represented as changes in gender behavior and sexuality is the subject being discussed. How many individuals were behaving in new ways or how much the representations were finally catching up to older behavior patterns are other matters.

41. Kathy Peiss, *Cheap Amusements: Working Women and Leisure in Turn-of-the-Century New York*, p. 34.

42. I. Wallerstein, *The Modern World-System*; Mike Featherstone, ed., *Global Culture: Nationalism, Globalization and Modernity*.

43. A discussion of the historiography for the period as of 1967 is in Irwin Unger, "The 'New Left' and American History: Some Recent Trends in United States Historiography."

44. May, *Screening Out the Past*, p. 31. Also see Michael Barton, "The Victorian Jeremiad: Critics of Accumulation and Display."

45. Besides May, see Stephen Kern, *Culture of Time and Space, 1880–1918*, pp. 200–201; Lewis A. Erenberg, *Steppin' Out: New York Nightlife and the Transformation of American Culture, 1890–1930*, pp. 16–22, 53–62.

46. F. A. MacKenzie, *The Trial of Harry Thaw*.

47. A whole series of foreign policy actions indicates a fresh militancy for expansion on the part of the U.S. government.

48. Unger, "The 'New Left,' " pp. 1247–48; Marilyn Blatt Young, "American Expansion, 1870–1900: The Far East," pp. 176–83.

49. The conditions for African-Americans in the South deteriorated. In the 1890s lynchings increased so that the *reported* number of cases for each year exceeded 100, with 161 recorded in 1892. The U.S. Supreme Court in *Plessy v. Ferguson* (1896) supported and legalized segregation of public spaces. Between 1898 and 1908 race riots occurred in Wilmington, North Carolina; New York City; New Orleans; Atlanta; and Springfield, Illinois. A "new abolitionism" responded, with the National Association for the Advancement of Colored People founded by 1910. James M. McPherson, "The Antislavery Legacy: From Reconstruction to the NAACP," pp. 137–57.

50. Oscar Handlin, ed., *Immigration as a Factor in American History*.

51. Protests organized against the Chinese in California occurred in the 1870s. By 1882, exclusionary laws directed toward Asians were passed. In 1891, the first attempts to regulate immigration began, and an Immigration Restriction League formed in Boston in that decade. By 1907, Roosevelt had negotiated with Japan to halt its flow of people to the West Coast. Jewish people also experienced the beginnings of exclusionary policies, and their response was the formation in 1906 of the American Jewish Committee and in 1913 the Anti-Defamation League of B'nai B'rith. Thomas F. Gossett, *Race: The History of an Idea in America*, pp. 287–90; John Higham, *Strangers in the Land: Patterns of American Nativism, 1860–1925*, pp. 68–10; Handlin, *Immigration*, pp. 171–82.

52. Higham, *Strangers in the Land*, p. 95.

53. Ibid., pp. 95–96, 143; Handlin, *Immigration*, pp. 178–82; Conn, *Divided Mind*, p. 140. Also see Allan M. Brandt, *No Magic Bullet: A Social History of Venereal Disease in the United States since 1880*, p. 7; "Mr. Roosevelt's Views on Race Suicide," *Ladies' Home Journal* 23, no. 3 (February 1906): 21. Higham notes that between 1905 and 1909 at least thirty-five articles on the subject of "race suicide" appeared in general periodicals.

54. Lears, *No Place of Grace*, p. 12.

55. T. J. Jackson Lears, "From Salvation to Self-Realization: Advertising and the Therapeutic Roots of the Consumer Culture, 1880–1930," p. 3.

56. Lears, *No Place of Grace*, p. 12. For the role that religion played in permitting this transition, see Barton, "The Victorian Jeremiad."

57. Lears, "From Salvation to Self-Realization," p. 4. Lears specifically references the Gramscian notion of hegemony as the theoretical frame for his perception of these events, a frame with which I agree. Hence, my use of "common sense" here is written with the full significance that it holds for Gramsci.

58. William Leiss, Stephen Kline, and Sut Jhally, *Social Communication in Advertising: Persons, Products and Images of Well-Being*, p. 247. Also see Susan Strasser, *Satisfaction Guaranteed: The Making of the American Mass Market*.

59. Emile Durkheim published *Suicide* in 1897.

60. William Leach, "Transformations in a Culture of Consumption," p. 333. An excellent discussion of this change is also in Alan Trachtenberg, *The Incorporation of America: Culture and Society in the Gilded Age*, pp. 130–39.

61. Beyond the threat of general alienation for the entire family should desire exceed radically its ability to purchase what it wanted, as shopping for manufactured goods took up more and

more time and moved the housewife into the marketplace, women cut down on domestic, church, and civic work. This change provides a partial rationale for the shift from religious institutions to other sources as the authority for behavior.

62. Leach, "Transformations in the Culture of Consumption," p. 337. A number of writers have compared the store window to the movie screen as a place into which to look for consumable goods. See most recently Hansen, *Babel and Babylon*; Jane Gaines, "The Queen Christina Tie-Ups: Convergence of Show Window and Screen."

63. Simon J. Bronner, "Reading Consumer Culture," pp. 17–20.

64. Annie Marion MacLean, "Two Weeks in Department Stores."

65. Robert H. Walker, *Reform in America: The Continuing Frontier*, p. 7. Although I would argue that sometimes a desire to *maintain* the status quo—and its *inequities*—may drive reform, recognition of diversity seems present in the cases I shall consider during this period.

66. Lears, *No Place of Grace*, p. 4. Also see Walker, *Reform*, p. 132, and Dick Hebdige, *Subculture: The Meaning of Style*, pp. 6–7.

67. Trachtenberg, *Incorporation of America*, pp. 173–81; Richard Hofstadter, *Age of Reform: From Bryan to F.D.R.*, pp. 48–80; Unger, "The 'New Left,' " pp. 1250–51.

68. Walker, *Reform*, pp. 132–34; Kenneth M. Roemer, *The Obsolete Necessity: America in Utopian Writings*, p. 2.

69. Charles J. Rooney Jr., *Dreams and Visions: A Study of American Utopias, 1865–1917*, p. 11.

70. Problems also existed for labor (long hours, low pay, no job security), in politics (corrupt public officials), in the environment (slums, air pollution, overpopulation, poor health), in social relations (inequality for women, intemperance, unhappy marriages), in education (illiteracy), and in religious life (declining morals).

71. Rooney, *Dreams and Visions*, pp. 42–47; Roemer, *Obsolete Necessity*, pp. 84–97.

72. Quoted in Chaim I. Waxman, "Perspectives on Poverty in Early American Sociology," p. 183.

73. Günther Brandt, *Origins of American Sociology: A Study in the Ideology of Social Science, 1865–1895*, abstract.

74. William F. Fine, *Progressive Evolutionism and American Sociology, 1890–1920*, pp. 7–12, 38–39; Waxman, "Perspectives on Poverty," pp. 184–85; Brandt, *Origins of American Sociology*, pp. 64–95.

75. Hofstadter, *Age of Reform*, pp. 148–64; Richard H. Pells, *Radical Visions and American Dreams: Culture and Social Thought in the Depression Years*, p. 3, summarizing Hofstadter and Robert H. Wiebe, *The Search for Order, 1877–1920*.

76. Conn, *The Divided Mind*, p. 2. Defining the terms and issues differently, some other historians perceive progressivism to perhaps even have hindered reform activities. If progressivism is theorized as the thoughts and values of a group or a set of institutions or even a political power, then some of the disagreements could be solved. However, progressivism can also be seen, as Wiebe argues, to be a general response to modernization. Thus, according to Peter G. Filene, progressivism was not a movement; it was an era in which great diversity existed among people interested in policies about monopolies, workers' rights, women's suffrage, nativism, and prohibition. Filene also insists that in this broad understanding of progressivism some upper-class individuals and laborers contributed to achieving specific goals.

77. Robert H. Wiebe, "The Progressive Years, 1900–1917"; Peter G. Filene, "An Obituary"; Hofstadter, *Age of Reform*, p. 131; Unger, "The 'New Left,' " pp. 1251–52.

78. Paul L. Murphy, *World War I and the Origin of Civil Liberties in the United States*, p. 25.

79. Samuel Haber, *Efficiency and Uplift: Scientific Management in the Progressive Era, 1890–1920*, p. x.

80. Hofstadter, *Age of Reform*, p. 280.

81. Conn, *The Divided Mind*, pp. 49–54; Hofstadter, *Age of Reform*, p. 186; Harold S. Wilson, *McClure's Magazine and the Muckrakers*, pp. 217–22; Christopher P. Wilson, "The Rhetoric of Consumption," p. 57. The muckraking by *McClure's* was to play a part in the disputes over regulation of moving pictures; it also provided the generic prototypes for *Traffic in Souls*.

82. Foucault, *The History of Sexuality*, pp. 17–24.

2: Sex O'Clock in America

1. Frank Luther Mott, *Golden Multitudes: The Story of Bestsellers in the United States*, p. 245 and *A History of American Magazines, 1885–1905*, vol. 4, pp. 122–23.

2. E. Ann Kaplan, in *Motherhood and Representation*, writes that recently scholars have studied so-called male-addressed versus female-addressed literature of the 1800s. Alfred Habegger, in *Gender, Fantasy and Realism in American Literature* (1982), argues that the "male realist novel [was] produced through reaction against the fantasy-laden and heavily escapist qualities of women's novels" (p. 72). Kaplan criticizes the idea that women's fiction is as simple as Habegger represents it, and I agree. Moreover, some "domestic feminism" produced novels that, in Kaplan's view, "articulate woman's oppressive positioning."

3. Terry Lovell, *Consuming Fiction*, p. 123.

4. This revision of the religious story of the fall of Adam and Eve is not, however, pronounced in the novel's aesthetic structure.

5. Cross-dressing is significant as a transgressive act confronting norms of femininity. Much current research discusses this, but see especially Jonathan Dollimore, *Sexual Dissidence: Augustine to Wilde, Freud to Foucault*, pp. 284–306. I shall briefly discuss some film examples in chapter 3. Here the novel's narrational voice ultimately seems to judge the stunt as too dangerous to use.

6. John C. Burnham, "The Progressive Era Revolution in American Attitudes about Sex," p. 889.

7. I am here indebted to the pioneering work of scholars such as Barbara Hobson, *Uneasy Virtue: The Politics of Prostitution and the American Reform Tradition*; Joanne J. Meyerowitz, *Women Adrift: Independent Wage Earners in Chicago, 1880–1930*; Judith Walkowitz, *City of Dreadful Delight: Narratives of Sexual Danger in Late-Victorian England*; Elizabeth Wilson, *The Sphinx in the City: Urban Life, the Control of Disorder, and Women*; and others mentioned elsewhere in these pages. My hope is simply to provide a more detailed and specific argument about the changing norms so that their arrival, coinciding with the advent of moving-picture regulation, can be seen to be as progressive as it ought to be relative to its time frame.

8. Although I would certainly not suggest that what has been produced for and by women in the twentieth century has freed us from patriarchy, I do consider certain aspects of the new discursive orders to have potential for improving women's situations as individuals in social formations. Thus, what I am discussing here is not only a specific historical transformation, but the process of transformation that has permitted feminists of the late twentieth century to discuss in our current terms our past and our future. Perhaps one of the best descriptions of the New Woman (and New Man) is in Peter G. Filene, *Him/Her/Self: Sex Roles in Modern America*, pp. 6–112, which I discovered late in my writing of this book. Filene's work supports the discussion I present, although his focus is less on the historical process and more on certain individual movements toward women's rights.

9. Barbara Welter, "The Cult of True Womanhood, 1820–1860," p. 152. Of course, this is a generalization in relation to the variety of specific images circulated during the period. However, Welter's work has been generally praised and is useful for understanding this period.

10. Stuart Ewen, *Captains of Consciousness: Advertising and the Social Roots of the Consumer Culture*, p. 126. Also see T. J. Jackson Lears, *No Place of Grace*, p. 15; Lynn D. Gordon, *Gender and Higher Education in the Progressive Era*, p. 13.

11. Furthermore, the ideology was attempting to regulate a behavior contrary to women's culture of earlier years or in different circumstances (such as pioneer and farm women who had to work in "public" places at this time). "Resistance" thus might be understood not only as a reaction to the domination but also as an attempt to continue other, older cultural and social practices.

12. Nancy Hewitt, "Yankee Evangelicals and Agrarian Quakers," p. 326; Carroll Smith-Rosenberg, "Writing History: Language, Class, and Gender."

13. Lisa Tickner, *The Spectacle of Women: Imagery of the Suffrage Campaign, 1907–14*, p. 266.

14. Karen Blair, *The Clubwoman as Feminist: True Womanhood Redefined, 1868–1914*, pp. 45, 73–74.

15. Gwendolyn Wright, *Building the Dream: A Social History of Housing in America*, p. 173; also see Peter Conn, *The Divided Mind*, p. 156, and Eleanor Flexner, *Century of Struggle: The Woman's Rights Movements in the United States*, pp. 184–86, 212–14.

16. Charlotte Perkins Gilman, *Women and Economics: A Study of the Economic Relation between Men and Women as a Factor in Social Evolution*, p. 21.

17. Rheta Childe Dorr, *What Eight Million Women Want*, pp. 287–300.

18. Nancy F. Cott, *The Grounding of Modern Feminism*, pp. 3, 10, 38. Howe was married to Frederic C. Howe, a "progressive municipal reformer"; the People's Institute was the civil organization that took on the task of regulating movies (see chapter 4).

19. Tickner, *The Spectacle of Women*, p. 266; Eric Trudgill, *Madonnas and Magdalens: The Origins and Development of Victorian Sexual Attitudes*, p. 271.

20. Dee Garrison, "The Tender Technicians: The Feminization of Public Librarianship"; Leslie Woodcock Tentler, *Wage-Earning Women: Industrial Work and Family Life in the United States*, p. 14.

21. Tentler, *Wage-Earning Women*, pp. 85, 109–11. Also see Elizabeth Ewen, "City Lights," p. S45.

22. Stuart Ewen, *Captains of Consciousness: Advertising and the Social Roots of the Consumer Culture*, pp. 113–17.

23. Margaret Marsh, "Suburban Men and Masculine Domesticity, 1870–1915," pp. 165–86.

24. Ronald Pearsall, *The Worm in the Bud: The World of Victorian Sexuality*, pp. xi–xiv; Carl N. Degler, "What Ought to Be and What Was: Women's Sexuality in Nineteenth Century America," p. 1477. Also see Jeffrey Weeks, *Sex, Politics, and Society: The Regulation of Sexuality since 1800*, p. 23; John D'Emilio and Estelle B. Freedman, *Intimate Matters: A History of Sexuality in America*, pp. 55–56.

25. Peter Gay, *The Bourgeois Experience: Victoria to Freud*; Degler, "What Ought to Be," pp. 1469–71.

26. Elizabeth Fee, "The Sexual Politics of Victorian Social Anthropology," p. 86.

27. For an example of such a recognition in 1914 by a social worker, see Ruth S. True, "The Neglected Girl." Also see Trudgill, *Madonnas and Magdalens*, pp. 34–35; Edward W. Said, *Orientalism*.

28. John S. Haller Jr. and Robin M. Haller, *The Physician and Sexuality in Victorian America*, pp. xii–xiii; Linda Gordon, "Voluntary Motherhood: The Beginnings of Feminist Birth Control Ideas in the United States," pp. 54–57; Ellen Carol DuBois and Linda Gordon, "Seeking Ecstasy on the Battlefield: Danger and Pleasure in Nineteenth-Century Feminist Sexual Thought," p. 39; Conn, *The Divided Mind*, p. 156.

29. D'Emilio and Freedman, *Intimate Matters*, pp. 56–84. Also see my chapter 7.

30. Haller and Haller, *The Physician and Sexuality*, pp. 77, 174–87; Lawrence Birken, *Consuming Desire: Sexual Science and the Emergence of a Culture of Abundance, 1871–1914*, pp. 81–82.

31. S. P. White, quoted by Haller and Haller, *The Physician and Sexuality*, p. 77; D'Emilio and Freedman, *Intimate Matters*, pp. 226–29.

32. Weeks, *Sex, Politics, and Society*, p. 38; Arnold I. Davidson, "Sex and the Emergence of Sexuality," p. 18. Also see Stephen Heath, *The Sexual Fix*, p. 7.

33. D'Emilio and Freedman, *Intimate Matters*, pp. 224–25; Cott, *The Grounding*, pp. 41–42.

34. Birken, *Consuming Desire*, pp. vii, 33–41, 49.

35. Cott, *The Grounding*, p. 43. For further examples from 1910 to 1920, see Percy Gamble Krammerer, *The Unmarried Mother: A Study of Five Hundred Cases*, pp. 211–13, and research by Dr. Celia Duel Mosher recounted in Degler, "What Ought to Be," pp. 1483–89.

36. Here I am interested in the history of descriptions of and prescriptions about prostitution, not the specific truths of its reality, which are often quite different from its representations.

37. Cora Kaplan, "Wild Nights: Pleasure/Sexuality/Feminism," p. 16; Leslie Fishbein, "Harlot or Heroine? Changing Views of Prostitution, 1870–1920." Descriptions of the facts of nineteenth-century prostitution are found in Judith Walkowitz and Daniel J. Walkowitz, " 'We Are Not Beasts of the Field': Prostitution and the Poor in Plymouth and Southampton under the Contagious Disease Act," pp. 192–93; D'Emilio and Freedman, *Intimate Matters*, pp. 171–83; Hobson, *Uneasy Virtue*. A classic study of this era's prostitution is Mark Thomas Connelly, *The Response to Prostitution in the Progressive Era*, which has influenced this entire section. An important recent study addressing prostitution in New York City is Timothy Gilfoyle's *City of Eros: New York City, Prostitution, and the Commercialization of Sex, 1790–1920*. Walkowitz and Walkowitz specifically note that the definition of a prostitute could be quite broad, even applying to women who accepted economic protection for cohabitation without marriage or who merely engaged in premarital sex. A period of active economic exchange for sexual favors might also be very short-lived.

38. DuBois and Gordon, "Seeking Ecstasy," pp. 32–33; Laura Hapke, *Girls Who Went Wrong: Prostitutes in American Fiction, 1885–1917*, pp. 17–18; Gilfoyle, *City of Eros*, pp. 270–97. Judith Walkowitz, *City of Dreadful Delight*, recounts a major media uproar in 1885 in London, England, when the *Pall Mall Gazette* published an exposé on women being drugged and violated. Her analysis of the narrative is particularly valuable as she notes how the *Gazette* combined and transformed conventions from melodrama, pornography, and fantasy literature.

39. Dorr, *What Eight Million Women Want*, pp. 198, 205.

40. It would also be useful to situate Lea Jacobs's discussion of the appearance of the "fallen woman" genre in light of this context (see her *Wages of Sin*, pp. 5–9).

41. Burnham, "The Progressive Era," p. 888.

42. Charles Parkhurst, *Our Fight with Tammany*, pp. 1–9; John Ensor Harr and Peter J. Johnson, *The Rockefeller Century*, pp. 106–15; Allen F. Davis, *Spearheads for Reform: The Social Settlements and the Progressive Movement, 1890–1914*, pp. 180–87; S. S. McClure, "The Tammanyizing of a Civilization"; Allan M. Brandt, *No Magic Bullet*, pp. 36, 41–42; Haller and Haller, *The Physician and Sexuality*, pp. 244–45; Gilfoyle, *City of Eros*, pp. 298–306.

43. George Kibbe Turner, "City of Chicago: A Study of the Great Immoralities," p. 582; Earnest A. Bell, *Fighting the Traffic in Young Girls; or, War on the White Slave Trade*.

44. See the evidence for this in chapter 6.

45. Brandt, *No Magic Bullet*, pp. 9–10, 31–41. Brandt also notes that around 1900, the idea that venereal diseases were spread by touching items in public spaces (such as water fountains) began to circulate. Brandt points out that this reinforced fears of other races and classes as dangerous (pp. 19–32).

46. Ibid., p. 26; Burnham, "The Progressive Era," pp. 887–902; Lears, *No Place of Grace*, p. 13.

47. Brandt, *No Magic Bullet*, pp. 19–20.

48. Some cities gave hotels favored treatment in securing liquor licenses to support their restaurant trade. However, saloons caught on to this, formed alliances with tenement houses, and provided a convenient arrangement for "cadets"—the period term for pimps—and their women.

49. Committee of Fifteen, *The Social Evil, with Special Reference to Conditions Existing in the City of New York*, p. 3. Material is also from Louis Filler, *Muckrakers*, pp. 286–94.

50. Prince Albert Morrow, quoted in Brandt, *No Magic Bullet*, p. 24; "The Common Welfare: National Merger to Fight White Slavery," *Survey* 27, no. 26 (30 March 1912): 1991–92; "The Bureau of Social Hygiene," *Outlook* 103, no. 6 (8 February 1913): 287–88; Burnham, "The Progressive Era," pp. 885–903.

51. Brandt, *No Magic Bullet*, pp. 37–38; George J. Kneeland, *Commercialized Prostitution in New York City: Publications of the Bureau of Social Hygiene*, pp. viii–xii.

52. Brandt, *No Magic Bullet*, p. 38; Kneeland, *Commercialized Prostitution*, p. ix; "Prostitution in Europe—Abraham Flexner's Study of Supply, Demand, Regulation," *Survey* 31, no. 16 (17 January 1914), 471–73; Abraham Flexner, *I Remember: The Autobiography of Abraham Flexner*, pp. 197–99.

53. Brandt, *No Magic Bullet*, p. 24; Christopher P. Wilson, "The Rhetoric of Consumption: Mass-Market Magazines and the Demise of the Gentle Reader, 1880–1920," p. 44; Mott, *A History*, p. 360; Helen Keller, " 'I Must Speak': A Plea to the American Woman," *Ladies' Home Journal* 16, no. 2 (January 1909): 6. *Ladies' Home Journal* did lose subscriptions as a result of some of its essays.

54. "The Common Welfare: Report of the Chicago Vice Commission," *Survey* 26 (15 April 1911): 99; Brandt, *No Magic Bullet*, p. 47; John D. Rockefeller Jr., "The Awakening of a New Conscience," *Medical Review of Reviews* 19 (May 1913): 289–91.

55. Burnham, "The Progressive Era," pp. 901–2; Steven Schlossman and Stephanie Wallach, "The Crime of Precocious Sexuality: Female Juvenile Delinquency in the Progressive Era," p. 86.

56. Charles W. Eliot, "New Methods for Grappling with the Social Evil," *Current Opinion* 54, no. 4 (April 1913): 308–9.

57. "Editorials," *Survey* 31 (28 February 1914): 682–83; Theodore Schroeder, "Our Prudish Censorship," *Forum* 53 (January 1915): 88.

58. Walter Lippmann, *A Preface to Politics*, pp. 148, 150.

59. Charlotte Perkins Gilman, *Women and Economics*, pp. 159–60; Margaret Deland, "The New Woman Who Would Do Things," *Ladies' Home Journal* 24, no. 10 (September 1907): 17.

60. Kathy Peiss, "Making Faces: The Cosmetics Industry and the Cultural Consumption of Gender, 1890–1930," pp. 152–53.

61. Miriam Formanek-Brunell, "Marketing a Campbell Kids Culture."

3: Troublesome Pictures

1. I am attempting here to recapture part of the public reception of these films. I have endeavored to see every film mentioned here, but many are lost. The filmography lists all the films mentioned in the text that I viewed, as well as the archive holding the print so that other researchers know which version (if several exist) I viewed. I would emphasize, however, that I am interested in the publicly stated impressions—both as an indication of what the people thought they saw and (but less so) as an influence on other people's viewing. It is questionable to what extent reviews had any effect on early audiences' reception of these films. Moreover, the papers had their own agendas, not the least of which was keeping the moving-picture trade alive. While

they might want to have producers adopt normative representational strategies, they might also be more willing than some middle-class people to "forgive" what they saw on the screen.

2. John Hagan, "Erotic Tendencies in Film, 1900–1906," p. 231.

3. Robert C. Allen, *Horrible Prettiness: Burlesque and American Culture*, pp. 26–27. For the mixed nature of entertainment in the early 1800s, see Lawrence W. Levine, "William Shakespeare and the American People: A Study in Cultural Transformation," and Paul DiMaggio, "Cultural Entrepreneurship in Nineteenth-Century Boston: The Creation of an Organizational Base for High Culture in America."

4. Timothy Gilfoyle, *City of Eros*, p. 127, describes *tableaux vivants* in New York City in the 1840s in which women may be wearing tights or transparent coverings, or they might even be naked.

5. Petter Gay, *The Bourgeois Experience*, vol. 1, opposite p. 182; Frank Luther Mott, *A History of American Magazines, 1885–1905*, p. 152. Also see Lois W. Banner, *American Beauty*, pp. 120, 152; Thomas Waugh, "Strength and Stealth: Watching (and Wanting) Turn of the Century Strongmen." Live performers wore tights. Apparently photographs had sufficient distance to permit actual nudity. Eadweard Muybridge's photographs—positioned as science—had such an ideology as well; see Linda Williams, "Film Body: An Implantation of Perversion," pp. 19–35.

6. Allen, *Horrible Prettiness*, pp. 225–36.

7. Ibid., p. 244.

8. Ibid., pp. 266–67; Tom Gunning, *D. W. Griffith and the Origins of American Film*, p. 156; Hagan, "Erotic Tendencies." Other examples from this time period in which women are partially or totally nude (without tights) are *The Draped Model* (AMB, 1902) and *The Pouting Model* (AMB, 1902). In both of these films the women pose nearly without movement.

9. Of course, other minor firms did continue to seek profits from these prohibited films.

10. See Janet Staiger, "Standardization and Differentiation: The Reinforcement and Dispersion of Hollywood's Practices," pp. 96–112, in David Bordwell, Janet Staiger, and Kristin Thompson, *The Classical Hollywood Cinema: Film Style and Mode of Production to 1960*.

11. "Houston Authorities Object to Picture of Thaw-White Tragedy," *Moving Picture World* 1, no. 7 (20 April 1907): 102 (hereafter cited as *MPW*).

12. "Trade Notes," *MPW* 1, no. 8 (27 April 1907): 119; "Trade Notes," *MPW* 1, no. 10 (11 May 1907): 153; "The Film Manufacturer and the Public," *MPW* 1, no. 12 (25 May 1907): 179. *The Unwritten Law* is variously referred to as "The Great Thaw Trial" or "The Thaw-White Case" in the trade papers and later accounts. As far as I can determine, only one film on the subject was produced around 1907, although later versions were manufactured. Ronald S. Magliozzi, ed., *Treasures from the Film Archives: A Catalogue of Short Silent Films Held by FIAF Archives*, lists only the first title as having prints existing. *Variety*, 30 March 1907, also reviewed the film, indicating that it featured the trial's "sensational points" and a "fairly complete exposition of Mrs. Harry Thaw's testimony," but the climax came too fast. Lubin, the manufacturing company, tended to push the boundaries more than other firms. This was neither the first nor the last time the firm would be called upon by the industry to tone down its movies.

13. *MPW* 1, no. 9 (4 May 1907): 143.

14. This is because, as I have suggested above, norms of representation quickly defined such films as unacceptable; hence, they went "underground" into men-only venues away from the nickelodeons and family exhibition sites.

15. "Three Points of View," *MPW* 1, no. 7 (13 April 1907): 89; "Public Opinion as a Moral Censor," *MPW* 1, no. 10 (11 May 1907): 147; [untitled], *MPW* 1, no. 13 (1 June 1907): 198. For a description of Hull House's operation, see "Wicked Five-Cent Theatres," *MPW* 1, no. 38 (23 November 1907): 615.

16. "Copy of Editorial in Chicago Tribune Referred to by Mr. Kleine/The Five Cent Theaters," *MPW* 1, no. 7 (20 April 1907): 101; "Trade Notes," *MPW* 1, no. 17 (29 June 1907): 263–64; "Trade Notes," *MPW* 1, no. 33 (19 October 1907): 524.

17. "Wake Up," *MPW* 1, no. 36 (9 November 1907): 575. Also see, for Cleveland, Ohio, "Trade Notes," *MPW* 1, no. 39 (30 November 1907): 629–30; "Trade Notes," *MPW* 1, no. 40 (7 December 1907): 645. For Nebraska City, Nebraska, see "Trade Notes," *MPW* 1, no. 40 (7 December 1907): 646.

18. Hans Leigh, "A Coffin for the Theatorium," *MPW* 2, no. 8 (23 February 1908): 135.

19. "A National Board of Censorship," *MPW* 4, no. 25 (19 June 1909): 825.

20. "Trade Notes," *MPW* 1, no. 11 (18 May 1907): 168; "Impelled to Slay by Picture Show," *MPW* 3, no. 7 (15 August 1908): 122. Promoters of movies, however, countered with evidence that youngsters could make up stories to appeal to judges. After the New York *World* attacked motion pictures in 1910 because of a young boy's "so-called confession," *Moving Picture World* turned up evidence that the child had "a record of several terms in the reformatory." The paper queried whether his answers would get him out of jail. "Childish Innocence Corrupted," *MPW* 7, no. 15 (8 October 1910): 805.

21. "Public Opinion," *MPW* 3, no. 16 (17 October 1908): 298.

22. The concern regarding effects on children continued. See, for instance, Lea Jacobs, "Reformers and Spectators: The Film Education Movement in the Thirties," regarding 1930s social scientific approaches to gauging children's responses to filmic images and specific organized attempts to teach children to be model spectators, including "improving popular taste" (p. 37).

23. *Moving Picture World* started reviewing films in the fall of 1908 as the difficulties with some reformers and legal authorities continued ("Comments on Film Subjects," *MPW* 3, no. 14 [3 October 1908]: 253). *Variety* started sporadically commenting on films in 1907. Exhibitors often wrote letters agreeing with or disputing reviewers' judgments. Hence, we have some evidence of correspondence (or lack of it) between exhibitors and reviewers. *Moving Picture World* was particularly sensitive to speaking for the exhibitors and supported their points of view (over the manufacturers) in most cases.

24. " 'An Unexpected Guest,' " *MPW* 5, no. 9 (28 August 1909): 283.

25. The review also jibes with the way realist and naturalist fiction and drama were being received at the time.

26. See the tracts and novels described in chapters 2 and 5.

27. "Comments on Film Subjects," *MPW* 4, no. 18 (1 May 1909): 556.

28. George Blaisdell, " 'The Scarlet Letter' (Kinema-Color)," *MPW* 16, no. 6 (10 May 1913): p. 599.

29. " 'The Call' (Biograph)," *Variety,* 20 January 1910.

30. John Bogart, "Another Exhibitor Registers a Kick," *MPW* 2, no. 23 (6 June 1908): 495. Also see Rush [pseud.], " 'Francesca di Rimini' (Dramatic)," *Variety,* 22 February 1908.

31. "Comments on the Films," *MPW* 10, no. 11 (16 December 1911): 905.

32. Having two reviews is unusual, suggesting some disagreement among the staff. The more positive review was published first.

33. "Facts and Comments," *MPW* 10, no. 13 (30 December 1911): 1052.

34. "Comments on Film Subjects," *MPW* 3, no. 14 (3 October 1908): 253; "Comments on Film Subjects," *MPW* 3, no. 26 (26 December 1908): 525.

35. The dates for these films are both 1908. In chapter 4 I discuss Richard Abel's research indicating that Pathé and other French films may well have been targets of U.S. manufacturers who, along with the National Board of Censorship, attempted to limit their economic success by using "American" standards of subject matter as barriers to exhibition. Both Abel ("The Perils of Ignoring Pathé") and Miriam Hansen (*Babel and Babylon*) discuss the *Moving Picture World* essay, "What Is an American Subject?" (22 January 1910), p. 82, as an explicit declaration of nativism. However, it is obvious that the subject matter and treatment of sexuality in French films had been troublesome prior to the formation of the board. That is not to say that the

film manufacturers did not take advantage of the board's creation and those conservative attitudes to try to limit Pathé's success in the U.S. market.

36. "Comments on the Films," *MPW* 12, no. 11 (15 June 1912): 1026.

37. "Comments on the Films," *MPW* 13, no. 9 (31 August 1912): 881.

38. Lux Graphicus [pseud.], "On the Screen," *MPW* 4, no. 22 (29 May 1909): 714.

39. "Comments on the Week's Films," *MPW* 5, no. 21 (20 November 1909): 719.

40. "Comments on the Films," *MPW* 14, no. 2 (12 October 1912): 124.

41. "Comments on the Films," *MPW* 12, no. 6 (11 May 1912): 527.

42. The review of *One Good Joke Deserves Another* in *Moving Picture World* does not correspond with the film from the Netherlands Filmmuseum shown at Pordenone Film Festival in 1987 under that title. See "Comments on the Films," *MPW* 17, no. 2 (12 July 1913): 204. I saw no other review during that period, however, that matched the plot. Neither did I find a review for *A Florida Enchantment* in *Moving Picture World*.

43. "Mr. Whitney Raymond," *MPW* 11, no. 8 (24 February 1912): 691.

44. See Allan Bérubé, *Coming Out under Fire*, pp. 71–76, on Julian Eltinge and female impersonation in the period 1900 to 1930.

45. " 'A Florida Enchantment,' " *Variety*, 14 August 1914.

46. Some historians of sexuality notice that homosexuality and cross-dressing become more obvious in the late 1800s. Perhaps at this point the threat to heterosexuality of such alternative practices was still insufficient to raise concerns requiring suppression. Cross-dressing, of course, remains a favorite comedy device throughout the twentieth century, although stereotypes and "realistic" representations of gays and lesbians would be prohibited by later representation codes.

47. "Comments on Film Subjects," *MPW* 4, no. 10 (6 March 1909): 269.

48. "Comments on the Films," *MPW* 17, no. 8 (23 August 1913): 845. Also see reviews for " 'When Women Win' (Lubin)," *Variety*, 27 November 1909, and " 'Just Like a Woman,' " *Variety*, 11 July 1908.

49. "Comments on the Films," *MPW* 17, no. 11 (13 September 1913): 1176.

50. "Comments on Film Subjects," *MPW* 3, no. 26 (26 December 1908): 526; "Comments on Film Subjects," *MPW* 3, no. 24 (12 December 1908): 476.

51. "Comments on the Films," *MPW* 12, no. 1 (6 April 1912): 40.

52. "Comments on the Films," *MPW* 14, no. 8 (23 November 1912): 769.

53. " 'Odd Pair of Limbs,' " *Variety*, 23 May 1908. The same sort of joke seems to occur in *A Queen of Burlesque*. " 'A Queen of Burlesque' (Edison)," *Variety*, 19 February 1910.

54. " 'The Gangsters,' (Keystone)," *MPW* 16, no. 9 (31 May 1913): 922.

55. " 'Lady Godiva' (Vitagraph)," *MPW* 10, no. 3 (21 October 1911): 214; "Comments on the Films," *MPW* 10, no. 5 (4 November 1911): 379; W. Stephen Bush, "Gauging the Public Taste," *MPW* 12, no. 6 (11 May 1912): 505.

56. Do note my discussion at the beginning of the chapter that photographs of nudes at this time were permitted.

57. Sime [pseud.], " 'The Hypocrites,' " *Variety*, 7 November 1914.

58. John Collier, "Censorship in Action, III," *Survey* 7 (August 1915): 426.

59. Hansen, *Babel and Babylon*, pp. 65–70, is excellent in describing examples of such calls for "uplift." Hansen continues to argue that not many of the films produced during this period (1907–12) actually tackled social issues of ethnicity or class. She also questions whether what I am about to describe as the "total-picture theory" about viewing worked. I would agree with her that it is very suspect to think spectators did what they were supposed to do. What I am examining here is what was being argued would work, who won in the argument, and why.

60. Christine Gledhill, "The Melodramatic Field: An Investigation"; Marcia Landy, "Introduction"; E. Ann Kaplan, *Motherhood and Representation*; Gledhill, "Between Melodrama and

Realism: Anthony Asquith's *Underground* and King Vidor's *The Crowd*." I shall be using the term *melodrama* here as it has been employed in literary and film criticism, not as it has been used by U.S. film reviewers. See the important discussion of the term *melodrama* in the trade press between 1930 and 1960 in Steve Neale, "Melotalk: On the Meaning and Use of the Term 'Melodrama' in the American Trade Press."

61. Gledhill, "Melodramatic Field," p. 16.

62. Ibid., pp. 17–23, following the work of Peter Brooks, Frank Rahill, and Nicholas Vardac.

63. As I have discussed elsewhere, rather than employ "wide gestures, large body movements, statuesque poses and highly-modulated voices"—the thespian choice for tragedy and melodrama—the new acting style emphasized "reducing extreme body movement and gestures, increasing work on facial gestures and developing peculiar, incidental, character details." Janet Staiger, " 'The Eyes Are Really the Focus,' " pp. 16–17. Numerous causes and events occurred to facilitate this; my account is abbreviated.

64. Gledhill, "Melodramatic Field," p. 34.

65. Horace Newcomb, *The Naturalist "Movement" in America*, p. 33.

66. Ibid., pp. 221–43.

67. Jay Martin, *Harvests of Change: American Literature, 1865–1914*, pp. 247–48.

68. John G. Cawelti, *Adventure, Mystery, and Romance*, p. 261.

69. Gledhill, "Between Melodrama and Realism," p. 165.

70. This argument has been influenced by reading Newcomb, *The Naturalist "Movement" in America*.

71. Gunning, *D. W. Griffith*, pp. 164–65.

72. Gunning states at the start of his book that he is studying a narrator system that Griffith used during the first two years of his filmmaking. However, as Gunning continues, he assumes the phrase "the narrator system." A casual reader might become confused, assuming that Griffith's system is equal to one evidenced in or directly leading to the classical Hollywood narrational system. However, Griffith's strategies are neither complete nor always a direct route to what would become standard practices. The same caution should be applied to Gunning's phrase "the moral voice."

73. As I have mentioned, "looking-into-keyhole" movies were gimmicks. *The 100-to-1 Shot* (Vitagraph, 1906) relies on point-of-view editing to convey the feelings of the protagonist as he watches his horse win the race. For other examples, see Kristin Thompson, "The Continuity System," in Bordwell, Staiger, and Thompson, *The Classical Hollywood Cinema*, pp. 198–99.

74. Ibid., pp. 174–93.

75. Besides Thompson, also see Janet Staiger, " 'The Eyes Are Really the Focus': Photoplay Acting and Film Form and Style."

76. It might be worth thinking through the implications of the fact that Anita Loos seems to have been the woman screenwriter who innovated the ironic-voice intertitle around 1915.

4: From Boston to Bombay

1. Usually a distinction is made between voluntary alteration of films on the advice of preview boards and the required elimination of material by boards or individuals authorized by law to insist upon those changes prior to exhibition. The voluntary process is termed *self-regulation;* the required procedure is called *censorship.*

2. The routine of attack by some minority group and a counterattack by the film industry would become habit. What occurred in New York City in 1908–9 also happened in the early 1920s and again in 1930 and 1934. In fact, even the "codes" of regulation in 1909 would be repeated by those who claimed that they would finally clean up the movies in 1922 and in the early 1930s. These codes were predominantly directed toward controlling representations of

crime and violence, preserving sensibilities of conservatives in regard to sexual mores, and protecting the dignity of (some) minorities who might take offense at stereotypes of themselves. Only the move after World War II to market segmentation and targeted, specialized audiences broke this pattern. Even now, certain remnants of the regulatory defense remain in the audience advisory rating system of X, R, PG-13, and so forth.

3. I am describing the situation in larger towns here. It was different in smaller places or rural areas. However, the activities of the business were significantly influenced by these more populous places.

4. Dan Quayle's problem with Murphy Brown having a child out of wedlock was not that she had the child, but that she was getting away with it—there was no moral or social retribution for her wrong choice.

5. Michael Budd, "The National Board of Review and the Early Art Cinema in New York," p. 11.

6. Epes Winthrop Sargent, *The Technique of the Photoplay*, p. 116.

7. "Sociological," *MPW* 8, no. 13 (1 April 1911): 709.

8. A study of Chicago's early cinema and its censorship is found in Kathleen McCarthy, "Nickel Vice and Virtue: Movie Censorship in Chicago, 1907–1915."

9. "Chicago Censorship," *MPW* 18, no. 11 (13 December 1913): 1265.

10. "The Censorship in Chicago," *MPW* 5, no. 15 (9 October 1909): 487.

11. "Trade Notes," *MPW* 1, no. 10 (11 May 1907): 153; "Trade Notes," *MPW* 1, no. 11 (18 May 1907): 170; Terry Ramsaye, *A Million and One Nights: A History of the Motion Picture through 1925*, pp. 473–75. Daniel Czitrom has recently published a good version of these events, "The Politics of Performance."

12. Here and elsewhere it is sometimes difficult to determine what films are being discussed, because titles are often not given. The film version of the Thaw-White trial that I discussed in chapter 3 was *The Unwritten Law* (Lubin, 1907). I can find no other versions of the incidents produced around 1907, although they may have been made by then. Ramsaye indicates that the film in question in this instance was *The Great Thaw Trial* (*A Million and One Nights*, p. 475) and Kevin Brownlow indicates the same but also discusses another film, *The Thaw-White Tragedy* (*Behind the Mask of Innocence*, pp. 4–5).

13. Lewis Jacobs, *The Rise of the American Film: A Critical History*, pp. 62–66; Jane Addams, "The House of Dreams," pp. 75–98. For more on Chicago and the events detailed below, see Ramsaye, *A Million and One Nights*, pp. 473–85; Richard Randall, *Censorship of the Movies: The Social and Political Control of a Mass Medium*, p. 12; Brownlow, *Behind the Mask*, pp. 4–8; Garth Jowett, *Film: The Democratic Art*, pp. 108–116. Chicago's City Council passed in 1907 a requirement for police inspection and licensing of films. This law was affirmed in *Block v. Chicago* by the Illinois Supreme Court in 1909.

14. "Trade Notes," *MPW* 1, no. 14 (8 June 1907): 214, 216; "Trade Notes," *MPW* 1, no. 15 (15 June 1907): 233.

15. "Moving Picture Combine," *MPW* 1, no. 14 (8 June 1907): 223; "Trade Notes," *MPW* 1, no. 17 (29 June 1907): 263–64.

16. "News of the Nickolets," *MPW* 1, no. 32 (12 October 1907): 502.

17. "Unity Is Strength," *MPW* 1, no. 37 (16 November 1907): 591; "The Manufacturers' and Film Renter's Conference," *MPW* 1, no. 38 (23 November 1907): 607; "The Pittsburgh Conference," *MPW* 1, no. 38 (23 November 1907): 608–10; *MPW* 1, no. 42 (21 December 1907): 677.

18. "Trade Notes," *MPW* 1, no. 40 (7 December 1907): 645; "The Sunday Situation in New York," *MPW* 1, no. 41 (14 December 1907): 667–68; "Trade Notes," *MPW* 1, no. 42 (21 December 1907): 683.

19. "Sunday Opening of Nickelodeons" and "Moving Picture Association," *MPW* 1, no. 43

(28 December 1907): 699, 700; "Trade Notes," *MPW* 2, no. 1 (4 January 1908): 708; "Moving Picture Exhibitors' Association," *MPW* 2, no. 4 (25 January 1908): 60.

20. "Will Eliminate Evil Pictures," *MPW* 2, no. 7 (15 February 1908): 116.

21. "Woman's League Investigates," *MPW* 2, no. 8 (23 February 1908): 137.

22. "Nickelodeon versus Saloon," *MPW* 2, no. 20 (16 May 1908): 433. Also see "Nickelodeons and Little Boys," *MPW* 2, no. 24 (13 June 1908): 511; "Moving Pictures Aid Temperance Movement," *MPW* 3, no. 1 (4 July 1908): 6–7; "The Masses Are Being Educated," *MPW* 3, no. 1 (4 July 1908): 7. Naturally, *Moving Picture World* was glad to publish these positive views of the films. What is important here is who is against and who is for moving pictures.

23. "Exhibitors: Keep Up the Standard of the Show," *MPW* 2, no. 11 (14 March 1908): 203. Also see "Those Moving Pictures," *MPW* 3, no. 16 (17 October 1908): 299; "Objectionable Vaudeville," *MPW* 6, no. 11 (19 March 1910): 415; "Low Grade Variety Act One Objection to Picture Shows," *MPW* 6, no. 11 (19 March 1910): 421. The oral, and hence transitory, nature of live acts made their regulation more difficult to handle.

24. "Injunctions against Police Vacated," *MPW* 2, no. 20 (16 May 1908): 437.

25. Tenements were large apartment buildings, not necessarily in poor shape.

26. "Are the Shows in Tenement Houses Doomed?" *MPW* 2, no. 26 (27 June 1908): 539; "Fox Again to the Rescue," *MPW* 3, no. 5 (1 August 1908): 81.

27. Sime [pseud.], " 'The Cracker's Bride,' " *Variety*, 27 March 1909.

28. "Greater New York Exhibitors in Trouble," *MPW* 3, no. 26 (26 December 1908): 523. The film was likely *The 100-to-1 Shot*, but it might also have been a rip-off such as *The Piker's Dream*. See *The Piker's Dream* review in *Variety*, 8 February 1908.

29. "The Christmas Present by Mayor McClellan to the Exhibitors of New York," *MPW* 4, no. 1 (2 January 1909): 3–4.

30. "Censorship for Moving Pictures," *Survey* 22 (3 April 1909): 8–9; Lewis E. Palmer, "The World in Motion," *Survey* 22 (5 June 1909): 364.

31. See Robert Bendiner, "Racketeers and Reformers in City Hall: Fifty Years of the New York Mayoralty," pp. 7–11, 55–56; John Ensor Harr and Peter J. Johnson, *Rockefeller Century*, pp. 106–15; Allan F. Davis, *Spearheads for Reform: The Social Settlements and the Progressive Movement, 1890–1914*, pp. 180–87; Louis Filler, *Muckrakers*, pp. 186–95; Harold C. Syrett, *The Gentleman and the Tiger: The Autobiography of George B. McClellan, Jr.*, pp. 169–235.

32. Charles Parkhurst, *Our Fight with Tammany*, pp. 1–9.

33. Syrett, *The Gentleman and the Tiger*, p. 200.

34. Ibid., pp. 201–2, 205.

35. Murphy had been pushing for a shift in the arenas where protection occurred and alliances were made, from vice to big businesses such as the docks, insurance, printing, and contracting. If one of the distinctions between the reform movement and the progressive movement as described in chapters 1 and 2 was a different sense of the cause of city corruption (either working class and ethnics or big business), the change might well have been due to a change in the crime system itself.

36. Lary May, *Screening Out the Past*, writes that Parkhurst and Anthony Comstock "asked for a public hearing on the movies" (p. 43). I have not been able to substantiate that in any documents from the period. In fact, it is more likely that Chase would have been the minister specifically involved in the situation, although the more general tenor of the reform movement can be attributed to Parkhurst.

37. Two kinds of licenses existed at this time: a $25 annual fee that could be revoked for cause by the license bureau and a $500 annual fee that required a court hearing. "Mayor McClellan's Action Declared Illegal," *MPW* 9, no. 2 (9 January 1909): 32; Lewis E. Palmer, "The World in Motion," *Survey*, 22 (5 June 1909): 364.

38. "The Christmas Present by Mayor McClellan to the Exhibitors of New York," *MPW* 4, no. 1 (2 January 1909): 3–4; "The Recent Closure—The Moral Aspect: Opinions of the Press," *MPW* 9, no. 2 (9 January 1909): 33; W. Stephen Bush, "The Question of Censorship," *MPW* 4, no. 2 (9 January 1909): 32.

39. Bush, "The Question of Censorship," 32.

40. "The Recent Closure—The Moral Aspect: Opinions of the Press," *MPW* 9, no. 2 (9 January 1909): 33; "Urge Law to Shut Shows to Young," *MPW* 4, no. 5 (30 January 1909): 117.

41. "To Reform Motion Pictures," *MPW* 4, no. 6 (6 February 1909): 139; "Censorship of Film Subjects," *MPW* 4, no. 7 (13 February 1909): 165.

42. See the files "National Board of Censorship" and "National Board of Review" at the New York Public Library (Forty-second Street). I have personally reviewed files under MFL, MFL+, and MWEX numbers, as well as clipping files. For background on the People's Institute and details of the board's work, see Robert J. Fisher, "Film Censorship and Progressive Reform"; Charles Matthew Feldman, *The National Board of Censorship (Review) of Motion Pictures, 1909–1922*; Nancy J. Rosenbloom, "Between Reform and Regulation: The Struggle over Film Censorship in Progressive America, 1909–1922"; Rosenbloom, "Progressive Reform, Censorship, and the Motion Picture Industry, 1909–1917"; and Rosenbloom, "In Defense of Moving Pictures: The People's Institute, the National Board of Censorship, and the Problems of Leisure in Urban America." Using the People's Institute papers at the New York Public Library and Cooper Union, Fisher notes that the board's reactions to films after 1916 are stated in publications, but few written opinions exist before then. Feldman provides good information about the internal strife on the board, although that material could use the benefit of papers from the People's Institute and the board that Rosenbloom employs. Tom Gunning, *D. W. Griffith*, pp. 159–60, reproduces some of the board's early reports to manufacturers, including one dated as early as 10 May 1909. William Uricchio and Roberta Pearson's work is in process.

43. Brownlow, *Behind the Mask of Innocence*, pp. 5–8.

44. "The Board of Censorship" and "The Censorship of Film Subjects," *MPW* 4, no. 10 (6 March 1909): 265–66, 266–67.

45. "The Censorship of Film Subjects," *MPW* 4, no. 10 (6 March 1909): 267.

46. "Exhibitors' Association of New York," *MPW* 4, no. 11 (13 March 1909): 300; "Censorship of Film Subjects," *MPW* 4, no. 12 (20 March 1909): 325; "Censorship for Moving Pictures," *Survey* 22 (3 April 1909): 8–9; "Editorial," *MPW* 4, no. 16 (17 April 1909): 467.

47. Howard T. Lewis, *Motion Picture Industry*, pp. 366–91; Frederick James Smith, "The Evolution of the Motion Picture: VIII: From the Standpoint of the Film Censor," *New York Dramatic Mirror* 70, no. 1807 (6 August 1913): 25, 33.

48. "The Progress of the Censorship," *MPW* 4, no. 16 (17 April 1909): 472.

49. Rush [pseud.], " 'The Romance of a Poor Girl' (Pathe)," *Variety*, 23 October 1909.

50. Walt [pseud.], " 'A Change of Heart' (Biograph)," *Variety*, 23 October 1909.

51. Eileen Bowser, ed., *Biograph Bulletins, 1908–1912*, p. 133.

52. Lewis E. Palmer, "The World in Motion," *Survey* 22 (5 June 1909): 363.

53. John Collier, "The Board of Censorship," *MPW* 4, no. 24 (12 June 1909): 797 (italics and capitalization in original). Also see "National Board of Censorship of Motion Pictures," *MPW* 5, no. 16 (16 October 1909): 524–25; letter from Fred'k N. Cooke, Jr., "The Moving Picture in the Church," *MPW* 5, no. 17 (23 October 1909): 577. The letter describes Collier addressing a meeting at the Church of the Ascension, calling for the use of films for education and "socialization."

54. Recall John Cawelti's remarks, recounted in chapter 3, that plausibility was still related to the triumph of virtue over vice.

55. Reported in Feldman, *The National Board of Censorship*, pp. 41–43.

56. Ramsaye, *A Million and One Nights*, pp. 483–84; and Brownlow, *Behind the Mask of Innocence*, p. 8. Ramsaye writes that both men used anti-Semitism in their criticisms; Brownlow, that Chase was "a supporter of the Ku Klux Klan."

57. "The National Censorship Bill," *MPW* 20, no. 2 (11 April 1914): 199.

58. *Mutual Film Corporation v. Industrial Commission of Ohio*, 236 U.S. 230–1. Also see Clarence L. Linz, "Picture Censorship Constitutional," *MPW* 23, no. 10 (6 March 1915): 1419–20.

59. Theodore Schroeder, "Our Prudish Censorship," *Forum* 53 (January 1915): 87–99.

60. John Collier, "Censorship; and the National Board," *Survey* 35 (2 October 1915): 9–14, 31–33, and "Censorship in Action," *Survey* 34 (7 August 1915): 423–27.

61. John Collier, "Censorship in Action," *Survey* 34 (7 August 1915): 425.

62. Ibid., p. 427.

63. Collier, "Censorship; and the National Board," p. 31.

64. Bendiner, "Racketeers," pp. 7–11, 55–56; William Russell Hochman, *William J. Gaynor: The Years of Fruition*, pp. 55–62; Davis, *Spearheads for Reform*, pp. 180–87; Syrett, *Gentleman and the Tiger*, p. 301; Martin J. Norden, "New York Mayor: William J. Gaynor and His City's Film Industry," pp. 78–91.

65. George Kibbe Turner, "Tammany's Control of New York by Professional Criminals," *McClure's Magazine* 33, no. 2 (June 1909): 117–34, and "The Daughters of the Poor: A Plain Story of the Development of New York City as a Leading Center of the White Slave Trade of the World, under Tammany Hall," *McClure's Magazine* 34, no. 1 (November 1909): 45–61; "Murphy and Gaynor Answer Vice Charge," *New York Times*, 25 October 1909, p. 2. Also see S. S. McClure, "The Tammanyizing of a Civilization," *McClure's Magazine* 34, no. 1 (November 1909): 117–28.

66. Turner, "The Daughters of the Poor," pp. 45–47.

67. "Gaynor Again Raps Mayor M'Clellan," *New York Times*, 26 October 1909, p. 2.

68. Lux Graphicus [pseud.], "On the Screen," *MPW* 5, no. 18 (30 October 1909): 602; "New York Exhibitors Endorse Gaynor," *MPW* 5, no. 18 (30 October 1909): 608; "Observations by Our Man about Town," *MPW* 5, no. 20 (13 November 1909): 679. Also see Norden, "New York Mayor," pp. 79–82.

69. "Observations by Our Man about Town," *MPW* 7, no. 5 (30 July 1910): 240; "Observations by Our Man about Town," *MPW* 7, no. 8 (20 August 1910): 404; "More Light on the Anti-I.M.P.A: A Discredited Organization," *MPW* 7, no. 14 (1 October 1910): 738; "The End of the Anti-Immoral Moving Picture Association," *MPW* 7, no. 17 (22 October 1910): 918. Commentators of the period recognized that some of the rationale behind the calls for banning the Jeffries-Johnson fight film was motivated by racism. As C. W. Lawford wrote in *Moving Picture World* (7, no. 5 [30 July 1910]: 236), "This national outburst is the culmination of a general disappointment because a white man could not hold the championship belt." On films and juveniles, Gaynor was quoted as saying, "I have seen the moving pictures repeatedly and find little fault with them; the faults [about juvenile crime] rather lie with the parents whose control of their children needs strengthening and to be made more vigilant." W. H. Jackson, "A Sociological Study," *MPW* 8, no. 15 (15 April 1911): 818.

70. "Moving Picture Inquiry in New York City," *MPW* 7, no. 27 (31 December 1910): 1532; Raymond B. Fosdick, "A Report on the Condition of Moving Picture Shows in New York, March 22, 1911," City of New York, 1911. Also see "Interesting Report," *MPW* 8, no. 19 (13 May 1911): 1056–57.

71. "Mayor Gaynor's Committee," *MPW* 8, no. 18 (6 May 1911): 995; "New York Picture Theatre Ordinance Discussed," *MPW* 10, no. 7 (18 November 1911): 543–45; "Another Picture Ordinance," *MPW* 10, no. 11 (16 December 1911): 891–93; John Collier, " 'Movies' and the Law," reprint from *Survey*, 20 January 1912, in the New York Public Library clipping file.

72. "Major Gaynor Wants Action," *MPW* 12, no. 6 (11 May 1912): 515; "New Censorship

Proposed," *MPW* 12, no. 3 (20 April 1912): 222; "Folks Ordinance Passed," *MPW* 14, no. 13 (28 December 1912): 1274.

73. "Mayor Gaynor's Veto," *MPW* 15, no. 2 (11 January 1913): 135. Also see W. Stephen Bush, "Mayor Gaynor on Censorship," *MPW* 15, no. 2 (11 January 1913): 134–35.

74. "Facts and Comments," *MPW* 17, no. 3 (19 July 1913): 295; "New York Picture Theater Ordinance," *MPW* 17, no. 5 (2 August 1913): 326–27.

75. "An Interesting Statement by Madame Alice Blache of the Solax Company," *Motion Picture News* 6, no. 26 (28 December 1912): 17.

5: The White Slave

1. "Sex O'Clock in America," *Current Opinion* 55, no. 2 (August 1913): 113.

2. All three films are also feature length, permitting an extended development of character and subplots. Thus, they are good articulations of the narrational methods in place by the early teens, methods that would develop into the classical Hollywood film.

3. This is an old proposition, taken from Vladimir Propp, the Russian Formalists, and the narratologists of the most recent generation of textual critics.

4. Jonathan Dollimore, *Sexual Dissidence*, pp. 86–87.

5. Annette Kuhn, *Cinema, Censorship and Sexuality, 1909–1925*, p. 113.

6. R[ichard] V. S[pencer], "Scenario Construction," *MPW* 8, no. 6 (11 February 1911): 294.

7. Kathleen Karr indicates that in films the "square-up" starts around 1912. The "square-up" was a "prefatory moralistic statement of apology for contemplating the discussion of nefarious subjects" (Karr, "The Long Square-Up: Exploitation Trends in the Silent Film," p. 108). This narrational strategy had a long history in literature.

8. E[pes] W[inthrop] Sargent, "Technique of the Photoplay," *MPW* 9, no. 6 (19 August 1911): 450. Also see Epes Winthrop Sargent, "Technique of the Photoplay," *MPW* 9, no. 2 (22 July 1911): 109; "Detroit Police Make Rules," *MPW* 9, no. 4 (5 August 1911): 279; Epes Winthrop Sargent, "The Scenario Writer," *MPW* 11, no. 4 (27 January 1912): 294.

9. Agnes Repplier, "Repeal of Reticence," p. 301.

10. John D. Rockefeller Jr., "The Awakening of a New Conscience," *Medical Review of Reviews* 19 (May 1913): 289–91.

11. A major source for the business background of *Traffic in Souls* is Terry Ramsaye, *A Million and One Nights*, pp. 612–19. Robert C. Allen, "Traffic in Souls," and Garth Jowett, *Film: The Democratic Art*, pp. 63–64, rely heavily upon Ramsaye for production and exhibition details. Kay Sloan, *The Loud Silents: Origins of the Social Problem Film*, pp. 80–86, gives a solid introduction and social context to the film, including the racist and antifamily fears generated by prostitution. See Kevin Brownlow, *Behind the Mask of Innocence*, pp. 70–85, for the most recent and best discussion of the film's production. Ben Brewster, "Traffic in Souls: An Experiment in Feature-Length Narrative Construction," analyzes to what degree the film is formally a feature-length narrative rather than one that retains traits of shorter constructions. For a slighter version of my thesis, see Shelley Stamp Lindsay, "Wages and Sin: Traffic in Souls and the White Slavery Scare." Lindsay took my course in American film in the fall of 1986 when I lectured on *Traffic in Souls* from the perspective of this book, introducing her to the connection between the film and its meanings within the context of American social change and representations of female sexuality. My interpretation has changed somewhat since then.

According to the American Film Institute catalog for feature films in the teens, Rockefeller asserted: "The use of my name in any such connection is absolutely unauthorized, and . . . I and those associated with me in this work [of the Bureau of Social Hygiene] regard this method of exploiting vice as not only injudicious but positively harmful." Quoted from the *New York Dramatic Mirror*, 17 December 1913, p. 944.

12. George Blaisdell, " 'Traffic in Souls,' " *MPW* 18, no. 8 (22 November 1913): 849.

13. At this time "white slavery" could be defined as broadly as prostitution in general or more narrowly as tricking, drugging, and imprisoning women in brothels. The narrow definition occurs first, widening to the larger meaning later.

14. Roy Lubove, "The Progressive and the Prostitute," p. 312; Louis Filler, *Muckrakers*, pp. 286–95.

15. Ellen Carol DuBois and Linda Gordon, "Seeking Ecstasy on the Battlefield" indicate that women reformers in the late 1800s attempted to raise the age of consent for sex for young girls. The age had been as low as nine or ten. This act produced a "new class of female offenders: teenage sex delinquents" (p. 38). Also see Steven Schlossman and Stephanie Wallach, "The Crime of Precocious Sexuality," who argue that the progressive reform, with its emphasis on using the state to regulate behavior, was a major contribution in making deviant previously acceptable levels of sexual exploration by women.

16. John Ensor Harr and Peter J. Johnson, *Rockefeller Century*, pp. 106–15; Raymond B. Fosdick, *John D. Rockefeller, Jr.: A Portrait*, pp. 137–40; Fosdick, *Chronicle of a Generation*, pp. 90–125. Fosdick reported that Gaynor had said of moral reformer Parkhurst: "He thinks he is pious when he is only bilious" (p. 91).

17. George Kibbe Turner, "The City of Chicago: A Study of the Great Immoralities," *McClure's Magazine* 28, no. 6 (April 1907): 575–92.

18. Ernest A. Bell, *Fighting the Traffic*, title page, pp. 25–26, 107–10, 289–304.

19. Clifford Roe, *Panders and Their White Slaves*, pp. 11–18, 26.

20. " 'Recruiting Stations of Vice,' " *MPW* 6, no. 10 (12 March 1910): 370–71.

21. "First Report Made on White Slave Traffic," *Survey* 23 (18 December 1909): n.p.

22. "The Common Welfare: Report of Chicago Vice Commission," *Survey* 26 (15 April 1911): 99; Graham Taylor, "The Story of the Chicago Vice Commission," *Survey* 26 (6 May 1911): 243; Vice Commission of Chicago, *The Social Evil in Chicago*, p. 25.

23. O. Edward Janney, *The White Slave Traffic in America*, pp. 66–67.

24. Vice Commission of Minneapolis, *Report of the Vice Commission of Minneapolis to His Honor, James C. Haynes, Mayor*, p. 76.

25. Florence Kelley, "The Economic Causes of Prostitution," *Social Diseases* 3, no. 3 (July 1912): 9; Arthur B. Spingairn, *Laws Relating to Sex Morality in New York City*, p. xiii; Jane Addams, *A New Conscience and an Ancient Evil*, p. 5; "Facts about the Department Store," *Nation* 97, no. 2509 (31 July 1913): 94–95. Also see Arthur W. Calhoun, *A Social History of the American Family, From Colonial Times to the Present*, pp. 89–90.

26. Vice Commission of Philadephia, *A Report on Existing Conditions with Recommendations to the Honorable Rudolph Blankenburg, Mayor of Philadelphia*, p. 16.

27. Laura Hapke, *Girls Who Went Wrong*, pp. 2–3, 17–18.

28. Clifford Roe, *Horrors of the White Slave Trade*, pp. 27–66. Also see, as an example of the woman-as-victim thesis, Arthur Gleason, "The Story of Rosalinda," *Collier's* 51 (10 May 1913): 16, 28, 30.

29. *"The Girl That Goes Wrong,"* *Survey* 27, no. 19 (10 February 1912): 1747–48.

30. As indicated above, the National Board of Censorship passed *Traffic in Souls* with several deletions and with some concern. Based on his research (unpublished), Mark Langer has indicated to me that he believes that the financial involvement by the Shuberts (theatrical producers) helped protect *A Traffic in Souls*. The Shuberts had good connections in New York City politics.

31. " 'The Past Forgiven' (Solax),—May 14," *MPW* 16, no. 8 (24 May 1913): 813.

32. Women could drug men, too. *How They Do Things on the Bowery* has an unsuspecting rube fooled by a city woman who steals his money after she has drugged him. In *Foul Play* (Vi-

tagraph, 1906), the trick is turned to the good when the wife is seeking information from her husband's friend to show that the friend framed her spouse. Also see *The Fatal Hour*.

33. David Shipman, *Caught in the Act: Sex and Eroticism in the Movies*, pp. 11–13.

34. "Comments on the Films," *MPW* 17, no. 11 (13 September 1913): 1177. Also see the manufacturer's notice: " 'A Fight against Evil' (Universal)," *MPW* 17, no. 13 (27 September 1913): 1396 (at this point Universal was a distributing company releasing films made by manufacturers such as Rex); "Comments on the Films," *MPW* 18, no. 5 (1 November 1913): 498.

35. "Comments on the Films," *MPW* 18, no. 10 (6 December 1913): 1152.

36. Ramsaye, *A Million and One Nights*, pp. 612–19.

37. The version of *Traffic in Souls* that I am referring to is a 16mm print distributed in the United States by Budget Films. Lauren Rabinovitz informs me that the National Film Archive print shown at the 1993 Pordenone film festival includes additional material at the end of the movie: a newspaper headline indicating that Trubus committed suicide and that his daughter had become insane and a scene in which Burke asks his captain for time off to wed Mary.

38. I shall refer to the characters as they are named in the intertitles of the film. An adaptation of the movie by Mabel Condon appears in *Photoplay*, Feb. 1914, pp. 33–44ff., which provides a name for Little Sister (Lorna) and other people in the film. The adaptation confirms the interpretations that I am giving to the denotative meanings of some of the events.

39. Many movies of this period make such jokes about do-gooders. See *The Deacon's Troubles* (Keystone, 1912).

40. " 'Traffic in Souls,' " *Variety*, 28 November 1913, p. 12. This may seem somewhat flimsy evidence, but I would argue that at least in New York City, Rockefeller's association with such activities might have easily produced this reception of the text. Moreover, making Rockefeller a villain is quite in line with his (and his father's) general image for the period. Brownlow, *Behind the Mask of Innocence*, also gives the reference credence in his discussion of the film.

41. See Aileen S. Kraditor, *The Ideas of the Woman Suffrage Movement 1890–1920*, p. 60.

42. The country girl, the Swedish immigrants, and the Bartons are Anglo-Saxons. I have not made a point about this, however, since all of the slavers are, as well. Thus, the Turner thesis about non-Anglo foreigners running the traffic is not being used in this film. One African-American does appear, and that is as a maid in the brothel. The minor appearance is not insignificant, since a thesis I mentioned was that blacks were forced to work in such places. However, no narrative attention is placed on the maid; she seems to exist as a realistic detail. The ideology and racism are explicit in that gesture of reducing the woman's existence to the level of a mere prop.

43. Numerous examples of this strong woman protagonist exist. One of my favorite reviews of this type of film is for *The Heroine of the Forge*. "The heroine is athletic but lovable, and one can see why the man whom she saves and his mother both fall in love with her." "Comments on Film Subjects," *MPW* 4, no. 4 (23 January 1909): 93. On the serial queen, see Ben Singer, "Female Power in the Serial-Queen Melodrama: The Etiology of an Anomaly." I'm not sure she *is* an anomaly.

44. Edison was perceived as an entrepreneur, although he was involved in large-scale research and design strategies and his companies were protected as patent monopolies. However, since he was publicly perceived as more the small businessman, the film might also be said to be contrasting Edison as cottage craftsperson with Rockefeller as monopoly capitalist.

45. According to *Moving Picture World*, there were to be three daily shows, but good business resulted in a fourth show in the afternoon. " 'Traffic in Souls' Makes Hit," *MPW* 18, no. 10 (6 December 1913): 1157.

46. Blaisdell, " 'Traffic in Souls,' " *MPW* 18, no. 8 (22 November 1913): 849; F [pseud.], [*Traffic in Souls*], *New York Dramatic Mirror* 70, no. 1822 (19 November 1913): 33. Also see Corb [pseud.], "Traffic in Souls," *Variety*, 28 November 1913, p. 12.

47. "The White Slave Films," *Outlook* 106 (17 January 1914): 120–22.

48. Allen, "Traffic in Souls," p. 52; Brownlow, *Behind the Mask of Innocence*, pp. 80–82.

49. Both prints that I viewed were quite jumbled in logic. This seems to be what happened. At any rate, no justice to the white slavers exists within the narrative logic of the movie (at least in either print that I saw).

50. " 'White Slave' Case for Jury Trial," *MPW* 19, no. 6 (7 February 1914): 684; "Facts and Comments," *MPW* 19, no. 12 (21 March 1914): 1503; "Facts and Comments," *MPW* 19, no. 4 (24 January 1914): 387.

6: The Vamp

1. Jason Joy, quoted by Lea Jacobs, *Wages of Sin*, p. 3.

2. In the 1890s, Kipling was a "craze" in the United States, according to Frank Luther Mott, *Golden Multitudes*, pp. 184–88. In particular, *The Vampire and Other Poems* had sales of around 90,000 (about one-sixth of one percent of the U.S. population at that point). The vampire was also the obsession of many paintings of that time. See Bram Dijkstra, *Idols of Perversity: Fantasies of Feminine Evil in Fin-de-Siècle Culture*, pp. 33–51. Dijkstra also reproduces (p. 350) Burne-Jones's "The Vampire" (circa 1897), which was the basis for Selig's 1910 version of the story.

3. Peter Milne, *Motion Picture News* 11, no. 3 (23 January 1915): 47; Margaret L. MacDonald, *MPW* 23, no. 5 (30 January 1915): 677.

4. "D," "*A Fool There Was*," *New York Dramatic Mirror* 73, no. 1883 (20 January 1915): 31. Also see " 'Vampire' Scores in Film Drama," *San Francisco Post*, 1 February 1915, n.p., [New York Public Library Clipping file]; "A Fool There Was," *Variety*, 12 March 1915, p. 24.

5. Rudyard Kipling, "The Vampire," p. 598.

6. Peter Gay, *The Bourgeois Experience*, vol. 1, pp. 200–213.

7. Robert Allen, *Horrible Prettiness*, p. 201.

8. Lewis A. Erenberg, *Steppin' Out*, p. 82.

9. Sumiko Higashi, *Virgins, Vamps, and Flappers*, p. 58.

10. In 1910 Selig produced *The Vampire*, but I have been unable to find a surviving print, and its review in *Moving Picture World* suggests that the plot was unclear: "An attempt to put into pictorial form Sir Edward Burne-Jones' picture and Rudyard Kipling's poem. Perhaps the attempt is successful in that it will be understood by those familiar with the picture and the poem. But what about those unfamiliar with them?" "Comments on the Films," *MPW* 7, no. 22 (26 November 1910): 1236.

11. "Manufacturers' Advance Notes," *MPW* 18, no. 1 (4 October 1913): 51; "Comments on the Films," *MPW* 18, no. 5 (1 November 1913): 496. For a photograph from and notes on the film, see Jay Leyda and Charles Musser, *Before Hollywood: Turn-of-the-Century Film from American Archives*, p. 152.

12. Porter Emerson Browne, *A Fool There Was*. I have read the novel but have been unable to find a copy of the play. Numerous intertexts for the film were available; I have tried to survey only the closest ones.

13. William L. O'Neill, "Divorce in the Progressive Era," p. 252. Also see Allan M. Brandt, *No Magic Bullet*, p. 7; Stuart Ewen, *Captains of Consciousness*, p. 120.

14. Elaine Tyler May, *Great Expectations: Marriage and Divorce in Post-Victorian America*, p. 4; O'Neill, "Divorce in the Progressive Era," pp. 252–53, 256; "The President," *Ladies' Home Journal* 23, no. 10 (September 1906): 17; Kay Sloan, *The Loud Silents*, pp. 78–79.

15. O'Neill, "Divorce in the Progressive Era," pp. 257–62; Arthur W. Calhoun, *A Social History of the American Family*, pp. 8–9.

16. The novel also has Elinor functioning as a critic of the double standard and advocating

divorce. At one point Elinor says, "There are no two codes of ethics. Right is right, and wrong is wrong; and there can be no compromise." Browne, *A Fool There Was*, p. 172.

17. "The Vampire of the Screen," *Green Book*, February 1916, pp. 263–65; Pauline L. Bara, "My Theda Bara," part 2, *Motion Picture Classic* 11, no. 5 (January 1921): 19–20, 79; untitled clipping, *Toledo Blade*, 23 February 1916, New York Public Library Clipping file.

18. Nixola Greeley-Smith, " 'Woman Must Choose to Love or Be Loved,' Says Vampire," *Peoria Journal*, 6 May 1915, New York Public Library Clipping file.

19. Ibid. For other versions of this declaration see Lary May, *Screening Out the Past*, p. 106; Nancy F. Cott, *The Grounding of Modern Feminism*, p. 13.

7: The Butterfly

1. Thorstein Veblen, *The Theory of the Leisure Class*, p. 126.

2. Elaine Tyler May, *Great Expectations*, pp. 77–91.

3. Kenneth M. Roemer, *The Obsolete Necessity: America in Utopian Writings, 1888–1900*, p. 126.

4. Jesse Lynch Williams, "The New Marriage," *Good Housekeeping* 58, no. 2 (February 1914): 181–82.

5. Ibid., p. 182 (italics in original).

6. Fredric Jameson, "Pleasure: A Political Issue," p. 4.

7. "Comments on the Films," *MPW* 14, no. 8 (23 November 1912): 769.

8. The film originally identified the oriental as Hishura Tori. As I shall discuss, tensions in California over racism directed against Japanese immigrants were extremely high at this time. After protests by the Japanese community, later prints of the film gave Tori the name Haka Arakau and labeled him "a Burmese ivory king." The prints I have seen use the Arakau intertitles, but since the period audiences saw the film originally as Hayakawa playing a Japanese individual, I will return to that ethnicity.

9. The film does indicate in a later scene that Richard becomes aware of Tori's attentions. In the scene in which Richard discovers that Edith is ignoring his commands, he sees, through point-of-view shots, Tori physically helping Edith from a car. Richard grabs at the curtain and then, upon Edith's arrival into the room, demands she return the gowns. One might well read his response as due equally to jealousy as to economic need. This recognition by Richard that Tori might be a rival for Edith is displayed elsewhere later in the film but also motivates Richard's following Edith to Tori's home. This permits Richard's appearance just after the shooting. Since Richard continues to allow Edith to behave as she does, this motivational line seems more for the convenience of the plot than really part of the dynamics of the ideology.

10. See particularly Judith Mayne, *The Woman at the Keyhole: Feminism and Women's Cinema*, pp. 31–42. Also see a rejoinder by Sumiko Higashi, "Ethnicity, Class, and Gender in Film: DeMille's *The Cheat*," pp. 112–39. Although I agree with Higashi that the film is "a statement about the impossibility of assimilating 'colored' peoples, no matter how civilized their veneer, and . . . warns against the horrors of miscegenation" (p. 130), I do not agree totally that the "fallen woman . . . is rehabilitated through objectification as spectacle, a strategy that reinforces sexual difference" (p. 130). As I shall stress, agency on Edith Hardy's part is crucial in the redemption.

11. Thomas F. Gossett, *Race: The History of an Idea in America*, pp. 287–90; Oscar Handlin, ed., *Immigration as a Factor in American History*, pp. 171–77.

12. Frank Luther Mott, *Golden Multitudes*, p. 245.

13. Elinor Glyn, *Three Weeks*, p. 275.

14. A letter from Rev. E. Boudinot Stockton complains about a recent film "in which a Queen commits adultery" to get an heir. "Prurient Pictures," *MPW* 21, no. 4 (24 October 1914): 465.

15. W. Stephen Bush, "The Cheat," *MPW* 26, no. 14 (25 December 1915): 2384.

16. Fred [pseud.], "The Cheat," *Variety*, 17 December 1915, p. 18.

17. "Fannie Ward as a Movie Tragedienne," *New York Times*, 13 December 1915, p. 13.

18. John D'Emilio and Estelle B. Freedman, *Intimate Matters*, pp. 231–33.

19. Annette Kuhn, *Cinema, Censorship and Sexuality, 1909–1925*, pp. 33–37. E. Ann Kaplan also provides a useful interpretation of the film in *Motherhood and Representation*, pp. 132–35.

20. Kevin Brownlow, *Behind the Mask of Innocence*, pp. 50–55.

Filmography and Bibliography

Filmography

Listed are the films that I viewed and that I discuss in the text. The abbreviations indicate the source of the print; some of the prints were seen at the various Giornate del Cinema Muto (Pordenone film festivals).

Budget. Budget Distributing Company.
DC 90. Domitor Congress, 1990.
EmGee. EmGee Distributing Company.
Everson. Collection of William K. Everson.
FA. Filmovy Archiv, Prague.
GEH. George Eastman House.
GV. Grapevine Video.
LOC. Library of Congress.
MoMA. Museum of Modern Art, New York, New York.
NF. Netherlands Filmmuseum, Amsterdam.
NFA. National Film Archive, England.
UCLA. University of California at Los Angeles Film and Television Archives.
UW. University of Wisconsin Center for Film and Theater Research.

By Man's Law. Biograph, 1913, W. Christy Cabanne, director; William E. Wing, screenplay. MoMA.
The Cheat. Jesse L. Lasky/Paramount, 1915. Cecil B. DeMille, director; Hector Turnbull and Jeanie Macpherson, screenplay; Alvin Wyckoff, cinematographer; Wilfred Buckland, art director; featuring Jack Dean, Sessue Hayakawa, Fanny Ward. Everson, EmGee.
The Corset Model. Biograph, 1903. LOC.
Dante's Inferno. Helios, 1912. DC 90.
The Draped Model. Biograph, 1902. LOC.
The Fatal Hour. Biograph, 1908. D. W. Griffith, director. LOC.
A Florida Enchantment. Vitagraph, 1914. Sidney Drew, director; Eugene Mullen and Marguerite Bertsch[?], screenplay; Robert A. Stuart, cinematographer; featuring Sidney Drew, Edith Storey, Charles Kent, Jane Morrow. LOC.
A Fool There Was. Fox/Box Office Attractions, 1915. Frank Powell, director; Roy L. McCardell, screenplay; George Schneiderman, cinematographer; featuring Theda Bara, Edward José, Mabel Fremyear, May Allison. MoMA.
Foul Play. Vitagraph, 1906. GEH.
Francesca di Rimini, or, the Two Brothers. Vitagraph, 1907. NFA.
The Gangsters. Keystone, 1913. Henry Lehrman, director. FA.
Hearts and Diamonds. Vitagraph, 1914. George D. Baker, director. GEH.
The Hypocrites. Bosworth/Universal, 1914. Lois Weber, director. LOC.
The Inside of the White Slave Traffic. Social Research Film Corp./Harry E. White, 1913. UW, LOC.

Lady Godiva. Vitagraph, 1911. Charles Kent(?), director. NFA, LOC.
The Lonely Villa. Biograph, 1909. D. W. Griffith, director. LOC.
The Lovesick Maidens of Cuddletown. Vitagraph, 1912. James Young, director. NFA.
Mr. Bolter's Infatuation. Vitagraph, 1912. George D. Baker(?), director. NFA.
Model Posing before a Mirror. Biograph, 1903. LOC.
The Mothering Heart. Biograph, 1913. D. W. Griffith, director. LOC.
The Musketeers of Pig Alley. Biograph, 1912. D. W. Griffith, director. LOC.
One Good Joke Deserves Another. Vitagraph, 1913. Wilfred North, director. NF.
The 100-to-1 Shot. Vitagraph, 1906. MoMA.
Open All Night. Famous Players/Paramount, 1924. Paul Bern, director. UCLA.
The Perils of Pauline. Eclectic Films, 1914. GV.
The Picture Idol. Vitagraph, 1912. NF.
The Pink Pajama Girl. Vitagraph, 1912. NFA.
The Pouting Model. Biograph, 1902. LOC.
Pull Down the Curtains, Suzie. Biograph, 1904. LOC.
Traffic in Souls. IMP/Universal, 1913. George Loane Tucker, director; Walter MacNamara and
     George Loane Tucker, screenplay; featuring June Gail, Ethel Grandin, Matt Morre, William
     Welsh. Budget.
Trapeze Disrobing Act. Edison, 1901. Edwin S. Porter, director. LOC.
An Unexpected Guest. Lubin, 1909. LOC.
The Unwritten Law: Thrilling Drama Based on the Thaw-White Case. Lubin, 1907. MoMA.
The Vampire. Kalem, 1913. Robert Vignola, director. LOC, GEH.
Where Are My Children? Universal, 1916. Lois Weber Smalley and Phillips Smalley, writers and
     producers; L. Payton and F. Hale, story source. LOC.

Journals

Current Opinion, 1913
Ladies' Home Journal, 1900, 1906–12, 1915
McClure's Magazine, 1907–9
Moving Picture World, 1907–17
Nickelodeon/Motography, 1909, 1912–14
Outlook, 1913–14
Photoplay, 1913–15
Survey, 1909–15
Variety (film reviews), 1907–10

Books and Articles

Abel, Richard. "The Perils of Ignoring Pathé." Unpublished paper, Drake University, 1993.
     Photocopy.
Addams, Jane. "The House of Dreams." In *The Spirit of Youth and City Streets.* 1909. Reprint.
     Urbana: University of Illinois Press, 1972.
_____. *A New Conscience and an Ancient Evil.* New York: Macmillan, 1912.
Allen, Robert C. *Horrible Prettiness: Burlesque and American Culture.* Chapel Hill: University of
     North Carolina Press, 1991.
_____. "Traffic in Souls." *Sight and Sound* 44, no. 1 (1975): 50–52.
Banner, Lois W. *American Beauty.* Chicago: University of Chicago Press, 1983.
Barton, Michael. "The Victorian Jeremiad: Critics of Accumulation and Display." In *Consuming*

Visions: Accumulation and Display of Goods in America, 1880–1920, edited by Simon J. Bronner, pp. 55–71. New York: Norton, 1989.

Baudry, Jean-Louis. "The Apparatus" [1975]. Translated by Jean Andrews and Bertrand Augst. *camera obscura*, no. 1 (Fall 1976): 104–26.

———. "Ideological Effects of the Basic Cinematographic Apparatus" [1970]. Translated by Alan Williams. *Film Quarterly* 28, no. 2 (Winter 1974–75): 39–47.

Bell, Ernest A. *Fighting the Traffic in Young Girls; or, War on the White Slave Trade*. N.p.: G. S. Ball, 1910.

Bendiner, Robert. "Racketeers and Reformers in City Hall: Fifty Years of the New York Mayoralty." *Park East*, September 1941, pp. 6–11, 55–56.

Bérubé, Allan. *Coming Out under Fire: The History of Gay Men and Women in World War Two*. New York: Free Press, 1990.

Birken, Lawrence. *Consuming Desire: Sexual Science and the Emergence of a Culture of Abundance, 1871–1914*. Ithaca, N.Y.: Cornell University Press, 1988.

Blair, Karen. *The Clubwoman as Feminist: True Womanhood Redefined, 1868–1914*. New York: Holmes and Meier, 1980.

Bordwell, David, Janet Staiger, and Kristin Thompson. *The Classical Hollywood Cinema: Film Style and Mode of Production to 1960*. London: Routledge and Kegan Paul, 1985.

Bowser, Eileen, ed. *Biograph Bulletins, 1908–1912*. New York: Octagon Books, 1973.

Brandt, Allan M. *No Magic Bullet: A Social History of Venereal Disease in the United States since 1880*. New York: Oxford University Press, 1985.

Brandt, Günther. *The Origins of American Sociology: A Study in the Ideology of Social Science, 1865–1895*. Ann Arbor, Mich.: University Microfilms, 1974.

Brewster, Ben. "Traffic in Souls: An Experiment in Feature-Length Narrative Construction." *Cinema Journal* 31, no. 1 (Fall 1991): 37–56.

Bronner, Simon J. "Introduction." In *Consuming Visions: Accumulation and Display of Goods in America, 1880–1920*, edited by Simon J. Bronner, pp. 1–11. New York: Norton, 1989.

———. "Reading Consumer Culture." In *Consuming Visions: Accumulation and Display of Goods in America, 1880–1920*, edited by Simon J. Bronner, pp. 13–53. New York: Norton, 1989.

Browne, Porter Emerson. *A Fool There Was*. New York: Grosset and Dunlap, 1909.

Brownlow, Kevin. *Behind the Mask of Innocence: Sex, Violence, Prejudice, Crime: Films of Social Conscience in the Silent Era*. New York: Knopf, 1990.

Budd, Mike. "The National Board of Review and the Early Art Cinema in New York: The Cabinet of Dr. Caligari as Affirmative Culture." *Cinema Journal* 26, no. 1 (Fall 1986): 3–18.

Burnham, John C. "The Progressive Era Revolution in American Attitudes about Sex." *Journal of American History* 59, no. 4 (March 1973): 885–908.

Butler, Judith. *Gender Trouble: Feminism and the Subversion of Identity*. New York: Routledge, 1990.

Calhoun, Arthur W. *A Social History of the American Family: From Colonial Times to the Present*. Vol. 3. Cleveland: Clark, 1919.

Cawelti, John G. *Adventure, Mystery, and Romance: Formula Stories as Art and Popular Culture*. Chicago: University of Chicago Press, 1976.

Committee of Fifteen. *The Social Evil, with Special Reference to Conditions Existing in the City of New York*. New York: Putnam, 1902.

Conn, Peter. *The Divided Mind: Ideology and Imagination in America, 1898–1917*. Cambridge: Cambridge University Press, 1983.

Connelly, Mark Thomas. *The Response to Prostitution in the Progressive Era*. Chapel Hill: University of North Carolina Press, 1980.

Cott, Nancy F. *The Grounding of Modern Feminism*. New Haven, Conn.: Yale University Press, 1987.

Crunden, Robert M. *Ministers of Reform: The Progressives' Achievement in American Civilizations, 1889–1920*. New York: Basic Books, 1982.

Curry, Lily. *A Bohemian Tragedy*. Philadelphia: Peterson, 1886.

Czitrom, Daniel. "The Politics of Performance: From Theater Licensing to Movie Censorship in Turn-of-the-Century New York." *American Quarterly* 44, no. 4 (December 1992): 525–53.

Daintrey, Laura. *Eros*. Chicago: Belford, Clarke, 1888.

Davidson, Arnold I. "Sex and the Emergence of Sexuality." *Critical Inquiry* 14, no. 1 (Autumn 1987): 16–48.

Davis, Allen F. *Spearheads for Reform: The Social Settlements and the Progressive Movement, 1890–1914*. New York: Oxford University Press, 1967.

Degler, Carl N. "What Ought to Be and What Was: Women's Sexuality in Nineteenth Century America." *American Historical Review* 79 (December 1974): 1467–90.

de Lauretis, Teresa. "Technologies of Gender." In *Technologies of Gender: Essays on Theory, Film and Fiction*, pp. 1–30. Bloomington: Indiana University Press, 1987.

D'Emilio, John, and Estelle B. Freedman. *Intimate Matters: A History of Sexuality in America*. New York: Harper and Row, 1988.

Dijkstra, Bram. *Idols of Perversity: Fantasies of Feminine Evil in Fin-de-Siècle Culture*. New York: Oxford University Press, 1986.

Di Lauro, Al, and Gerald Rabkin. *Dirty Movies: An Illustrated History of the Stag Film, 1915–1970*. New York: Chelsea House, 1976.

Dimaggio, Paul. "Cultural Entrepreneurship in Nineteenth-Century Boston: The Creation of an Organizational Base for High Culture in America." *Media, Culture and Society* 4, no. 4 (January 1982): 33–50.

Dollimore, Jonathan. *Sexual Dissidence: Augustine to Wilde, Freud to Foucault*. Oxford: Clarendon Press, 1991.

Dorr, Rheta Childe. *What Eight Million Women Want*. Boston: Small, Maynard, 1910.

DuBois, Ellen Carol, and Linda Gordon. "Seeking Ecstasy on the Battlefield: Danger and Pleasure in Nineteenth-Century Feminist Sexual Thought." In *Pleasure and Danger: Exploring Female Sexuality*, edited by Carole S. Vance, pp. 31–49. London: Routledge and Kegan Paul, 1984.

Eagleton, Terry. *Literary Theory: An Introduction*. Minneapolis: University of Minnesota Press, 1983.

Erenberg, Lewis A. *Steppin' Out: New York Nightlife and the Transformation of American Culture, 1890–1930*. Westport, Conn.: Greenwood Press, 1981.

Ewen, Elizabeth. "City Lights: Immigrant Women and the Rise of the Movies." *Signs* 5, no. 3 (1980): S45–S65.

Ewen, Stuart. *Captains of Consciousness: Advertising and the Social Roots of the Consumer Culture*. New York: McGraw-Hill, 1976.

Featherstone, Mike, ed. *Global Culture: Nationalism, Globalization and Modernity*. London: Sage, 1990.

Fee, Elizabeth. "The Sexual Politics of Victorian Social Anthropology." In *Clio's Consciousness Raised: New Perspectives on the History of Women*, edited by Mary Hartman and Lois W. Banner, pp. 86–102. New York: Harper and Row, 1974.

Feldman, Charles Matthew. *The National Board of Censorship (Review) of Motion Pictures, 1909–1922*. New York: Arno Press, 1977.

Filene, Peter G. *Him/Her/Self: Sex Roles in Modern America*. 2nd ed. Baltimore, Md.: Johns Hopkins University Press, 1986.

———. "An Obituary for the Progressive Movement." *American Quarterly* 22 (1970): 22–34.

Filler, Louis. *Muckrakers*. University Park: Pennsylvania State University Press, 1976.

Fine, William F. *Progressive Evolutionism and American Sociology, 1890–1920*. Ph.D. diss., University of Iowa, 1975.

Fishbein, Leslie. "Harlot or Heroine? Changing Views of Prostitution, 1870–1920." *Historian* 43, no. 1 (November 1980): 23–35.

Fisher, Robert J. "Film Censorship and Progressive Reform: The National Board of Censorship of Motion Pictures, 1909–1922." *Journal of Popular Film* 4 (1975): 143–56.

Fishman, Robert. *Urban Utopias in the Twentieth Century*. New York: Basic Books, 1977.

Flax, Judith. "Postmodernism and Gender Relations in Feminist Theory." In *Feminism/Postmodernism*, edited by Linda J. Nicholson, pp. 39–62. New York: Routledge, 1990.

Flexner, Abraham. *I Remember: The Autobiography of Abraham Flexner*. New York: Simon and Schuster, 1940.

Flexner, Eleanor. *Century of Struggle: The Woman's Rights Movements in the United States*. Cambridge: Harvard University Press, 1959.

Formanek-Brunell, Miriam. "Marketing a Campbell Kids Culture." *Civitas: Cultural Studies at MIT* 2, no. 3 (Spring 1993): 1–5.

Fosdick, Raymond B. *Chronicle of a Generation: An Autobiography*. New York: Harper, 1958.

———. *John D. Rockefeller, Jr.: A Portrait*. New York: Harper, 1956.

Foucault, Michel. *The History of Sexuality: An Introduction*. Vol. 1 [1970]. Translated by Robert Hurley. New York: Vintage Books, 1978.

———. *The Use of Pleasure: The History of Sexuality*. Vol. 2 [1984]. Translated by Robert Hurley. New York: Vintage Books, 1986.

Gaines, Jane. "The Queen Christina Tie-Ups: Convergence of Show Window and Screen." *Quarterly Review of Film and Video* 11, no. 1 (1989): 35–60.

Garrison, Dee. "The Tender Technicians: The Feminization of Public Librarianship, 1876–1906." In *Clio's Consciousness Raised: New Perspectives on the History of Women*, edited by Mary Hartman and Lois W. Banner, pp. 158–78. New York: Harper and Row, 1974.

Gay, Peter. *The Bourgeois Experience: Victoria to Freud*. Vols. 1 and 2. New York: Oxford University Press, 1984–86.

Gilfoyle, Timothy. *City of Eros: New York City, Prostitution, and the Commercialization of Sex, 1790–1920*. New York: Norton, 1992.

Gilman, Charlotte Perkins. *Women and Economics: A Study of the Economic Relation between Men and Women as a Factor in Social Evolution*. 1898. Reprint. New York: Source Book Press, 1970.

Ginzburg, Carlo. *The Cheese and the Worms: The Cosmos of a Sixteenth-Century Miller* [1976]. Translated by John and Anne Tedeschi. Middlesex, England: Penguin Books, 1982.

Gledhill, Christine. "Between Melodrama and Realism: Anthony Asquith's *Underground* and King Vidor's *The Crowd*." In *Classical Hollywood Narrative: The Paradigm Wars*, edited by Jane Gaines, pp. 129–67. Durham, N.C.: Duke University Press, 1992.

———. "The Melodramatic Field: An Investigation." In *Home Is Where the Heart Is: Studies in Melodrama and the Woman's Film*, edited by Christine Gledhill, pp. 5–39. London: BFI, 1987.

Glyn, Elinor. *Three Weeks*. 1907. Reprint. New York: Macaulay, 1924.

Gordon, Linda. "Voluntary Motherhood: The Beginnings of Feminist Birth Control Ideas in the United States." In *Clio's Consciousness Raised: New Perspectives on the History of Women*, edited by Mary Hartman and Lois W. Banner, pp. 54–71. New York: Harper and Row, 1974.

Gordon, Lynn D. *Gender and Higher Education in the Progressive Era*. New Haven, Conn.: Yale University Press, 1990.

Gossett, Thomas F. *Race: The History of an Idea in America*. Dallas, Tex.: Southern Methodist University Press, 1963.

Grand, Madame Sarah. *The Heavenly Twins*. New York: Cassell, 1893.

Gunning, Tom. "The Cinema of Attraction: Early Film, Its Spectator and the Avant-Garde." *Wide Angle* 8, nos. 3 and 4 (1986): 63–70.

———. *D. W. Griffith and the Origins of American Narrative Film: The Early Years at Biograph.* Urbana: University of Illinois Press, 1991.

Haber, Samuel. *Efficiency and Uplift: Scientific Management in the Progressive Era, 1890–1920.* Chicago: University of Chicago Press, 1964.

Hagan, John. "Erotic Tendencies in Film, 1900–1906." In *Cinema 1900–1906: An Analytical Study by the National Film Archive (London) and the International Federation of Film Archives,* edited by Roger Holman, pp. 231–38. Vol. 1. Brussels: FIAF, 1982.

Haller, John S., Jr., and Robin M. Haller. *The Physician and Sexuality in Victorian America.* Urbana: University of Illinois Press, 1974.

Handlin, Oscar, ed. *Immigration as a Factor in American History.* Englewood Cliffs, N.J.: Prentice-Hall, 1959.

Hansen, Miriam. "Adventures of Goldilocks: Spectatorship, Consumerism and Public Life." *camera obscura,* no. 22 (January 1990): 51–71.

———. *Babel and Babylon: Spectatorship in American Silent Film.* Cambridge: Harvard University Press, 1991.

Hapke, Laura. *Girls Who Went Wrong: Prostitutes in American Fiction, 1885–1917.* Bowling Green, Ohio: Bowling Green State University Popular Press, 1989.

Harr, John Ensor, and Johnson, Peter J. *The Rockefeller Century.* New York: Scribner, 1988.

Haskell, Molly. *From Reverence to Rape: The Treatment of Women in the Movies.* 2nd ed. Chicago: University of Chicago Press, 1987.

Heath, Stephen. *The Sexual Fix.* London: Macmillan, 1982.

Hebdige, Dick. *Subculture: The Meaning of Style.* London: Methuen, 1979.

Hewett, Nancy. "Yankee Evangelicals and Agrarian Quakers: Gender, Religion, and Class in the Formation of a Feminist Consciousness in Nineteenth-Century Rochester, New York." *Radical History Review,* nos. 28–30 (1984): 326–42.

Higashi, Sumiko. "Ethnicity, Class, and Gender in Film: DeMille's *The Cheat.*" In *Unspeakable Images: Ethnicity and the American Cinema,* edited by Lester D. Friedman, pp. 112–39. Urbana: University of Illinois Press, 1991.

———. *Virgins, Vamps and Flappers: The American Silent Movie Heroine.* St. Albans, Vt.: Eden Press Women's Publications, 1978.

Higham, John. *Strangers in the Land: Patterns of American Nativism, 1860–1925.* New Brunswick, N.J.: Rutgers University Press, 1955.

Hobson, Barbara. *Uneasy Virtue: The Politics of Prostitution and the American Reform Tradition.* New York: Basic Books, 1987.

Hochman, William Russell. *William J. Gaynor: The Years of Fruition.* Ph.D. diss., Columbia University, 1955.

Hofstadter, Richard. *The Age of Reform: From Bryan to F.D.R.* New York: Random House, 1955.

Jacobs, Lea. "Reformers and Spectators: The Film Education Movement in the Thirties." *camera obscura,* no. 22 (January 1990): 28–49.

———. *The Wages of Sin: Censorship and the Fallen Woman Film, 1928–1942.* Madison: University of Wisconsin Press, 1991.

Jacobs, Lewis. *The Rise of the American Film: A Critical History.* Rev. ed. New York: Teachers College Press/Columbia University, 1948.

Jameson, Fredric. "Pleasure: A Political Issue." In *Formations of Pleasure,* edited by Formations Editorial Collective, pp. 1–14. London: Routledge and Kegan Paul, 1983.

Janney, O. Edward. *The White Slave Traffic in America.* New York: National Vigilance Committee, 1911.

Jowett, Garth. *Film: The Democratic Art.* Boston: Little, Brown, 1976.

Kaplan, Cora. "Wild Nights: Pleasure/Sexuality/Feminism." In *Formations of Pleasure*, edited by Formations Editorial Collective, pp. 15–35. London: Routledge and Kegan Paul, 1983.

Kaplan, E. Ann. *Motherhood and Representation: The Mother in Popular Culture and Melodrama.* London: Routledge, 1992.

Karr, Kathleen. "The Long Square-Up: Exploitation Trends in the Silent Film." *Journal of Popular Film* 3, no. 2 (Spring 1974): 107–28.

Kauffman, Reginald Wright. *The Girl That Goes Wrong.* New York: Moffat, Yard, 1911.

————. *The House of Bondage.* New York: Moffat, Yard, 1911.

Keller, Helen. " 'I Must Speak' ": A Plea to the American Woman." *Ladies' Home Journal* 16, no. 2 (January 1909): 6.

Kern, Stephen. *The Culture of Time and Space, 1880–1918.* Cambridge, Mass.: Harvard University Press, 1983.

Kipling, Rudyard. "The Vampire." In *The Best Loved Poems of the American People*, edited by Hazel Zelleman, pp. 598–99. 1936. Reprint. Garden City, N.Y.: Garden City Books, 1960.

Kneeland, George J. *Commercialized Prostitution in New York City: Publications of the Bureau of Social Hygiene.* New York: Century, 1913.

Kraditor, Aileen S. *The Ideas of the Woman Suffrage Movement, 1890–1920.* New York: Norton, 1965.

Krammerer, Percy Gamble. *The Unmarried Mother: A Study of Five Hundred Cases.* Criminal Science Monograph, no. 3. Boston: Little, Brown, 1920.

Kuhn, Annette. *Cinema, Censorship and Sexuality, 1909–1925.* London: Routledge, 1988.

Landy, Marcia. "Introduction." In *Imitations of Life: A Reader on Film and Television Melodrama*, edited by Marcia Landy, pp. 13–32. Detroit, Mich.: Wayne State University Press, 1991.

Leach, William. "Transformations in a Culture of Consumption." *Journal of American History* 71, no. 2 (September 1984): 319–42.

Lears, T. J. Jackson. "From Salvation to Self-Realization: Advertising and the Therapeutic Roots of the Consumer Culture, 1880–1930." In *The Culture of Consumption: Critical Essays in American History, 1880–1980*, edited by T. J. Jackson Lears and Richard Wightman Fox, pp. 1–38. New York: Pantheon, 1983.

————. *No Place of Grace: Antimodernism and the Transformation of American Culture, 1880–1920.* New York: Pantheon Books, 1981.

Leiss, William, Stephen Kline, and Sut Jhally. *Social Communication in Advertising: Persons, Products and Images of Well-Being.* Toronto: Methuen, 1986.

Lentricchia, Frank. "Foucault's Legacy—The New Historicism?" In *The New Historicism*, edited by H. Abram Vesser, pp. 231–42. New York: Routledge, 1989.

Levine, Lawrence W. "William Shakespeare and the American People: A Study in Cultural Transformation." *American Historical Review* 89, no. 1 (February 1984): 34–66.

Lewis, Howard T. *The Motion Picture Industry.* New York: Van Nostrand, 1933.

Leyda, Jay, and Charles Musser, eds. *Before Hollywood: Turn-of-the-Century Film from American Archives.* New York: American Federation of the Arts, 1986.

Lindsay, Shelley Stamp. "Wages and Sin: *Traffic in Souls* and the White Slavery Scare." *Persistence of Vision*, no. 9 (1991): 90–102.

Lippmann, Walter. *A Preface to Politics.* New York: Mitchell Kennerley, 1914.

Lovell, Terry. *Consuming Fiction.* London: Verso, 1987.

Lowe, Donald M. *History of Bourgeois Perception.* Chicago: University of Chicago Press, 1982.

Lubove, Roy. "The Progressive and the Prostitute." *Historian* 24, no. 3 (May 1962): 308–30.

McCarthy, Kathleen. "Nickel Vice and Virtue: Movie Censorship in Chicago, 1907–1915." *Journal of Popular Film* 5, no. 1 (1976): 37–55.

McClure, S. S. "The Tammanyizing of a Civilization." *McClure's Magazine* 34, no. 1 (November 1909): 117–28.

Mackenzie, F. A., ed. *The Trial of Harry Thaw*. London: Geoffrey Bles, 1928.

MacLean, Annie Marion. "Two Weeks in Department Stores." *American Journal of Sociology* 4, no. 6 (May 1899): 721–41.

McPherson, James M. "The Antislavery Legacy: From Reconstruction to the NAACP." In *Towards a New Past: Dissenting Essays in American History*, edited by J. Barton Bernstein, pp. 126–57. New York: Random House, 1967.

Magliozzi, Ronald S., ed. *Treasures from the Film Archives: A Catalogue of Short Silent Films Held by FIAF Archives*. Metuchen, N.J.: Scarecrow Press, 1988.

Marsh, Margaret. "Suburban Men and Masculine Domesticity, 1870–1915." *American Quarterly* 40, no. 2 (June 1988): 165–86.

Martin, Jay. *Harvests of Change: American Literature, 1865–1914*. Englewood Cliffs, N.J.: Prentice-Hall, 1967.

May, Elaine Tyler. *Great Expectations: Marriage and Divorce in Post-Victorian America*. Chicago: University of Chicago Press, 1980.

May, Lary. *Screening Out the Past: The Birth of Mass Culture and the Motion Picture Industry*. Chicago: University of Chicago Press, 1980.

Mayne, Judith. "Immigrants and Spectators." *Wide Angle* 5, no. 2 (1982): 32–41.

———. "Uncovering the Female Body." In *Before Hollywood: Turn-of-the-Century Film from American Archives*, pp. 63–67. New York: American Federation of Arts, 1986.

———. *The Woman at the Keyhole: Feminism and Women's Cinema*. Bloomington: Indiana University Press, 1990.

Mencken, H. L. "The Flapper." *Smart Set* 45, no. 2 (January 1915): 1–2.

Metz, Christian. *The Imaginary Signifier: Psychoanalysis and the Cinema*. Translated by Celia Britton, Annwyl Williams, Ben Brewster, and Alfred Guzzetti. Bloomington: Indiana University Press, 1982.

Meyerowitz, Joanne J. *Women Adrift: Independent Wage Earners in Chicago, 1880–1930*. Chicago: University of Chicago Press, 1988.

Michelson, Annette. "On the Eve of the Future: The Reasonable Facsimile and the Philosophical Toy." *October*, no. 29 (Summer 1984): 3–21.

More, Sir Thomas. *Utopia* [1517]. Translated by Peter K. Marshall. New York: Washington Square Press, 1965.

Mott, Frank Luther. *Golden Multitudes: The Story of Bestsellers in the United States*. New York: Macmillan, 1947.

———. *A History of American Magazines, 1885–1905*. Vols. 4 and 5. Cambridge: Harvard University Press, 1957–68.

Murphy, Paul L. *World War I and the Origin of Civil Liberties in the United States*. New York: Norton, 1979.

Neale, Steve. "Melotalk: On the Meaning and Use of the Term 'Melodrama' in the American Trade Press." *Velvet Light Trap*, no. 32 (Fall 1993): 66–89.

Newcomb, Horace M. *The Naturalist "Movement" in America*. Ph.D. diss., University of Chicago, 1969.

Norden, Martin J. "New York Mayor William J. Gaynor and His City's Film Industry." *Film Reader*, no. 6 (1985): 78–91.

O'Neill, William L. "Divorce in the Progressive Era." In *The American Family in Socio-Historical Perspective*, edited by Michael Gordon, pp. 251–66. New York: St. Martin's Press, 1973.

Parkhurst, Charles H. *Our Fight with Tammany*. New York: Scribner, 1895.

Pearsall, Ronald. *The Worm in the Bud: The World of Victorian Sexuality*. London: Weidenfeld and Nicolson, 1969.

Peiss, Kathy. *Cheap Amusements: Working Women and Leisure in Turn-of-the-Century New York.* Philadelphia: Temple University Press, 1986.

———. "Making Faces: The Cosmetics Industry and the Cultural Consumption of Gender, 1890–1930." *Genders*, no. 7 (March 1990): 143–69.

Pells, Richard H. *Radical Visions and American Dreams: Culture and Social Thought in the Depression Years.* Middletown, Conn.: Wesleyan University Press, 1973.

Rabinovitz, Lauren. "Temptations of Pleasure: Nickelodeons, Amusement Parks, and the Sights of Female Sexuality." *camera obscura*, no. 23 (May 1990): 71–88.

Ramsaye, Terry. *A Million and One Nights: A History of the Motion Picture through 1925.* 1926. Reprint. New York: Simon and Schuster, 1965.

Randall, Richard S. *Censorship of the Movies: The Social and Political Control of a Mass Medium.* Madison: University of Wisconsin Press, 1968.

Repplier, Agnes. "The Repeal of Reticence," *Atlantic Monthly* 113 (March 1914): 297–304.

Rives-Chauler, Amélie. *The Quick or the Dead? A Study.* Philadelphia: Lippincott, 1888.

Roe, Clifford. *The Great War on White Slavery.* 1911. Reprint. New York: Garland, 1979. Also known as *Horrors of the White Slave Trade.*

———. *Horrors of the White Slave Trade: The Mighty Crusade to Protect the Purity of Our Homes.* London: n.p., 1911.

———. *Panders and Their White Slaves.* New York: Revell, 1910.

Roemer, Kenneth M. *The Obsolete Necessity: America in Utopian Writings, 1888–1900.* Kent, Ohio: Kent State University Press, 1976.

Rogin, Michael. " 'The Sword Became a Flashing Vision': D. W. Griffith's *The Birth of a Nation.*" *Representations*, no. 9 (Winter 1985): 150–95.

Rooney, Charles J., Jr. *Dreams and Visions: A Study of American Utopias, 1865–1917.* Westport, Conn.: Greenwood Press, 1985.

Rosen, Philip. "Introduction." In *Narrative, Apparatus, Ideology: A Film Theory Reader*, edited by Philip Rosen, pp. 281–85. New York: Columbia University Press, 1986.

Rosenbloom, Nancy J. "Between Reform and Regulation: The Struggle over Film Censorship in Progressive America, 1909–1922." *Film History* 1, no. 4 (1987): 307–25.

———. "In Defense of Moving Pictures: The People's Institute, the National Board of Censorship, and the Problems of Leisure in Urban America." *American Studies* 33, no. 2 (Fall 1992): 41–61.

———. "Progressive Reform, Censorship, and the Motion Picture Industry, 1909–1917." In *Popular Culture and Political Change in Modern America*, edited by Ronald Edsforth and Larry Bennett, pp. 41–59. Buffalo: SUNY, 1991.

Said, Edward W. *Orientalism.* New York: Random House, 1978.

Sargent, Epes Winthrop. *The Technique of the Photoplay.* 2nd ed. New York: Moving Picture World, 1913.

Scheiber, Harry N., Harold G. Vatter, and Harold Underwood Faulkner. *American Economic History.* 9th ed. New York: Harper and Row, 1976.

Schlossman, Steven and Stephanie Wallach. "The Crime of Precocious Sexuality: Female Juvenile Delinquency in the Progressive Era." *Harvard Educational Review* 48, no. 1 (February 1978): 65–94.

Schroeder, Theodore. "Our Prudish Censorship." *Forum* 53 (January 1915): 87–99.

"Sex O'Clock in America." *Current Opinion* 55, no. 2 (August 1913): 113–14.

Shipman, David. *Caught in the Act: Sex and Eroticism in the Movies.* London: Elm Tree Books, 1985.

Singer, Ben. "Female Power in the Serial-Queen Melodrama: The Etiology of an Anomaly." *camera obscura*, no. 22 (January 1990): 91–129.

Sklar, Robert. *Movie-Made America: A Cultural History of American Movies*. New York: Vintage Books, 1975.

Slade, Joseph W. "Violence in the Hard-Core Pornographic Film: A Historical Survey." *Journal of Communication* 34, no. 3 (Summer 1984): 148–63.

Sloan, Kay. *The Loud Silents: Origins of the Social Problem Film*. Urbana: University of Illinois Press, 1988.

Smith-Rosenberg, Carroll. "Writing History: Language, Class, and Gender." In *Feminist Studies/Critical Studies*, edited by Teresa de Lauretis, pp. 31–54. Bloomington: Indiana University Press, 1986.

Spingairn, Arthur B. *Laws Relating to Sex Morality in New York City*. New York: Century, 1915.

Staiger, Janet. " 'The Eyes Are Really the Focus': Photoplay Acting and Film Form and Style." *Wide Angle* 6, no. 4 (1985): 14–23.

———. *Interpreting Films: Studies in the Historical Reception of American Cinema*. Princeton, N.J.: Princeton University Press, 1992.

Strasser, Susan. *Satisfaction Guaranteed: The Making of the American Mass Market*. New York: Pantheon Books, 1989.

Syrett, Harold C. *The Gentleman and the Tiger: The Autobiography of George B. McClellan, Jr.* Philadelphia: Lippincott, 1956.

Tentler, Leslie Woodcock. *Wage-Earning Women: Industrial Work and Family Life in the United States*. New York: Oxford University Press, 1979.

Thernstrom, Stephan. "Urbanization, Migration, and Social Mobility in Late Nineteenth-Century America." In *Towards a New Past: Dissenting Essays in American History*, edited by Barton J. Bernstein, pp. 158–75. New York: Random House, 1967.

Tickner, Lisa. *The Spectacle of Women: Imagery of the Suffrage Campaign, 1907–14*. Chicago: University of Chicago Press, 1988.

Trachtenberg, Alan. *The Incorporation of America: Culture and Society in the Gilded Age*. New York: Hill and Wang, 1982.

Trudgill, Eric. *Madonnas and Magdalens: The Origins and Development of Victorian Sexual Attitudes*. New York: Holmes and Meier, 1976.

True, Ruth S. "The Neglected Girl." In *West Side Studies*, edited by Pauline Goldmark. New York: Russell Sage Foundation, 1914.

Turner, George Kibbe. "The City of Chicago: A Study of the Great Immoralities." *McClure's Magazine* 28, no. 6 (April 1907): 575–92.

———. "The Daughters of the Poor: A Plain Story of the Development of New York City as a Leading Center of the White Slave Trade of the World, under Tammany Hall." *McClure's Magazine* 34, no. 1 (November 1909): 45–61.

———. "Tammany's Control of New York by Professional Criminals." *McClure's Magazine* 33, no. 2 (June 1909): 117–34.

Unger, Irwin. "The 'New Left' and American History: Some Recent Trends in United States Historiography." *American Historical Review* 72, no. 4 (July 1967): 1237–63.

Veblen, Thorstein. *The Theory of the Leisure Class*. 1899. Reprint. New York: Mentor, 1953.

Vice Commission of Chicago. *The Social Evil in Chicago*. 1911. Reprint. New York: Arno Press and the New York Times, 1970.

Vice Commission of Minneapolis. *Report of the Vice Commission of Minneapolis to His Honor, James C. Haynes, Mayor*. 1911. Reprinted in *The Prostitute and the Social Reformer*. New York: Arno Press, 1974.

Vice Commission of Philadelphia. *A Report on Existing Conditions with Recommendations to the Honorable Rudolph Blankenburg, Mayor of Philadelphia*. 1913. Reprinted in *The Prostitute and the Social Reformer*. New York: Arno Press, 1974.

Volosinov, V. N. *Marxism and the Philosophy of Language* [1929]. Translated by Ladislav Matejka and I. R. Titunik. New York: Seminar Press, 1973.

Walker, Robert H. *Reform in America: The Continuing Frontier*. Lexington: University Press of Kentucky, 1985.

Walkowitz, Judith. *City of Dreadful Delight: Narratives of Sexual Danger in Late-Victorian London*. Chicago: University of Chicago Press, 1992.

Walkowitz, Judith, and Daniel J. Walkowitz. " 'We are Not Beasts of the Field': Prostitution and the Poor in Plymouth and Southampton under the Contagious Disease Act." In *Clio's Consciousness Raised: New Perspectives on the History of Women*, edited by Mary Hartman and Lois W. Banner, pp. 192–225. New York: Harper and Row, 1974.

Wallerstein, I. *The Modern World-System*. 2 vols. New York: Academic Press, 1974.

Waugh, Thomas. "Strength and Stealth: Watching (and Wanting) Turn of the Century Strongmen." *Canadian Journal of Film Studies* 2, no. 1 (1992): 1–20.

Waxman, Chaim I. "Perspectives on Poverty in Early American Sociology." In *Ethnicity, Identity, and History: Essays in Memory of Werner J. Cahuman*, edited by Joseph B. Maier and Chaim I. Waxman, pp. 183–98. New Brunswick, N.J.: Transaction Books, 1983.

Weeks, Jeffrey. *Sex, Politics and Society: The Regulation of Sexuality since 1800*. London: Longman, 1981.

Welter, Barbara. "The Cult of True Womanhood, 1820–1860." *American Quarterly* 18, no. 2 (1966): 151–57.

Wiebe, Robert H. "The Progressive Years, 1900–1917." In *The Reinterpretation of American History and Culture*, edited by William H. Cartwright and Richard L. Watson Jr., pp. 425–42. Washington, D.C.: National Council for the Social Studies, 1973.

———. *The Search for Order, 1877–1920*. New York: Hill and Wang, 1967.

Williams, Linda. "Film Body: An Implantation of Perversions." *Ciné-Tracts* 3, no. 4 (Winter 1981): 19–35.

———. *Hard Core: Power, Pleasure, and the "Frenzy of the Visible."* Berkeley: University of California Press, 1989.

Wilson, Christopher P. "The Rhetoric of Consumption: Mass-Market Magazines and the Demise of the Gentle Reader, 1880–1920." In *The Culture of Consumption: Critical Essays in American History, 1880–1980*, edited by T. J. Jackson Lears and Richard Wightman Fox, pp. 39–64. New York: Pantheon, 1983.

Wilson, Elizabeth. *The Sphinx in the City: Urban Life, the Control of Disorder, and Women*. Berkeley: University of California Press, 1991.

Wilson, Harold S. *McClure's Magazine and the Muckrakers*. Princeton, N.J.: Princeton University Press, 1970.

Wright, Gwendolyn. *Building the Dream: A Social History of Housing in America*. New York: Pantheon, 1981.

Young, Marilyn Blatt. "American Expansion, 1870–1900: The Far East." In *Towards a New Past: Essays in American History*, edited by Barton J. Bernstein, pp. 176–201. New York: Random House, 1967.

Index

Janet Staiger is a professor of radio, television, and film at the University of Texas at Austin. She has also taught at New York University and the University of Delaware and has been a visiting professor at the University of California–Los Angeles and the China Film Association in Beijing. She is author of *Interpreting Films: Studies in the Historical Reception of American Cinema* and coauthor with David Bordwell and Kristin Thompson of *The Classical Hollywood Cinema: Film Style and Mode of Production to 1960*. She was president of the Society for Cinema Studies from 1991 to 1993.

BOWMAN LIBRARY
MENLO SCHOOL AND COLLEGE

791.43
S 782

PN 1995.9 .W6 S73 1995
Staiger, Janet.
Bad women

$49.95

DATE			

BAKER & TAYLOR